Colorado's

Newest & Best Wildflower Hikes

**Boulder • Breckenridge • Colorado Springs • Denver
Fort Collins • Rocky Mountain National Park • Vail**

TEXT BY

PAMELA IRWIN

PHOTOGRAPHY BY

DAVID IRWIN

WESTCLIFFE PUBLISHERS

bigearthpublishing.com

ISBN: 978-1-56579-597-6

EDITOR: Alisa Geiser
DESIGN: Rebecca Finkel

PUBLISHED BY: Westcliffe Publishers
a Big Earth Publishing company
3005 Center Green Drive, Suite 220
Boulder, Colorado 80301

PRINTED IN: Printed in China through World Print Ltd.

9 8 7 6 5 4 3 2 1

LIBRARY OF CONGRESS CATALOGING-IN-PUBLICATION DATA:
data on file

PLEASE NOTE:
Risk is always a factor in backcountry and high-mountain travel.
Many of the activities described in this book can be dangerous,
especially when weather is adverse or unpredictable, and when
unforeseen events or conditions create a hazardous situation.
The author has done her best to provide the reader with accurate
information about backcountry travel, as well as to point out some
of its potential hazards. It is the responsibility of the users of this
guide to learn the necessary skills for safe backcountry travel,
and to exercise caution in potentially hazardous areas, especially
on glaciers and avalanche-prone terrain. The author and publisher disclaim any liability for injury or other damage caused by
backcountry traveling, or performing any other activity described
in this book.

The author and publisher of this book have made every effort to
ensure the accuracy and currency of its information. Nevertheless,
books can require revisions. Please feel free to let us know if
you find information in this book that needs to be updated,
and we will be glad to correct it for the next printing. Your
comments and suggestions are always welcome.

*For more information about other fine
books and calendars from Westcliffe
Publishers, a Big Earth Publishing
company, please contact your local
bookstore, call us at (800) 258-5830,
or visit us on the Web at*
bigearthpublishing.com

COVER PHOTO:
Red paintbrush on Betty
and Bob Lakes Trail

Acknowledgments

The highest reward for a man's toil is not what he gets for it,
but what he becomes by it. —JOHN RUSKIN

Many unsung heroes and heroines go into the making of a book. And when that book is full-color, nonfiction, and loaded with photos, maps, directions, and supplemental information, it takes a team. It is with great pleasure and appreciation that I acknowledge those teammates:

Firstly, my boon companion and irreplaceable husband and photographer, David Harlan Irwin.
Cherish your visions and your dreams, as they are the children of your soul—
the blueprints of your ultimate achievement. —NAPOLEON HILL

Gratitude goes to the superb publishing team of:
Linda Doyle, my dear mentor and lively lady who wears many publishing hats, including that of Big Earth Publishing's vice president of sales and marketing, and who makes book things happen.
We make a living by what we get, but we make a life
by what we give. —NORMAN MACEWAN

Ali Geiser, my delightful and thorough Westcliffe managing editor, who guided *Colorado's Newest and Best Wildflower Hikes* to fruition by dealing with my penchant for "flowery" verbiage and,,, over-commatization.
There's nothing quite as irksome as someone else's mess. —SUE GRAFTON

Rebecca Finkel, madam of maps, great graphics, and photograph massaging.
The best way to get people to think out of the box
is not to create the box in the first place. —MARTIN COOPER

Janet Heisz, Westcliffe competent comptroller, who has seen the five Irwin-authored-and-photographed books through the numbers.
Work is a slice of your life. It's not the whole pizza. —JACQUELYN MITCHARD

Molly Hazelrig, cheery director of sales, who sees that the books get to where they should be, and, ultimately, into the readers' hands.
People rarely succeed at anything unless they have fun doing it. —LA ROCHEFOUCAULD

Best friends who happen to love wildflowers and are willing to lace up boots and slurp from water bottles are special. Thank you, Pat Whittall and Jan Richings. Then, of course, there is David . . . the "Mule" who slings 30 pounds of photographic gear and overnight survival equipment, including snacks and copious amounts of water, on his back.
A friend may well be reckoned the masterpiece of nature. —RALPH WALDO EMERSON

And a final thank-you to you, the reader who understands:
But indeed it is not so much for its beauty that the forest makes a claim upon men's hearts,
as for the subtle something, that quality of air, that emanation from the old trees, that so
wonderfully changes and renews a weary spirit. —ROBERT LOUIS STEVENSON

Dedication

To my mother

with love and joyous gratitude

for all the doors she flung wide…

*"Thankfulness is the soil
in which joy thrives."*

Colorado's

Newest & Best Wildflower Hikes

Symbols in this legend are used in the maps for each hike.

– – – Trail	Lake
----- Adjoining Trail	○ Point of Interest
—— Road	TH Trailhead
----- Dirt Road	P Parking
—— River	▲ Campground
.... Continental Divide	① Wildflower Hike

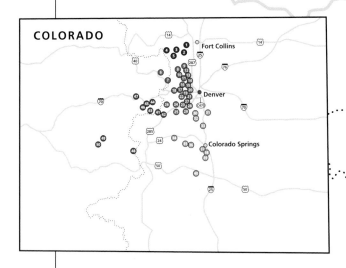

COLORADO

Fort Collins

Denver

Colorado Springs

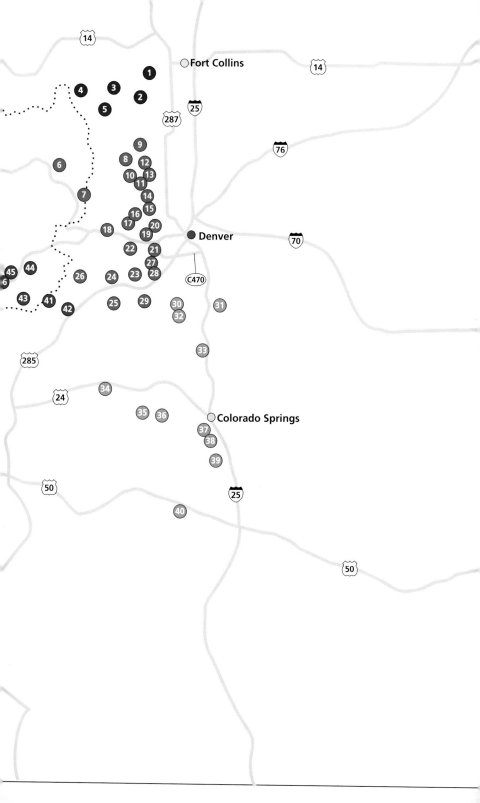

Table of Contents

Wildflower Profiles (arranged alphabetically)
Common name (*Latin name*)

Blue Columbine, Colorado's state flower since 1899.

Introduction

COLORADO. The very name evokes images of snow-creased peaks jutting into an impossibly blue sky. It calls to mind rushing rivers and serene lakes; lush meadows and dense forest; thrusting red rock and yawning canyons; pastoral valleys and mountains of sand; molten gold aspen and vast grasslands . . . and a wonderment of wildflowers.

The astounding array of wildflowers offered within the state's borders curls, like a rainbow ribbon, to bind Colorado sky and earth. As the snow recedes in the high country, early spring has come and gone on the plains; foothills are far into their bloom season; and montane flowering is underway. Everywhere, trails rife with wildflowers await your exploration.

The state boasts some 10,000 miles of trail that bring hikers into the realm of blooming plants. Expect those in the plains life zone to bloom early, soon to be followed by those in the foothills, and so on. Geared to the average hiker, the treks within this book vary from about 1 mile up to 9 miles; most fall in the 2 to 5 mile category, and about half are loop trails. All 50 hikes in this book are day-hikes.

So many choices, so little time. For the wildflower aficionado, as well as the outdoor enthusiast, this book, *Colorado's Newest and Best Wildflower Hikes,* along with its three companion volumes—*Colorado's Best Wildflower Hikes: The Front Range, Colorado's Best Wildflower Hikes: The High Country,* and *Colorado's Best Wildflower Hikes: San Juan Mountains*—offers direction for finding Colorado's finest wildflowering areas.

This volume focuses mainly on an expanded Front Range radius that extends north to Boulder and Fort Collins, west to Vail and the Dillon-Frisco-Breckenridge region, and then south and west into the Colorado Springs area. The exceptionally floristic Crested Butte region contributes a few trails as well.

Selected wildflower species encountered along each trail appear in boldface type. To further the aficionado's education, each chapter highlights one or more wildflowers in "profiles" that include a color photo as well as information such as description, Latin name, and trivia.

Each hike in this book fits into one of five broad-based life zones, determined by elevation, which are as follows:

Plains:	below 6,000 feet
Foothills:	6,000-8,000 feet
Montane:	8,000-10,000 feet
Subalpine:	10,000-11,500 feet
Alpine:	above 11,500 feet

Though these life zones help us predict which flora and fauna we will find at a particular elevation, keep in mind that when and where a flower will bloom is also influenced by other factors, such as aspect (a slope angled 5 degrees to the north makes for the equivalent of traveling 300 miles north), altitude (each 100-foot elevation gain equals a day longer to bloom), snowpack (the amount can hasten or delay bloom by weeks), moisture (cold, wet, or hot, dry weather influences flowering), and wind (direction, duration, and power can be noted in a plant's growth). Let's not leave out Mother Nature's other capricious agents, including but not limited to animal and insect appetite, fire, germinating forces, disease, and even us. But never mind all that—walk somewhere out there and you will find wildflowers. *Colorado's Newest and Best Wildflower Hikes* will further your goals.

Before you set out on any hike, make sure you are prepared. Arrive at the trailhead equipped with maps, a whistle, a compass, snacks, and plenty of water. Your hiking gear should incorporate weatherproof outerwear, a hat, sturdy hiking boots, sunscreen, and sunglasses. You should familiarize yourself not only with your destination, but also with lightning activity and other hazards unique to an area or season. Never underestimate the need to be fully informed, especially when afoot. Common sense, say the French, is not so common. It is your best ally—carry a generous supply with you at all times.

That said, it is a privilege and pleasure to welcome you to the wonderful world of Colorado wildflower hiking. Consider this book an invitation to explore the inner and outer reaches of the best areas. Enjoy the allure of open air, fine scenery, and inspiring wildflowers. Learn a little about wildflowers and, perhaps, a lot about yourself.

> We conserve what we love
> We love what we know
> We know what we are taught.
> —BABA DIOUM

> *The charm of a woodland road lies*
> *not only in its beauty but in anticipation.*
> *Around each bend may be a discovery,*
> *an adventure.* —DALE REX COMAN

> *Happy hiking among Colorado's munificent wildflowers!*
> —PAMELA IRWIN

Wildflower Hike 1

Well Gulch Nature Loop

A seasonal creek burbles along beside the Well Gulch Nature Loop.

Trail Rating	easy
Trail Length	1.6-mile loop
Location	Lory State Park/Fort Collins
Elevation	5,500 to 5,860 feet
Bloom Season	April to October
Peak Bloom	June
Directions	From Fort Collins, take US 287 north. Turn left onto County Road 52 for 1 mile, then left onto County Road 23 for 2 miles. Turn right onto County Road 25G and proceed 1.5 miles to the Lory State Park entrance gate. Park at the Eltuck picnic area. Fee required. Horses and bikes prohibited.

LORY STATE PARK, just 20 minutes west of Fort Collins, offers close-in foothills serenity. The park's 1.6-mile Well Gulch Nature loop is a great kickoff for the wildflower hike season. Beginning gently up Well Gulch drainage, the trail tightens toward an overlook of Horsetooth Reservoir before dropping to the site of the old Howard family homestead, now a picnic area. The loop finishes on the horse trail paralleling the entrance road.

In addition to about six dozen wildflower species, Well Gulch offers striking views and diverse habitats, ranging from riparian to dry scrubland to ponderosa parkland. Keep an eye out for poison ivy—even petting a dog that has encountered this plant may cause a reaction in sensitive people.

The generous parking area is shared with picnickers.

From the parking lot, head west across the entrance road to the trailhead. If you like, pick up a self-guided Well Gulch Nature Trail brochure; the interpretive blurbs inside correspond with numbered posts along the way.

As you pass through grassland scrub, note **threeleaf sumac** or **lemonadebush**, whose tacky orange-red fruits were once valued for making a refreshing beverage. Nearby, perfumed **wild plum** thickets typically produce flowers before producing leaves.

The grassy slope ahead features purple-blue spires of **silvery lupine** and **tall larkspur**, which complement **prairie coneflower** and **bush sunflower**, a rough-foliaged perennial. On the left, look for **spiderwort**, **scorpionweed**, and **prickly pear cactus**.

Head into a ravine, passing **wild geranium** and **beebalm**, a magnet for hummingbirds, bees, butterflies, and other winged pollinators. Look for **showy milkweed**, whose interesting globular heads of dusty pink flowers mature into silk-stuffed pods. Rock outcrops adorned with bright **spiderwort** jut up where the trail crosses a drainage.

Juniper and ponderosa pine appear as the trail crosses a trickle rife with pink **wild geranium** and attendant butterflies. Lory State Park tallies 100 different butterfly species. The

WESTERN VIRGIN'S BOWER
Clematis ligusticifolia

Another charming name for this rambling, scrambling, thin, woody vine is **traveler's joy.** Floaty clusters of whitish sepals decorate this member of the buttercup family in late summer, followed by clouds of pale feathery seed plumes. Resourceful Native Americans used the bark for making shampoo and to treat sore throats; they also used the plant as a tonic and to treat headaches and wove nets from its tough fibers. When clematis was introduced to England from Spain, Elizabeth I, the Virgin Queen, was on the throne — hence, perhaps, the name **virgin's bower.**

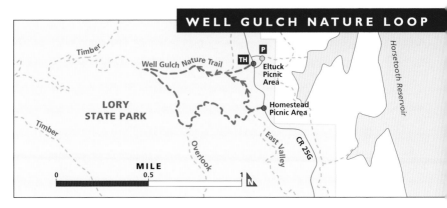

brush hereabout is hung with the thin woody vines of **western virgin's bower** or **white clematis**.

As the path starts rising, **smooth goldenrod** appears. Farther along, **prickly pear** shows up. Though its big blooms don't last long, **prickly pear**'s buds keep up a succession of translucent yellow petals surrounding a green pistil and tactile-reactive stamens that, when touched by a pollinating insect, begin to slowly move inward.

Blocky boulders curb the path as it leads to plush patches of poison ivy. Leaves of three, leave them be . . . advice well heeded.

The little streamlet widens to a silver sheet running down a bedrock terrace to moisten **water speedwell**. Speedwell's lavender-blue, four-petaled flowers, like those of all veronicas, are edible.

Up to the right a low, rugged cliff displays a patchwork of orange, chartreuse, and gray lichen—a symbiosis of rock-clinging fungus and food-gathering algae. **Leafy cinquefoil**, like five-petaled pats of butter, softens the trail's edges.

The path smooths where **wild rose** and **wild geranium** attract fleets of butterflies, then rises over a rocky tread where **waxflower** shrubs grace overhanging outcrops. Tucked into the rocks are clumps of yellow **stonecrop** and **harebell**. At their feet, alien **houndstongue**'s forget-me-not-like flowers sit upon the hefty, rough-textured leaves that give this plant its common name.

Scoured and polished rock sends the trail above the waterway and through **ninebark** bushes, whose billowing white clouds of blossoms appear in June. Cicadas may be buzzing in the warming air.

The trail brings us back alongside the creek, where refreshingly scented **mint** is nourished beside white **meadow anemone**, rangy **bur avens**, and **beebalm**.

At the entrance to a rocky ravine, ponderosa pine and Rocky Mountain maple shelter shade-loving **Canada violet**. After crossing a creek flanked by overhanging willows and dark red-barked river birch, look for **cow parsnip**. Two subsequent crossings in the rocky ravine find **speedwell** and more **mint** growing in the water.

The trail passes heavily scented **wild rose** as it climbs onto a dry, south-facing slope where **candle anemone** and **harebell** watch rampant **wild foxgrape** send out curling tendrils. Look for **golden banner** in the early season. Pass head-high **meadowrue** before coming to a small hillside of **wild licorice**, **silvery lupine**, and upcoming **beebalm**.

When you reach a junction, follow the sign inscribed "Homestead Picnic Area via Well Gulch Trail," but not before noting the patriarch ponderosa with **western virgin's bower** or **white clematis** climbing clear to its top. Also called **traveler's joy**, this tangled woody vine of creamy flowers once served as a veritable pharmacy for Native Americans. For a **blue columbine** fix, travel a short way up the Arthur's Rock Trail to see Colorado's lovely state flower before doubling back to the junction.

Leaving the little creek, the loop rises on stone steps, passing **northern bedstraw** to traverse the ponderosa pine belt. Glance eastward for a view of the red-sandstone-cradled Horsetooth Reservoir, Fort Collins, and the high plains.

As the path wends gently up, keep an eye out for **spotted coralroot**. This orchid is unable to produce chlorophyll. Its perfect flowers, with their signature spotted lip, deserve a look with a hand lens.

S-curve into **mountain mahogany** and **threeleaf sumac** scrub as the route levels through ponderosa parkland. Switchbacks send you higher and drier, leading to a ravine of **golden aster, fleabane daisy, pale comandra, scarlet gaura,** and **prickly pear**. Farther along, a grassy hillside offers more views of Horsetooth Reservoir.

Drop now through **snowberry** and **lupine** toward a plum thicket. **Locoweed** forms pods as a junction continues the loop straight ahead into open skies. The declining path reveals **yarrow**, reportedly used to stanch bleeding and for its antiseptic qualities.

Watch your step at a ledgy downhill section of the trail. Patches of **Fendler buckbrush**, its frothy clusters consisting of minuscule starry flowers protected by branchlet spines, dot the dry slope. Stone waterbars assist your descent and facilitate observation of spidery **scarlet gaura, stonecrop, locoweed,** and **penstemon**. The pine-studded, xeric hillside also yields **death camas** and **northern bedstraw**. As you come into a small ravine, avoid the poison ivy cloaking the right bank.

The trail levels out past generous **prickly pear** blossoms, then dips over mica-speckled loose rock and pink-tinged white tiers of **whorled monarda**. Also called **white monarda**, this blushing cousin of beebalm is an annual.

Crossing a rocky, pine-shaded ravine full of **ninebark, chokecherry, hawthorn, wild plum, wild raspberry,** and **wild rose**—all in the rose family—brings you alongside a ledgy rock outcrop. Here, dangling lavender **harebell** and brilliant yellow **sulphurflower** follow early-blooming **bluemist penstemon** and white **sand onion**.

The mica-glittered track smoothes out as it heads into scrub, passing more **sulphurflower** and **golden aster**. **Blanketflower**, or **gaillardia**, with its toothed yellow rays and burnt red disc florets, contrasts with bright blue **Geyer larkspur** and vibrant magenta **locoweed**.

Switchbacks head down through a field of **fleabane daisies** interspersed with **showy Townsendia**. Check occasionally under bushes for earlier-blooming **sugarbowls**, their platinum seed plumes arranged like troll hairdos. **Harebells** and a specimen or two of collared **purple prairie clover** inhabit an expanse of **lupine**.

A trail intersection just above the Homestead picnic area turns the loop left (north) back toward the parking lot. In the early season, **Drummond milkvetch** filled the grass and **lupine** thick fields through which you now travel.

Wildflower
Hike 2

Crosier Mountain East

Begin your hike along the Crosier Mountain East Trail by passing through a colorful meadow.

Trail Rating   moderate

Trail Length   3.0 miles out and back

Location   Estes Park

Elevation   6,600 to 7,360 feet

Bloom Season   late May to September

Peak Bloom   mid- to late June

Directions   Take US 34 west from Loveland. When you reach the town of Drake, turn right onto County Road 43. Continue for 2.4 miles to the small Garden Gate parking area on the left side of the road.

THIS EASTERN SECTION OF THE CROSIER MOUNTAIN TRAIL, accessed by a scenic backroad, beckons crowd-weary wildflowerists. The objective of this aerobic 3-mile trek is a huge flower-bedecked meadow stretching out from a jutting granite monolith. The Crosier Mountain Trail continues on to summit 9,250-foot Crosier Mountain.

About 80 wildflower species, representative of several plant communities and habitats, thrive along Crosier Mountain Trail. In late June, the hillside near the trailhead is a mass of vivid Lambert's locoweed. This sight is best enjoyed in late afternoon light.

Parking is limited to the extreme, allowing room for a only a couple of vehicles.

Close the trailhead gate behind you and ascend through fruiting **skunkbrush** or **lemon-adebush**, more officially known as **threeleaf sumac**. In its shelter grow **wild geranium**, **wire** and **Drummond milkvetches**, and Lambert's locoweed. Nearby, alien **houndstongue** sends up a surfeit of foliage for such little flowers.

Juniper and mountain mahogany introduce twining **virgin's bower** or **white clematis** as well as fading **chiming bells** and fresh **harebells**. More vivid magenta **Colorado** or **Lambert's locoweed** and off-white **Drummond milkvetch** bloom beside bright-headed **sulphurflower**. Arrive at the trailhead sign for Crosier Mountain/Drake. In late June, be on the lookout for a specimen or two of uncommon bright-pink **nipple ball cactus**.

Evening out, the trail turns back on itself, flanked by an entire hillside mantled in **locoweed**. Fragrant globes of **purple field milkvetch** appear alongside **prairie cinquefoil**. An old ponderosa pine

LAMBERT'S OR COLORADO LOCOWEED
Oxytropis lambertii

Lambert's locoweed presents vivid violet-magenta flowers on bare stems rising over silvery, ladder-like leaves. This spring bloomer is also known as **purple locoweed, Colorado loco,** and **Lambert's crazyweed,** or just plain **loco.** *Loco,* meaning "crazy" in Spanish, describes this legume family member's ability to collect selenium in its tissues; consumption of this chemical causes poisoning in livestock. Horses, which are especially susceptible to addiction to this plant, get the blind staggers if they consume too much. Both common and Latin specie names salute British botanist A. B. Lambert. Cousins include **Rocky Mountain locoweed** (*Oxytropis sericea*) and **drop-pod loco** (*Oxytropis deflexa*).

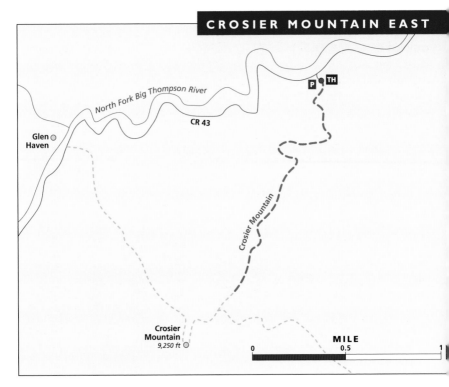

CROSIER MOUNTAIN EAST

North Fork Big Thompson River

CR 43

Glen Haven

Crosier Mountain

Crosier Mountain
9,250 ft

MILE
0   0.5   1

harbors **boulder raspberry, blanketflower,** and a couple of leathery-tepaled **sugarbowls**. Plumy **pasqueflower** seedheads are in evidence if they haven't been nipped off by wildlife.

S-curve up toward more ponderosa pine and Douglas fir, watching for golden tubes of **many-flowered puccoon,** named by Native Americans, who found that certain puccoon roots make a fine reddish-purple dye. Narrowing and rockier, the trail edges across a slope to meet **prickly pear cactus'** silky yellow blossoms and **showy Townsendia's** white, daisy-like blooms. Mats of **pussytoes** lead into a stony ravine where shrubs of **waxflower,** a relictual hydrangea family member, and **ninebark,** of the rose clan, flourish.

Sounding like wind rushing in the valley below, the North Fork Big Thompson River can be heard off to the north. Outcrops sport crevice-loving **bracted alumroot** and mats of **dotted** or **moss saxifrage,** with its minutely spotted petals.

Assisted by peeled log waterbars, the mica-glittered path comes to a mining shaft. It then lifts steeply before gentling near ragged, pinkish granite, where **bush sunflower, winged buckwheat,** and **showy Townsendia** bask in the light of an open, dry slope. Also featured are yellow **blanketflower, stonecrop,** and **sulphurflower.**

Up on the right, a monolithic outcrop sustains an aspen copse, whose dappled shade nurtures brackenfern and **northern bedstraw**. Check the far right edge of the outcrop for the pink heads of **Geyer onion**, named for plant collector Carl Geyer who followed the Oregon Trail west in 1844. As the trail prepares to climb, keen eyes may pick out pale, lavender-blue **blue rock clematis** vines to the left. A bit of showy **mountain penstemon** accents the rising trail.

The trail levels, passing through an area looted by fire but revitalized by **golden banner**, **fleabane daisy**, **whiskbroom parsley**, and a few flames of **scarlet paintbrush**. Earlier in the season, **wavyleaf false dandelion** bloomed where **Fendler sandwort** now suspends white stars along the trail. Look among the myriad rocks on the left for uncommon **Venus' looking-glass**, a bellflower exhibiting small, cupped lavender corollas cradled by stem-clasping leaves.

Wending through the burn, the trail finds protected bits of **early larkspur** and, in spring-damp places, the gold heads of **meadow arnica**. Teaming up to brighten a big, fire-ravaged ponderosa are **American hawkweed** and **Geyer onion**. Along the disturbed trail margins, **silvery** or **woolly cinquefoil**, one of over two dozen cinquefoil or potentilla species along the Front Range, blooms in yellow, as does nearby **bladderpod**.

The route is marked by stone cairns now. The first one, stacked with quartz samples, may harbor satiny pink flares of **mountain ball cactus**. Look around nearby for rare and unusual **false pimpernel**, or **blue toadflax**, a penstemon and paintbrush relation in the snapdragon family. This slender, erect plant with delicate-lobed and -lipped lavender-blue flowers deserves a search.

Another rock cairn sends you toward a huge meadow parkland gilded with **meadow arnica**. Centering the expanse is an imposing thrust of granite with what looks like a parrot or a bent-billed woodpecker, maybe even a penguin, clinging to its south side.

Drift into the soothing meadow, where a plethora of **Geyer onion** accompanies **blue-eyed grass**, **silvery lupine**, and **purple field milkvetch**. Take time to absorb the beauty here before turning around and returning to your car.

Wildflower Hike 3

North Fork/Dunraven to Deserted Village

The North Fork of the Big Thompson River provides musical company.

Trail Rating	easy
Trail Length	6.0 miles out and back
Location	Comanche WA/RMNP/Estes Park/Drake
Elevation	7,960 to 8,160 feet
Bloom Season	June to October
Peak Bloom	June
Directions	From Estes Park, where US 36 becomes N St. Vrain Ave., turn right onto Wonderview Ave., then right again onto Mac Gregor Ave. Continue 0.8 mile, then turn right at Devil's Gulch Rd./CR 43. Continue for 9 miles. Turn left at County Road 51B and continue 2.2 miles to the trailhead.

EASYGOING NORTH FORK/DUNRAVEN TRAIL travels beside the North Fork of the Big Thompson River and is within Comanche Peaks Wilderness for most of its length. Not far from Rocky Mountain National Park's east boundary, the trail reaches a broad meadow that contained a hunting resort in the late 1800s. Only a tumbledown cabin remains today.

The wildflower species count reaches about six dozen in mid- to late June. Early to mid-June offers the alluring possibility of calypso orchids in deep conifer duff.

Parking is generous at the trailhead. Don't forget the possibility of feisty summer afternoon thunderstorms that can brew up a pot of trouble in a flash.

The North Fork/Dunraven Trail starts out behind restrooms on a decomposed granite surface. Look for a trailhead sign that reads "Deserted Village." Evergreens such as ponderosa pine, Douglas fir, and Rocky Mountain juniper flank the rising trail, passing **boulder raspberry** and **bitterbrush** shrubs. Under them, smatterings of drought-tolerant **leafy cinquefoil**, **mouse-ear**, **silvery lupine**, and **whiskbroom parsley** represent typical foothills life zone denizens.

Soon, a sign announcing entry into Comanche Peak Wilderness sends the trail on a descent. Joined by river sounds to the south and golden granite underfoot, you will drop through little rock gardens containing **skullcap**, **senecio**, **stonecrop**, and **cutleaf fleabane daisy**. Other rockeries harbor **bluemist penstemon**, **wallflower**, **Fendler senecio**, and a spire or two of **miner's candle**.

A seep, vaunting plush **shooting stars**, makes for a pleasant surprise along this dry, lithic ridge. Continue down through sweet-smelling **wild rose**. Water sounds build as the trail reaches a small sign saying, succinctly, "RMNP" Rocky Mountain National Park—to the right. The trail curves west here to meet **waxflower** and **wax currant** bushes, and, within riparian influence, **white geranium**.

Amber-bedded North Fork Big Thompson River rushes like a canyon wind as the track comes up on **fireweed**, **blue columbine**, and **twinberry honeysuckle**, whose red bracts cup paired dull gold tubes ready to mature into side-by-side unpalatable black berries. Check shaded soil for the odd **spotted coralroot**, a saprophyte that depends on decaying organic matter in lieu of chlorophyll to nourish its tiny, perfect orchids.

A monstrous boulder resembling the surfacing head of Moby Dick anchors the river in the vicinity of saprophytic **pinedrops** dressed in rusty wool. This plant's slender stalks, hung with sticky bells, rise from pine needle duff, as does **heartleaf arnica**. Trailside, **northern bedstraw**'s white froth contrasts with nononsense **black-eyed Susan**.

Wild rose wafts its heavenly breath as the trail reveals its horse traffic with muddy hoof prints and "meadow muffins." Alder, aspen, and towering Colorado blue spruce enjoy moist soil, while, on the right, well-named **candle anemone**'s cone of disk flowers elongates as it matures. What appears to be a lanky cinquefoil is actually **bur avens**, named for its hooked seedhead. In the vicinity, moisture gives height to tall **coneflower** or **goldenglow** as well as **tall chiming bells**.

Cross a short boardwalk through lush vegetation to arrive at a footbridge spanning the river. A rugged outcrop nurtures rose-like **boulder raspberry**. A brief segment along the south bank quickly gives way to a bridge-assisted return to the north bank and a chance to look for **blue-eyed grass**, an iris relation.

The muddy trail curves around a huge outcrop featuring **waxflower, bracted lousewort**, and both **common** and **bracted alumroot**. Hairy stinging nettles issue a warning. Later, **beebalm** will send out a minty fragrance from a fountain of rosy-purple tubes.

A small peninsula momentarily quiets the river as the tread becomes rockier in the environs of downed timber. Damp soil welcomes big-leaved, big-headed **cow parsnip**. Watch for **wild strawberry**'s white blossoms, which will later morph into delicious fruits for wildlife, including late-summer hikers. Golden yellow snowflakes of **mountain parsley** are easy to spot, but it takes concentration to spot the pea-type, subtle white blooms of **Parry milkvetch**.

A forest campsite precedes a third bridge crossing North Fork Big Thompson. **Brookcress** relishes wet feet on the near shore. A sign posted in the shadowy earth claims private property for the next 0.25 mile. Look for **blue columbine** and **heartleaf arnica** in the dappled shade. Rising slightly, the track passes mats of **dotted** or **moss saxifrage**, their white petals marked with warm spectrum spots.

Private property respect is reinforced with the appearance of log buildings and a corral. Along here, the tight track introduces minuscule, sparsely clustered white stars of **highbush cranberry**, a member of the honeysuckle family bearing tiny edible fruit later in the summer.

The muddy trail runs close to the noisy river, entering a wet area that is home to **green bog orchid**. To the left, a moss-cloaked outcrop supports **waxflower**, an ancient relict shrub with flowers so perfectly formed they appear to be molded from porcelain. **Bracted alumroot** can be found in the rock crevices as well. **Tall chiming bells** and **twisted-stalk**, its flared bells dangling on a kinked stalk, appreciate the outcrop's damp foot. The trail rises above the river, coming upon the shiny red berries of toxic **baneberry**.

As the fourth bridge comes into view, look left, in a mossy glade between dark

BITTERBRUSH
Purshia tridentata

Bitterbrush, or **antelope-brush,** a favorite food of mule deer, is long-lived and drought-tolerant. Its fragrant, light yellow flowers are set off by subtle green, tri-toothed leaves that resemble duck feet. This branchy rose family member is common in Front Range foothills. The genus name recalls Frederick Pursh, the German botanist who catalogued the extensive plant collection of the 1804–1806 Lewis and Clark Expedition.

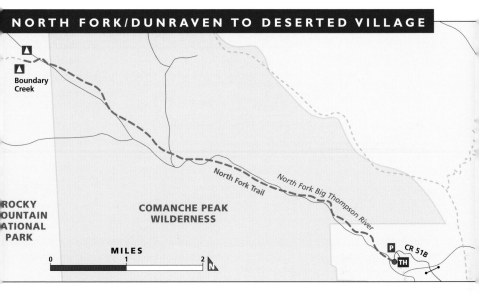

conifers, for exquisite **calypso orchid**. Alternately but endearingly named
fairyslipper orchid, these shy beauties are a find in duff-rich soil. Picking one
signs its death warrant.

On the north bank of the clear river, a sign points our route left, toward
Rocky Mountain National Park and Lost Lake, continuing our route to Deserted
Village. The cruising, road-wide track sees dark, smooth-barked river birch
guarding some bright pink **shooting stars**. Nearby, aspens abide in a Colorado
blue spruce–studded meadow, as the intoxicating fragrance of **wild rose** wafts
from a boss of many stamens surrounded by five pink petals.

Back on national forest land, the level trail runs through ponderosa pine
and open spaces that nourish **columbine, locoweed, golden banner,** and **parsley**.
Forced between closer banks, the North Fork nurtures a few **shooting stars**.
Watch for **spotted coralroot** in the ponderosa-lodgepole duff. Open spaces
encourage **wild iris, blue-eyed grass,** and spreading **pussytoes**.

Alternating between dry and wet footing, the trail comes to a fifth bridge,
returning you to the south side, which means a cooler, damper north exposure.
Pass more **heartleaf arnica**, noting that it produces few flowers. In the shaded
vicinity, a few more peerless **calypso orchids** linger.

Continue past a horse ford, finding more **coralroot orchid** and more secretive
calypsos. The next footbridge presents elegant **blue columbine**. Backcountry
campsites and another footbridge lead to an expansive meadow studded with
aspen and evergreens. The trail is reduced to a single track in the thick grasses.
This parkland sports an occasional prickly gooseberry patch, accented by **tall
Jacob's ladder**. **Wild iris** and **golden banner** adorn the sea of green.

On the far end of this broad meadowland, a lone log building—all that
is left of Lord Dunraven's 1870s hunting complex—rests its history-weary
bones. This makes a good place to turn around.

Wildflower Hike 4 ## Mount Chapin Vista Overloo

High-country splendor in Rocky Mountain National Park.

Trail Rating	moderate to strenuous
Trail Length	2.0 miles out and back
Location	Rocky Mountain National Park/Estes Park
Elevation	10,640 to 11,580 feet
Bloom Season	July to September
Peak Bloom	late July to early August
Directions	From Estes Park, take Wonderview Ave./US 34 bypass to Rocky Mountain Nation Park's Fall River entrance station. Head west on the US 34 bypass and continue 2 miles until the pavement ends. Continue 6.4 miles on Old Fall River Rd. (one-way road) to the trailhead. Park along the roadway. Fee required.

EVEN GETTING TO THE TRAILHEAD for Chapin Pass and Mount Chapin is interesting. Beginning at Endovalley on Rocky Mountain National Park's east side, Old Fall River Road winds one-way only: west and up. Hike the short, floristic trail, then drive another 2.4 miles up Old Fall River Road to the Alpine Visitors' Center. Return to Estes Park via Trail Ridge Road.

This short trail climbs immediately to Chapin Pass. After some rugged hills, the trail eases before heading up the gentle west flank of Mount Chapin to reach a fantastic overlook.

At least 70 species of wildflowers may be found along this 1-mile stretch of trail. These range from subalpine spruce-fir forest shade lovers to open-tundra sun lovers.

Even though the road is one-way, parking at the trailhead is competitive, especially on weekends.

Tall chiming bells, broadleaf arnica, arrowleaf senecio, and aptly named frosty ball thistle grow down a steep embankment near the parking area on the left side of the road. Nearby, purple fringe and Whipple penstemon cling to disturbed soil. A roadside trail kiosk sign apprising you of weather and hazards precedes a wide path shaded by big Engelmann spruce. Peeled log waterbars lift the rocky trail to a pocket garden of senecio, king's crown, blueleaf cinquefoil, and bistort. Low-growing, pink-starred pygmy bitterroot and a brush-stroke or two of rosy paintbrush add interest.

The incline lessens, but rocky and rooty best describes the trail. Subalpine firs mix in with the spruce. Barely blue delicate Jacob's ladder, off-white sickletop louse-wort, black-headed daisy, and intense, midnight blue-purple subalpine larkspur enjoy their shade.

Having climbed the couple hundred yards to Chapin Pass, find a sign directing you right (east), toward Mount Chapin. The trail drifts down to a small meadow where a few rosy paint-brush swabs survive the heavy

BLACK-HEADED DAISY
Erigeron melanocephalus

Small **black-headed daisy** may be the most common high-country fleabane. Underneath the white, narrow-rayed head, a soft collar of purplish-black hairs explains the common name. Two-to six-inch hairy stems support the solitary flowers. **One-headed daisy,** a cousin tundra dweller with reddish-purple woolly hairs and lavender rays, is sometimes found with **black-headed daisy.**

grazing by elk that frequent the area.

Cross a hewn log bridge and begin a forested climb, passing **birdfoot butter-cup**. Continue up a sidehill where **subalpine buttercup**'s poppy-type foliage frames glossy petals.

Stone steps assist an ascent where **black-headed daisy** buds display signature purplish-black hairs. Golden granite introduces elegant **Colorado blue columbine**, the state flower since 1899. **Frosty ball** or **woolly thistle** and **tall chiming bells** also bloom here.

The track eases for a look north to the Chapin Creek drainage, where elk like to graze. Head up stone steps to encounter short **greenleaf chiming bells** in intense matte blue, complemented by sunny **alpine avens**, **yellow paintbrush**, and a few **king's crown**.

Talus creates an ideal home for buns and cushions such as pink **moss campion**. A member of the pink or carnation clan, this pioneer plant may reach a decade old before blooming. **Alpine sandwort**, affectionately called **sandywinks**, creeps over and around rocks, presenting little white flowers held close to foliage so dense it feels hard. Neighboring snow willow is a prostrate creeper as well.

The narrow, rugged trail climbs steeply. A drop-off on the left calls for caution. Pause to observe the binding mastery of **whiproot clover**. Vivid orange and chartreuse lichen cling to a ragged outcrop whose crevices and pockets feature gold **pygmy tonestus**, **yellow stonecrop**, a bit of **moss campion**, and needle-leaved mats of **moss** or **dotted saxifrage**.

The trail eases past a little rockery starring creamy, typically eight-petaled **mountain dryas**, also called **white avens** and **alpine rose**. This valuable knitter of unstable lithic soil forms low, woody-stemmed mats. Its scalloped leaves are favored by ptarmigan.

Mountain or **wild candytuft** ushers in a leveling of the route. Wrap around a hill for a Mummy Range vista to the north. A meadow spattered with **orange agoseris**, **Parry clover**, **one-headed daisy**, **senecio**, and white batons of **American bistort** thrives under open skies, as do **little pink elephants** and **Whipple** or **dusky penstemon** adorning a small seasonal pond.

Continue along, looking for bright blue **greenleaf chiming bells** and ivory **narcissus-flowered anemone** decorating spruce krummholz, charmingly referred to as elfinwood. Search nearby for the delicate, glistening cups of **alplily**. The crystalline texture of its almost translucent white petals is best appreciated with a hand lens. Leave the stunted spruce to encounter a few stray **elephants**.

Weave through **horned dandelion**, **alpine avens**, and **hawkweed**. Continue along a south exposure matted with **alpine sandwort**, **clovers**, and **yarrow**, even some **harebells**. Composites abound before the trail resumes an ascent. Nearby, **elephants** and **rosy paintbrush** color a damp spot.

MOUNT CHAPIN VISTA OVERLOOK

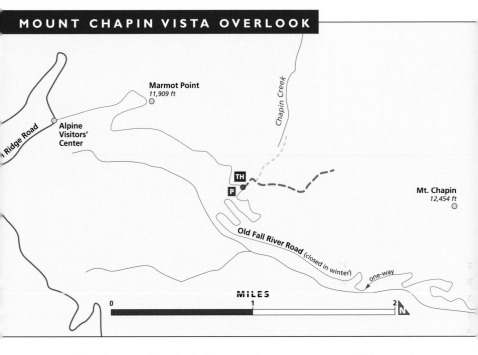

A social trail veers off to the left. Stay right to arrive at a small basin where early-season hikers found **marsh marigolds**. The rising path passes lavender **one-headed daisies** in addition to ground-hugging **alpine** and wiry **Fendler sandworts**, the latter waving white stars high above grass-like leaves.

A wildflower-strewn hillside offers more **blue columbine** and **greenleaf chiming bells**. **Alpine avens**, **whiproot clover**, and **mountain dryas** also bloom here. **Dwarf sulphurflower** puts in a matted appearance with its congested, bright umbels.

Mount Chapin's gentle west flank angles above you, while outcrops, backed by flagged spruce, send you left along a social trail to reach panoramic views. While there, look among the rocks for **bracted alumroot**, **stonecrop**, and **pygmy tonestus** as well as inch-high, creeping yellow **draba**. Up on Mount Chapin, **old man of the mountains** guards the scene with huge east-facing sunflower heads, the size of which result from many seasons' energy-gathering for its swansong blooming.

Take in the sweeping vista for a grand way to experience, at a glance, the beautiful northern reaches of Rocky Mountain National Park. Then turn around and return the way you came.

Wildflower Hike 5

Lily Lake Loop

Rocky Mountain National Park's Lily Lake.

Trail Rating	easy
Trail Length	1.0-mile loop
Location	Rocky Mountain National Park/Estes Park
Elevation	8,880 feet
Bloom Season	June to September
Peak Bloom	mid- to late June
Directions	From Estes Park, head south on CO 7 for 6 miles. Park at the visitors' center adjacent to Lily Lake.

NOT FAR SOUTH OF THE RESORT TOWN OF ESTES PARK, serene Lily Lake—repository of endangered native greenback cutthroat trout—reposes in an eastern extension of Rocky Mountain National Park. Wildflowers start blooming around mid-June, and the greenback cutthroat trout, Colorado's state fish, are in full mating hues between mid-May and mid-June. The small lake also boasts a visitors' center and views of 11,006-foot Estes Cone and 14,259-foot Longs Peak, Rocky's only fourteener. Well-sited lakeside benches invite visitors to relax.

The nearly flat 1-mile lakeside loop rests on crusher fines that, with perseverance, accommodate wheelchairs and strollers. Boardwalk planks take the path over swampy areas. Summer programs at Rocky Mountain National Park include ranger-led wildflower walks around Lily Lake.

The easy stroll, all of which concerns water or lack of it, discovers a surprising 60 species of wildflowers in late June and early July.

On weekends, parking is at a premium. Picnickers, fishermen involved in catch-and-release, and other visitors spill from a tight mass of vehicles. Late evening or early morning affords the best light and parking places. On summer afternoons, thunderstorms often brew up in the high peaks to the west.

Travel around the lake counter-clockwise by heading across a stout bridge on the right. Look in the salmon-colored granite for **boulder raspberry**, a member of the rose family whose insipid fruit—called drupes—do not live up to the snowy blossoms' promise. Gaze higher to consider the character of twisted limber pine clinging to precarious rootholds. **Wild geranium**, once sought as a birth control source by Native Americans, blooms in clear pink. Yellow is represented by **wallflower**, **golden banner**, and **cinquefoils** such as **leafy**, **beauty**, and **shrubby**. Continue into a ponderosa pine parkland of dry, open spaces spattered

CHOKECHERRY
Padus virginiana ssp. melanocarpa

In spring, rose family member chokecherry bears long, pendulous clusters of creamy-white flowers, each maturing into glossy, black berries by late summer. They are best left for wildlife such as birds and bears because the pits contain a potent cyanide agent called hydrocyanic acid, which, reportedly, can cause poisoning. Growing up to 12 feet tall, choke-cherry suckers into a shrub-like clump whose wood was once sought for musical instruments. The fruit pulp was sometimes included in pemmican. A relative is wild plum (*Prunus americana*).

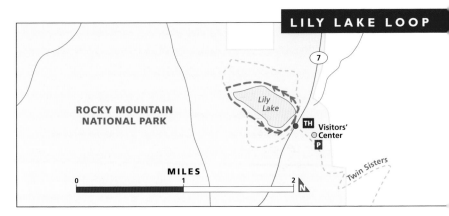

with the **sulphurflower**, more **leafy cinquefoil**, **blanketflower**, and charming white **mouse-ear**, each cleft lobe mimicking a pair of pert ears. Sporadic **silver-leaf scorpionweed** and spikes of **miner's candle** call on **scarlet paintbrush** and **locoweed** for accent.

Beyond an olfactory wealth of **wild rose**, stunted aspen and **chokecherry** lead the eye to **harebells** and **many-rayed goldenrod**. An artistic grouping of boulders introduces vermilion arrows of **narrow-leaved paintbrush**, each vivid bract spouting a green tongue—the true flower. Closer in, **northern bedstraw** froths up in white as **nodding onion** bows cool pink umbels. Indicating a restful bench, **pussytoes**, both **white** and **rosy**, emphasize a view of lofty Longs Peak.

As you curve above the water along the north shore, more **wild roses** promise perfume. **Alumroot** finds shelter in lichened outcrop crevices under a big Douglas fir.

Round another corner to reach a hefty bench located below a rugged outcrop where aptly named **waxflower** thrives in decomposing granite soil. This pink-budded, white-blossomed hydrangea family relict is sometimes called **Jamesia** in honor of Dr. Edwin James, a physician and botanist who traveled with the 1820 Stephen Long Expedition.

Another bench, this one built into a rock wall, invites you to contemplate the sheer, diamond-shaped east face of majestic Longs Peak, reflected here in Lily Lake's calm waters.

Wild strawberries adorn the wetter west shore of Lily Lake, where **white geranium** and **blue columbine** may abide. On the right, **wild blue flax** flourishes in drier soil. Its sky-blue blossoms are best seen in the early hours or on cloudy days. Native Americans used the tough stem fibers for weaving and snares.

Dry shade along the south shore suits annual **golden smoke**. Also imaginatively called **scrambled eggs**, this member of the oft-toxic fumitory clan sports poppy-like foliage and odd yellow tubes.

Continue around the lake, passing short spires of blue **lupine**. Early-season visitors found delicate pink **spring beauties** and **pasqueflowers** in this area.

A swampy area leads to yet another bench where a lakeside rock pile full of **chokecherry** and **wild rose** brings forth flat, white heads of **yarrow**. Yarrow is connected with Achilles, the Greek warrior-prince, through its Latin name *Achilles*. Legend has it that Achilles' army marched from Sparta to rescue the lovely Helen, who'd been abducted by Paris, son of the king of Troy. During a decade of fighting, Achilles made good use of yarrow's medicinal properties, using it to stanch bleeding and as an antiseptic for wounded soldiers. Yarrow's qualities were not strong enough to stem the blood flowing from our hero's vulnerable heel where Paris shot him—nevertheless, the healing herb became **woundwort**, and Achilles a legend.

Out in the open marshland, a rusty trickle supports **tall chiming bells**, **big-leaved** or **bur avens**, and perhaps a hot pink **shooting star** or two. Pause along the planks here and look back into the inner sanctum of Rocky Mountain National Park's cadre of impressive peaks. A fishing landing cues a watch for complementary **wild iris** and **golden banner**. Mid-summer conjures up **fireweed** as you conclude the Lily Lake circuit.

Crusher fines line the Lily Lake loop.

Wildflower Hike 6

Cascade Creek

Cascade Creek boasts a pair of grand waterfalls.

Trail Rating	moderate
Trail Length	9.6 miles out and back
Location	Arapaho National Recreation Area/Indian Peaks Wilderness/Granby
Elevation	8,340 to 9,500 feet
Bloom Season	June to September
Peak Bloom	July
Directions	From Denver, head west on I-70. Take exit 232 for US 40 W. Merge onto County Road 255, then make a slight right at US 40 and continue 46.5 miles to make a right at US 34, just past the town of Granby. Travel 5.5 miles, then go right on Frontage Road 125/Arapaho Bay Rd. for 9.4 miles to reach the Monarch Lake trailhead.

CASCADE CREEK TRAIL not only spotlights a pair of spectacular waterfalls, but also qualifies as a "century" hike, with well over 100 wildflower species. Boots make water and rock hazards easier to navigate. This 4.8-mile trek begins with a flat cruise past Monarch Lake and its surrounding meadows. The trail then begins rising through forest and gets increasingly steeper and rockier, reaching the plunging lower falls at 3.5 miles. Expect an even steeper push to Upper Cascade Falls. Parking at this popular trailhead comes at a premium for late arrivals.

From the parking area, stroll to a huge sign at the head of Monarch Lake, listing Cascade Creek Falls 4.5 miles ahead. The singletrack trail starts wildflowering off with **mountain parsley, heartleaf arnica,** and **Colorado blue columbine.** Willows nurture **white geranium, tall chiming bells,** and, among archaic horsetails, **shooting stars** and rosy **shortstyle onion.** Look in aspen and evergreen shade for **wintercress.**

As you pass by deep conifer duff, look for reddish-stemmed **spotted coralroot,** its miniature orchids sporting a red-spotted white lip. Unable to produce chlorophyll, the contorted coral-like roots derive nourishment from soil fungi, as do late-emerging **pinedrops.**

Trickling rills touch the path where **white bog orchid** rises tall and fragrant in the company of **yellow monkeyflower,** whose leaves were once used as salad greens and to make rope burn ointment, and **pink pyrola,** whose straight stalk dangles scalloped parasols.

Boulders shaded by lodgepole pines are garnished with dainty **twinflower**'s paired, blushed bells rising on wiry stems over round-leaved mats. Overlooking the lake, a slope of pink **wild rose** wafts intoxicating perfume.

Red-osier dogwood's sleek red bark contrasts with its minuscule white flower clusters where the trail negotiates an elfin waterfall. A tumbled rock slope towers over sparkling Monarch Lake, which reflects the rugged, snow-creased Continental Divide. Outcrops on the left support **bluemist penstemon, bracted alumroot,** and **creamy buckwheat.** Nearby, look for **highbush cranberry** and **chokecherry.** A rugged prow is anchored by tall, rosy **wand penstemon.**

Look low in the ensuing forest for **green-flowered wintergreen** rising from rounded basal leaves. Upcoming aspen offer **green gentian,** or **monument plant.** A little farther on, Buchanan Creek pours into the lake's east end.

Clumps of purple-budded **cutleaf fleabane daisy** decorate a dark rockfall as the trail rises to view the amber creek, which almost qualifies as a river. After passing **false Solomon's seal, dogbane,** and budding **fireweed,** the track descends to river level. Crossing a bog on stones reveals **brookcress** and **twistedstalk.**

Spruce gives way to meadow, encouraging **showy loco**'s display of hot pink beaks. By an Indian Peaks Wilderness sign, late summer finds **Parry** or **Rocky Mountain gentian**'s deep blue chalices. Nearby, **alpine milkvetch** trails pea-type flowers tinged steely purple. Look in deep, spruce-shaded duff for **calypso orchid**, an exquisite early bloomer.

Following Buchanan's curving waters, the trail pulls up, undulating as it passes proud **aspen sunflowers** and wild **sarsaparilla**. An outcrop garlanded in mats of delicate **twinflower** cradles **bracted alumroot**. Look left for more **blue columbine.**

At a junction where Southside Trail goes right, continue straight ahead on Cascade Creek Trail. S-curves take our route up and away from the water. Damp forest openings foster rosy-red **shortstyle onion**, joined by **monkshood**, **green bog orchid**, and **purple avens**.

A drier area introduces **mountain death camas**, bent like a shepherd's crook in bud, straightening in full bloom. Trailside, leafy **thimbleberry**, parsimonious with its white blossoms, shelters demure **Canada violet.**

The stream returns in a white fury to accompany the ascending trail. Switchbacks herald the water's rush through a narrow gorge. Continue along dry slopes featuring **narrow-leaved paintbrush**, **harebells**, **creamy buckwheat**, and **wand penstemon**. Scraggly aspens share terrain with **velvety buckbrush.**

Cross a sturdy bridge spanning a stream from Hell Canyon. Dancing aspens replace stolid evergreens as switchbacks curve the trail past a brook. Look for **blue rock clematis** sprawling on its far side.

Cruise beside Buchanan Creek after more switchbacks. Giant boulders form a heavy landscape where tiger swallowtails and fritillaries flutter lightly. Lodgepole pines make way not only for **blue columbine**, but

BROWNIE LADY'S SLIPPER
Cypripedium fasciculatum

Brownie lady's slipper is uncommon, endangered, and hard to spot in deep coniferous shade, making it quite a find. Often hiding under a pair of substantial, broad, polished leaves about 6 inches long, the brownish-purple, veined flowers, each with a lower-petal sac, appear in clusters of two to four, hence the alternate name **clustered lady's slipper.** The Latin genus name *Cypripedium,* derived from the Greek words for Venus (*Kypris*) and foot (*pes*), arrives at a third moniker: **Venus' Slipper.** Also uncommon—and rapidly becoming more so—is cousin **yellow lady's slipper** (*Cypripedium calceous ssp. parviflorum*).

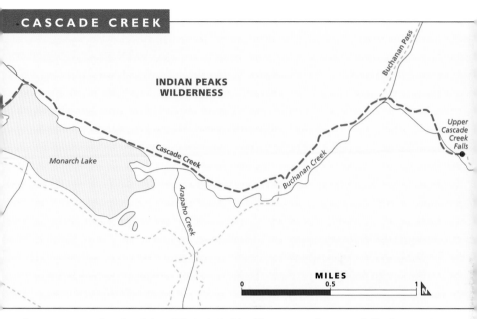

also **western red columbine**. Their hybrid offspring are large and display pink tints. Among **candle anemones**, multitudes of feathery seed plumes relate **pasqueflower**'s early bloom.

Willow and alders lead to Stone Shelter wilderness campsite, where **mule's ears'** resin-shiny, emerald leaves frame their sunflower faces. Watch for a junction sign continuing our Cascade Creek Trail straight ahead. Buchanan Pass Trail goes left.

A bit stony underfoot, Cascade Creek Trail passes **pearly everlasting** and golden snowflakes of **mountain parsley** before reaching a bridge over noisy Buchanan Creek. Before crossing, pause to look for blooms on a **mountain ash** tree bending over **tall chiming bells**.

The trail leaves Buchanan Creek behind and picks up Cascade Creek. The roaring waterway squeezes through a narrow gorge, creating thundering waterfalls. Exercise caution when maneuvering to view them.

As whitewater courses down, the trail grinds up over a brief, steep, rocky segment before easing to rise past a willow-choked meadow trumpeting **little pink elephants**. **Mountain blue violets** lead to a pocket of unforgettable **calypso orchids** on the left. In deep spruce shade, the keen eye may spot rather rare **brownie lady's slipper**, sporting outsized glossy leaves. Each cluster of purplish-brown flowers also suggests the name **clustered lady's slipper**.

From above, the snarling falls are pussycat quiet as the gold-bedded creek heralds an ascent to a meadow of **tall chiming bells**, **white geranium**, and **white bog orchid**. Flanking the track are tall **larkspur** and ferny-leafed **Porter's lovage**, a veritable pharmacy for early native peoples. Look for **blue columbine**'s large blooms and sweet white **mouse-ear**'s small ones.

Mountains poke teasingly above the treetops while cool **western paint-brush** leads toward a specimen or two of **purple fringe** and fading **bracted lousewort**. Pass a beaver dam, keeping an eye out for **pink-headed daisies**. Arcs of glossy-leaved **false Solomon's seal** are harbingers of the ragged ramparts to come.

Pass a sign that reads, "No campfires beyond this point." Progress to a log bridge overlooking a gilded waterway set with gem islands sparkling in whites of **brookcress** and **bog orchid** along with pinks of **elephants** and **pink willowherb**.

Beavers are responsible for a trailside pond reflecting a stiff outcrop enriched by **scarlet paintbrush**. In view of the next cascade, vegetation crowds the rocky track as it climbs under open skies.

Upper Cascade Creek Falls are simply smashing. Embraced as they are by 11,938-foot Thunderbolt Peak and 12,649-foot Mount Achonee, the falls epitomize high-country energy.

The falls' foreground plateau area accommodates **blue columbine**, **subalpine daisy**, **paintbrush**, and **blue rock clematis**. Dotting the soil are the distinctive tri-parted seed capsules of early-blooming **glacier lily**. The thundering falls of Cascade Creek signal the turnaround point.

Calypso orchids are also called fairyslippers.

High Lonesome/ Betty and Bob Lakes

Wildflower Hike 7

Stunning floral displays define this trail, which passes by three lakes.

moderate to strenuous	**Trail Rating**
3.6 miles out and back	**Trail Length**
Rollins/Corona Pass/Winter Park	**Location**
11,220 to 11,671 feet	**Elevation**
July to September	**Bloom Season**
late July to early August	**Peak Bloom**
From Denver, take I-70 west. Exit north on US 40. Just past Winter Park Ski Area, turn right on dirt Moffat Rd./Frontage Road 149. Trailhead is 15 miles ahead, at Rollins Pass.	**Directions**

IN MID- TO LATE SUMMER the hike to Betty and Bob Lakes is a trek through a beautiful wildflower kingdom. Located east of Winter Park near the Continental Divide, this route passes three lovely lakes. A whole season's worth of flora may be viewed along the way.

The trail begins atop Corona Pass and eases along High Lonesome/Continental Divide Trail before descending quickly to King Lake. It then snakes down to a creek before ascending to Betty Lake. A final uphill push takes you to Bob Lake. Gains and losses at high elevation earn this hike a more strenuous rating. Boots are a boon.

About 80 species of high-country wildflowers grace the trek during peak bloom.

Parking is generous at historic Rollins Pass.

Except during its brief gem-like bloom in early summer, the tundra beyond the trail kiosk sign displays brave old standbys such as **American bistort** and yellow **paintbrush**. Tidy-clumped lavender **cutleaf fleabane daisy**, long-blooming **alpine avens**, and tight-mounded **alpine sandwort** appear as well.

Walk north along the wide, stony path, passing tenacious buns of pink **moss campion** and little-noticed **sibbaldia** patches with strawberry-like leaves. Erect **little rose gentian** decorates the rocky ground.

An old foundation on the right precedes an Indian Peaks Wilderness sign. As the track flattens, a stolid gray ridge, sutured by the High Lonesome Trail, appears ahead. **Parry clover** bloom by **yellow paintbrush**, alpine avens, **bistort**, and bicolored, soil-knitting **whiproot clover**. You might hear that rabbit relative and rockpile resident, the pika, a pip-squeak with an attention-getting voice.

A second sign aims you right, down to King Lake, now visible below. Early-blooming **sky pilot** lines the descending, rocky path. Lingering snowbanks suit **snow buttercup**. Spikes of rock-loving, brick-red **alpine sorrel** sport rounded, kidney-shaped leaves—an ultra-sour, vitamin C–charged snack.

GOLDBLOOM SAXIFRAGE
Hirculus serpyllifolius ssp. chrysantha

Goldbloom saxifrage is found in gravelly soil at elevations of 11,000 feet and above. Its smooth leaves form solid mats. Vivid yellow cups are centered with a pedestal pistil that begins cool yellow, then ripens to a strong red. The erect blossoms sport an orange dot on each sepal.

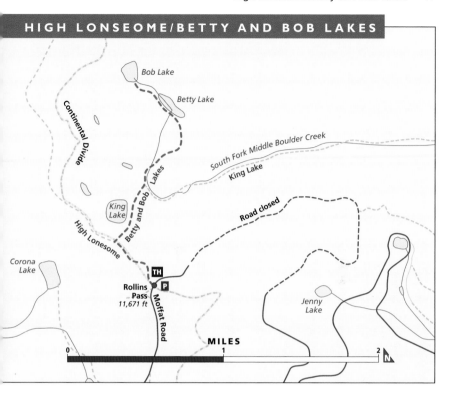

HIGH LONSEOME/BETTY AND BOB LAKES

Plush clump grasses may tout a **little pink elephant** or two as well as the most common fleabane of the high country: woolly-collared **black-headed daisy**. **Alpine** or **single harebell** also blooms here. The sharp eye may discover tender-white **alplily**, with its six crystalline petals and improbably narrow leaves.

Small rivers of coarse stones flow down to trailside banks overhung with **moss campion**, **alpine sandwort**, and **pygmy tonestus**. Patches of subshrub **mountain dryas** or **white avens** serve as tundra armor.

The descent toward King Lake presents a hillside plethora of summer's last hurrah, **arctic gentian**. Its almost translucent white chalices are striated dark purple on the outside, giving it a striped appearance. In the vicinity, look for **goldbloom saxifrage**, **king's crown**, and **greenleaf chiming bells**.

Granite boulders' bases are places to look for **moss campion**, **delicate Jacob's ladder**, and **bigroot** or **alpine spring beauty**. The latter may have a root 2–3 yards long to accommodate the shifting of its rocky roothold.

Evening out through willow and spruce krummholz on a north exposure, the trail reveals late bloomers such as gold **whiplash saxifrage** and cousin **moss** or **dotted saxifrage**. Outcrops suit **king's crown**, **greenleaf chiming bells**, **blue columbine**, **alpine avens**, and **bracted alumroot**. A tad of power-pink **Parry primrose** and **frosty ball thistle** join in for a mosaic effect.

Great sweeps of **rosy paintbrush** zing the lake's grassy south edge. The path is fairly level now, passing ungiving mounds of yellowish-green **nailwort**. As you pass into spruce krummholz, the sound of the lake's outlet babbles into little King Lake. Above it all, the Continental Divide forms a 180-degree pewter arc.

Drop on rockier footing along an s-curve, passing **whiproot clover, yellow stonecrop**, and **old man of the mountains**. Pocket rock gardens lead to a great overlook where **goldenrod** supplants early-blooming **sky pilot**.

The trail, trough-like now, leads to cool pink **subalpine daisy**. Before another s-curve arrives, look in a marshy zone for **little pink elephants** heralding tall **bracted lousewort, arrowleaf senecio, tall chiming bells**, and lovely **blue columbine**. A little meadow fills with **tall scarlet paintbrush, rosy paintbrush**, and their hybrid offspring.

WHIPLASH SAXIFRAGE
Saxifraga flagellaris

Bright red runners and bristly hairs outlining rosetted leaves are diagnostic of golden-yellow **whiplash saxifrage.** This denizen of gravelly, rocky tundra does not depend on seeds alone, but roots its stolons at the tips. Ripe seed capsules are red.

Colorful, lush glades accompany a steepening descent and rougher footing. Look for globular, off-green bursts of **Grays angelica**. The trail levels a bit where delicate **Jacob's ladder** and **sickletop lousewort** bloom among flagged spruce. Talus brings on **arrowleaf senecio** and **tall chiming bells**. **Black-headed daisies** and **pygmy bitterroot** also bloom here, soon to be followed by **fireweed**.

Step down to burbling Middle Boulder Creek. Head downstream to cross on well-aligned stones. Step past islands of lacy **cowbane**, hairy **subalpine arnica**, and plain **bog saxifrage** and its airy cousin, **brook saxifrage**. **Rosy paintbrush** and **bistort** bloom creekside.

A sign sends you left, up toward Betty and Bob Lakes. In the vicinity, check for **little pink elephants, subalpine arnica, bracted lousewort**, and **homely buttercup**.

Look along disturbed trailsides for smaller flowers, such as both **milky** and **pink willowherbs**, blue **alpine veronica**, and **alpine violet**. Among boulders, look for **subalpine buttercup** with its poppy-like foliage. Both cool pink **subalpine** daisy and **pink-headed daisy**, along with **mouse-ear**, **alpine chickweed**, and **alpine bistort**, accompany the rising trail.

Wind up through **tall scarlet paintbrush** and **Whipple penstemon**, creamy-mauve here. Push through contorted, stunted spruces and willow to top a ridge decorated with a rock garden of buns, mats, and cushions. Sneak a glimpse of Lake Betty's serene waters through boggy willow where **little pink elephants**, dusky purple **star gentian**, and rosy-pink **queen's crown** thrive. Crossing the stream that feeds Betty Lake can be a challenge.

The lake's west shore features more willows and stunted spruce along with **elephants**, **cinquefoil**, **senecio**, and cool yellow **western paintbrush**. About halfway along the level stretch above Betty Lake, find a **scarlet paintbrush** pocket near a water-filled pit of jumbled rock on the left. A cairn to the right keeps you on track. Stay left of the cairn and climb a brief incline with no discernible trail.

Once on top of the short pitch, regain the faint trail accessing Bob Lake. Where snowbanks lingered, look for penstemon-related **snowlover** sporting eggshell-hued tubes with singed tips. A majestic granite wall rises over a thousand feet above the lake; a corniced snowfield feeds the icy waters. Rock interspersed with grassy tundra gives way to **little pink elephants, yellow paintbrush, bistort, alpine avens, subalpine daisy,** and **tall chiming bells**. After you've stopped to smell the flowers, return the way you came.

Scarlet paintbrush lead the way north to Betty and Bob Lakes.

*Wildflower
Hike 8* Ceran St. Vrain

*In early June,
calypso orchids
bloom just
beyond the
footbridge span-
ning South
St. Vrain Creek.*

THE CERAN ST. VRAIN TRAIL was named after Ceran St. Vrain, an
accomplished Colorado mountain man and trader who lived from 1802 to
1870. It parallels South St. Vrain Creek, named for the same man. Located
not far from Boulder, in the Roosevelt National Forest, this hike is known
for early-season calypso orchid displays and student camping. Early to mid-
June is the time to look for orchids, while later June or early July brings on
about five dozen wildflower species.

Parking is adequate on weekdays, but on weekends, walk-in
campers and hikers can fill the lot quickly.

Trail Rating	easy to moderate
Trail Length	4.0 miles out and back
Location	Roosevelt National Forest/Boulder/Jamestown
Elevation	8,000 to 8,300 feet
Bloom Season	June to October
Peak Bloom	June to July
Directions	From Boulder, head north on US 36 for 5 miles. Turn left down Lefthand Canyon Dr. Stay right on County Road 94 when the road forks at about 5 miles. Continue for 4.5 miles, passing through Jamestown. About 0.5 mile after the pavement ends, take a right onto James Canyon Dr. and continue for 0.25 mile to the trailhead.

Robust with spring runoff, South St. Vrain Creek surges over bedrock at the trailhead, scouring the granitic stone smooth. A handsome, sturdy bridge spans the waterway, putting hikers on the shaded north bank. Rugged outcrops present intoxicating **wild rose**, while forest duff exhibits saprophytic **pinedrops**. The same duff habitat suits **spotted coralroot orchid**, also unable to produce chlorophyll and dependent on decaying organic material for nutrients. Early-season hikers encounter **mountain blue violet** and **cutleaf fleabane daisy** in this rich environment.

The deep duff also nurtures a goodly number of unforgettable **calypso** or **fairyslipper orchids** in early June. Each pink confection secretes a light fragrance, perhaps like its namesake, Calypso, the Greek sea nymph of Homer's *Odyssey*. Individual bulbs have two divisions: one half produces the single leaf, the other half the blossom. Picking a calypso bloom destroys the whole plant.

Down to the right, look for a little island sporting any number of wildflower species, such as **cow parsnip**, **brookcress**, and less common **purple avens**, a member of the rose clan. Also anchoring the island's marshy end are **tall chiming bells** and **shooting stars**.

Follow the trail down to a lush hillside of lovely **blue columbine**, each blossom exuding a sweet honeysuckle scent. Petal spurs ending in nectar-filled knobs make burglars out of bees, which have been known to nip a hole in the bulb to steal the sweet liquid without paying the favor of pollination. Hummingbird bills are perfect for the rewarding chore of fertilization. **Fireweed** will inflame this hillside later in the summer. It is said that baby eagles fledge when fireweed blooms.

The trail rises gently, passing moss-and-lichen-cloaked boulders whose niches and crannies are crammed with **bracted alumroot** and shrubs of lightly fragrant **waxflower**, a member of hydrangea's ancient family lineage. Lightly scented **twinflower** creeps along the forest floor in round-leaved mats, its paired, pink-blushed bells dangling from bare, thin, forked stems. In the vicinity, look for wintergreen **prince's pine**, or **pipsissewa**, its baby-pink parasols perching over dark, leathery leaves.

Lodgepole pine, particularly in doghair density, usually creates a poverty-stricken understory. Here it supports **heartleaf arnica** and **coralroot** as the track pulls up and away from the creek. The steep, mossy upside slope is luxuriated in early-blooming **calypsos**, each maturing into a round seed capsule.

Head down a steep pitch toward the fast-moving water. The towering outcrop wall tucks **waxflower**, **bracted alumroot**, and fern into its crevices. **Wild rose** adds its perfume.

A rivulet trickles in from the left where **Canada violet** flourishes. Ascend a rocky segment, where the dry high side nurtures **stonecrop**, **whiplash fleabane daisy**, and velvety purple **skullcap**. Midsummer will add **goldenrod** to the list. Where the track undulates along, **pasqueflowers** bloomed earlier, leaving visible evidence in plumy seedheads.

Alder-dappled shade near a second little seasonal tributary exhibits blowzy **cow parsnip** and, later, a profusion of vivid **fireweed**. Look along dry sections for **spreading dogbane**, an oleander

WAXFLOWER
Jamesia americana

Waxflower is found most often in the foothills and montane life zones, typically in the company of rocks. Leaf fossils provide evidence of this shrub's 35-million-year-old origins. This lanky member of the hydrangea family produces delicately fragrant, porcelain-perfect flowers of five petals and ten stamens. Matte leaves that turn soft rosy-red in fall are distinctly veined, almost puckered; underneath, they are white. **Waxflower's** genus name honors Edwin James, a young surgeon and naturalist who collected plants on the 1820 Major Stephen Long Expedition. Not only did Dr. James discover a plethora of new plants—including the Colorado state flower, **blue columbine**—but he was also the first white man to summit 14,110-foot Pikes Peak.

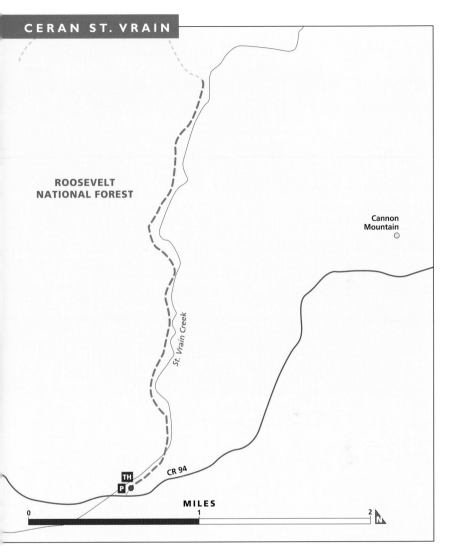

CERAN ST. VRAIN

ROOSEVELT
NATIONAL FOREST

Cannon
Mountain

St. Vrain Creek

TH
P

CR 94

MILES

0   1   2   N

relation with dainty, blushed bells. Other nearby xerics include **sulphurflower**, **blanketflower**, and **scorpionweed**. Damper places nurture **black-eyed Susan**, **homely buttercup**, **meadow anemone**, and even **pink pyrola**.

The trail drops to talkative South St. Vrain Creek's inviting shore, where an old road crosses a ford. This makes a good turnaround point.

Wildflower Hike 9

Sleepy Lion Loop

Acres of milkvetch and magenta locoweed reward the elevation gain along Sleepy Lion Loop.

Trail Rating	moderate to strenuous
Trail Length	5.5-mile balloon loop
Location	Button Rock Preserve/Lyons
Elevation	5,940 to 6,650 feet
Bloom Season	June to September
Peak Bloom	mid-June
Directions	Head north out of Boulder on US 36/CO 7. Continue on US 36 until you are about 4 miles past Lyons. Take a left on CR 80 and continue 2.8 miles to the trailhead.

A TRAIL OF VARIED TERRAIN AND FLORAL SURPRISES, Sleepy Lion Loop at Button Rock Preserve is a bit challenging in places and feels longer than its 5.5 miles might suggest. However, this foot-traffic-only trail sees less use than many foothills life zone trails, and that in itself is gratifying to the wildflower lover.

The trail begins riverside on a wide roadway, then turns uphill sharply, crossing a flowery table to zigzag down to a rugged drainage before rejoining the roadway on its return. This loop gains its "strenuous" designation due to a short streamside segment. Wear sturdy boots, and be prepared for wet, uneven footing.

Over 80 species of wildflowers grow along the Sleepy Lion Trail. A peak-bloom hike during a sufficiently wet year is highlighted by a tableland crossing flanked with a nonstop display of locoweed and milkvetch.

The preserve's popularity makes parking difficult on good-weather weekends. Arrive early to secure a spot and beat afternoon thunderstorm activity.

With the rush of North St. Vrain Creek—more like a river here—in your ears, pass a metal gate and stroll down the broad gravel roadway paralleling the water. **Bush sunflower** and dark blue **larkspur** light up the granite along the north bank.

Drystack stone walls support an old aqueduct as it shoulders its way through the rocky canyon. Later in the summer **bouncing Bet**, an import soapwort, will smother the rainbow lichens now seen covering the sheer cliff near a spillway depression.

To your right, **chokecherry** blooms wane as snowy blossoms of **boulder raspberry** flourish beside Longmont Reservoir's serene waters. Sculpted outcrops on the left tuck **waxflower** shrubs into their worn crevices.

Pass the reservoir, continuing along the red-bedded river. **Boulder raspberry**, **waxflower**, **chokecherry**, and **ninebark** glisten in a dark canyon to your right. In the meadowy vale to your left, lichened formations overlook **bluemist penstemon**, **mountain parsley**, and beautiful **blue columbine**.

At the 1-mile point, Sleepy Lion Trail leaves the road and climbs left (south) up a gulch. North St. Vrain Creek sounds fade as the trail climbs steadily. Look for pink **wild geranium** at a broad hairpin turn.

The route traces an old wagon road supported by drystack stone walls. Near ponderosa pines, look for **tall pussytoes** and **James starwort**. Later in the season, **silvery cinquefoil** will bloom trailside. Clinging to rough, crumbling granite, **antelope** or bitterbrush puts out numerous pale yellow flowers among duckfoot-shaped leaves.

Come alongside a saddle arrayed in vivid **Lambert's** or **Colorado locoweed**, which is toned down by **death camas** and pale **lupine**. Look trailside for ground-hugging **pussytoes**. Nearby, deeply divided palmate leaves and dusty pink, plumed seedheads attest to **pasqueflowers'** past purple glory. Farther along, an occasional subtle white **Drummond milkvetch** or bright white **mouse-ear** accents a golden hillside of **meadow arnica** and **cinquefoil**.

Your effort is about to be rewarded as the trail pitches up steeply, then bursts from the pines onto a glorious tableland tapestry. Acres of pale ivory **Drummond milkvetch** team up with hot magenta **locoweed** for a pea family reunion. When **meadow arnica** fades, electric blue **Geyer larkspur** will charge the accent scheme. Granite formations and forest frame the flower-filled landscape.

Passing pink granite boulders, the track slowly rises to meet orange-barked ponderosas again. A sniff of the tree's bark hints at vanilla—the scent reportedly repels marauding insects.

DRUMMOND MILKVETCH
Astragalus drummondii

Drummond milkvetch's bushy, profusely hairy, gray-green foliage supports racemes of off-white pea-type flowers cupped by hairy sepals. Xeric habitats suit this prolific milkvetch, one of 100 or so in its family to be found in the Rockies; there are over 1,600 species of milkvetch worldwide. This wild-flower gets its name from Scotsman Thomas Drummond, a plant collector from Canada who gathered specimens while exploring with the Franklin Party in the early 1800s.

Rocks dominate as the trail drops from a ridge through stunted pines and a few Douglas firs. The roughening path dips only to rise again, passing **blue-mist penstemon** and **skullcap**. Listen for the muffled growl of rushing water as you pass pocket rock gardens dotted with strong-smelling **canyon aletes**, a low-growing yellow member of the parsley family.

Switchbacking and rolling hills lead to a vantage point far above the Button Rock Dam and the green waters of Ralph Price Reservoir. Follow hiker-icon posts through iron gates and to an old road headed down-hill. Decomposed granite takes over trailside as the road turns, passing more **aletes, Fendler senecio**, and **wallflower**—all blooming yellow.

The descending path follows a creek shaded by aspen and lush vegetation. **Boulder raspberry** and **ninebark** flourish in this stream-watered ravine. Keep an

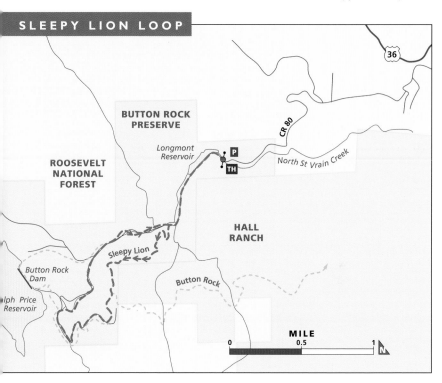

eye out for **wild sarsaparilla**, a member of the ginseng family spouting emerald fireworks. The spherical flowering head bursts over a bare stalk like a green Sputnik.

As you continue along the rockbound descent, look for **few-flowered false Solomon's seal**, or more succinctly **star Solomon's seal**, prospering in shady environs. Wet places are preferred habitat for the exotic arrows of bright pink **shooting stars**. Carefully pick your way down, choosing between wet rocks and old concrete steps—footing is slippery here.

The trail emerges from the ravine near the thundering dam outflow—a rage of impounded fury shooting concentrated whitewater like a gargantuan fire hose. A 2-mile saunter down the level road takes you back to your vehicle.

Canyon Loop at Betasso Preserve

Flurries of Rocky Mountain phlox settle beside the Canyon Loop trail in June.

Trail Rating	easy to moderate
Trail Length	2.75-mile loop
Location	Betasso Preserve/Boulder
Elevation	6,000 to 6,600 feet
Bloom Season	May to September
Peak Bloom	late May to June
Directions	From Denver, take CO 36 into Boulder. Turn left (west) onto Canyon Blvd./CR 119. After about 6 miles, go right on Sugarloaf Rd./County Road 122. Take another right onto Betasso Rd. Park at the eastern trailhead.

BOULDER COUNTY purchased what is now the Betasso Preserve from the ranching Betasso family in 1976. The undulating land cradles varied plant communities and makes a fine place for an early-season hike. It is underlain by one of the oldest rock types in Boulder County—1.7 billion-year-old Boulder Creek granodiorite, famed for its rich mineral deposits.

Canyon Loop offers 50 or so wildflower species on its 2.75-mile circuit, including stellar late-spring displays of Rocky Mountain phlox.

At the east trailhead, parking space is shared with picnickers. Early arrivals get choice spaces and avoid rambunctious afternoon thunderstorms. It also behooves the hiker to keep a sharp eye and ear out for rocketing mountain bikers.

Head north on Canyon Loop Trail along a declining slope. A view of the University of Colorado at Boulder's red roofs opens to the east. Drift down a wide, pine-flanked path of decomposing Boulder Creek granodiorite, where pink **Rocky Mountain phlox** and perky white **mouse-ear** create a fairyland flowerscape. **Bluemist penstemon**, **early larkspur**, **chiming bells**, **cutleaf fleabane daisy**, **whiskbroom parsley**, **yellow violets**, and **wallflower** provide accent colors.

As the path continues through the pine shade, watch for **spotted coralroot orchid**. Warming days bring on **sulphurflower** and **golden aster**, followed by **bush sunflower**, a sandpapery perennial. **Wild rose** perfumes summer breezes, which riffle plumed seedheads of early-blooming **pasqueflower**. Other early birds in the vicinity—**sand lilies**, **mountain** or **wild candytuft**, and daisy-like **early Townsendia**—bloom in white. **Golden banner** adds its pea-type flowers. Usually the first spring foothills life zone wildflower to bloom is refined pink **spring beauty**, a member of the purslane clan.

WHORLED MONARDA
Sidalcea candida

Whorled monarda's whorls of two-lipped flowers look like a circle of white geese about to take flight from a bristly merry-go-round. This mint family member shares lineage with sage, rosemary, and thyme. Serving as a cough and skin ailment remedy, monarda honors Nicolas Monardes, a Spanish physician and botanist who wrote about medicinal herbs in the 16th Century. **Spotted beebalm,** an additional common name, refers to golden glands of volatile oils that dot the leaves.

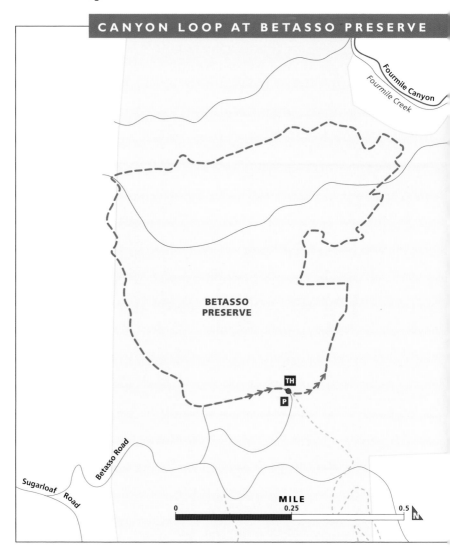

CANYON LOOP AT BETASSO PRESERVE

Fourmile Canyon

Fourmile Creek

BETASSO
PRESERVE

TH
P

Betasso Road

Sugarloaf Road

MILE
0   0.25   0.5
N

    The trail follows a gentle slope, replete with fragrant **phlox** and **ninebark** shrubs. It then narrows and passes through a small open area where the scented heads of pastel **purple field milkvetch** decorate the right side of the path. Heading west now, pass a north slope featuring Douglas fir. A seasonal trickle waters the brief but bright blooming of hot pink **shooting stars**.

    The gradient increases, passing shade-loving **Canada violet** and **snowball saxifrage**. Nearby, flurries of **Rocky Mountain phlox** sprinkle the earth with pastel stars on mats of needle-like leaves. Pass by shallow draws where graceful **chokecherry** racemes follow the cloying perfume of **wild plum**, which typically blooms before leafing out; chokecherry leafs out before it flowers.

Follow alongside a dry, south-facing slope where **sand onion**, **spiderwort**, **yellow violets**, and **wild blue flax** grow. Early in the day—or all day if it is cool and cloudy—the latter's five fragile petals look like azure silk; heat drops them, but numerous buds open over a long period.

Prickly pear cactus, **yucca**, and **whorled monarda**, an annual beebalm cousin, also thrive on this xeric hillside. Watch trail edges for tiny-flowered **pinnate-leaf** or **sticky gilia**.

After topping a short, steep section of the trail, catch your breath by a stand of ponderosa pines, keeping an eye out for clear magenta **Lambert's locoweed**, sunny yellow **cinquefoil**, and luminous **orchid penstemon**. In the summer, look for **beebalm**.

The trail heads uphill to arrive at a sprawling view of Boulder Valley and a junction with an abandoned road. Turn left. Under wide skies, follow the waterbar-assisted trail toward a broad grassy meadow. Look for signs letting you know that the Canyon loop is still underfoot.

Proceed to a junction. Turn left (east) down Betasso Road to return to your vehicle. An ethereal garden of sweet-smelling **phlox** and notch-petaled **mouse-ear** accompany you along this final stretch.

Rocky Mountain phlox presents pink stars in spring.

Wildflower Hike 11

Anne U. White

The scenic Anne U. White Trail is practically on Boulder's north doorstep.

Trail Rating	easy
Trail Length	3.5 miles out and back
Location	Boulder County Open Space/Boulder
Elevation	6,040 to 6,540 feet
Bloom Season	May to October
Peak Bloom	late May to early June
Directions	From Boulder, head north on North Broadway. Turn left down Lee Hill Dr. and continue 1 mile. Head left for 1 mile down Wagon Wheel Gap. Turn left at mailbox/"no outlet" sign. Continue 0.1 mile to trailhead. Park on the right (north) side of the road, being mindful of the private property. Biking prohibited on trail.

ANNE U. WHITE is a pretty, water-accompanied surprise of a trail. Practically on Boulder's north doorstep, this pleasant hike leads up Fourmile Canyon beside the creek of the same name. This 1.75-mile long trail is named for local environmentalist Anne U. White, who was instrumental in preserving access land flanking Fourmile Canyon Creek.

The mostly flat trail's challenge is its nearly two dozen crossings of said creek. Boots help grip slippery stones strategically placed in the stream. The Anne U. White Trail ends at a boundary sign with private property behind it.

Late May offers about four dozen wildflower species, while early June may add another dozen. Playing leapfrog with the creek brings about encounters with both riparian species and those preferring drier habitats.

Parking is extremely limited. Try for a hike on a weekday. Be mindful of the private residence at the trailhead.

Granite slopes studded with ponderosa pines greet you at the trailhead. Look up the decomposed granite bank on the right for rich blue **spiderwort**, **orchid penstemon**, and sunny **wallflower**. Respecting the private property sign, check near its base for bushy, palmate-leaved **Geyer larkspur**, an electrifying blue June bloomer. The Anne U. White trailhead signpost is encircled by alien **bouncing Bet**, a weedy soapwort escapee from old miners' gardens.

Accompanied by creek sounds, head west into the snug canyon. Pink **wild geranium**, once prized as a potherb, talks color with **wallflower**, a scented mustard tinted yellow, gold, and burnt orange. By mid-summer, mint tribesman **beebalm**'s rosy-lilac fountainheads will attract bees and butterflies.

Plush patches of **wild raspberry** guarded by poison ivy flank the trail as it approaches the Fourmile Canyon Creek. **Bluemist penstemon** and later-blooming **prickly pear cactus** find a footing on tweed-textured granite outcrops. As you saunter along, be on the lookout for white "sports" or mutants of **bluemist penstemon**. Looking like thick antlers, **smooth sumac** harbors colonies of fuzzy-foliaged **waterleaf** and **few-flowered false Solomon's seal** or **star Solomon's seal**. **Meadow anemone**'s demure, white, five-petaled cups top long-necked stems rising from a collar of dark green, deep-toothed leaves.

The trail's decomposed granite foot bed makes for good walking even after a rain. Tenacious poison ivy's characteristic three-part glossy leaves are evident, emerging bronze before turning green. Heed the saying . . . "leaves of three, leave them be."

Golden banner complements **early larkspur** as the trail comes up on huge granite outcrops splotched with gray, greenish, and orange lichens. A partnership of algae and fungus, lichen produces an acid that slowly breaks down rock.

Across the creek, outcrops turn out lax-petaled **serviceberry** bushes; later in the season, **waxflower** shrubs will display flowers so perfect as to appear to have been cast from porcelain. Ferns flourish in the mossy northern exposure. Look trailside for **silvery cinquefoil** and the occasional woody-vined **blue rock clematis**.

Tea-worthy mint thrives along the burbling waterway. Pass through multi-trunked Rocky Mountain maples to reach a big Douglas fir tree sheltering a bright colony of **heartleaf arnica**. Big tiger swallowtail butterflies may be flitting overhead and tiny blue melissa butterflies, sometimes called blue skippers, puddle for moisture and minerals.

The roadway winds with the stream toward a great mossy outcrop, where May hikers inhale the spring-in-the-country scent of a couple of feral **apple trees**, thick with blushed blossoms as brief as they are beautiful. Follow the curving trail to view a north-facing bank where more **waxflower** shares billing with **boulder raspberry** and glossy-leaved arcs of creamy-racemed **false Solomon's seal**, or **Solomon's plume**.

MEADOW ANEMONE
Anemonidium canadense

Meadow anemone's five pristine white sepals cradle myriad yellow stamens above a dark green ruff of deeply cut leaves. Fond of moist soil, this colonizing member of the buttercup clan vaunts single flowers on long, slender stalks. Native Americans found anemone roots to be powerful medicine for healing wounds and lockjaw. Cousins include **red globe anemone** (*Anemone multifida ssp. globosa*) and **narcissus-flowered anemone** (*Anemonastrum narcissiflorum ssp. zephyrum*).

Along this flat segment of the trail, watch for spindly-stemmed **sticky gilia** in the decomposed granite soil on the right. The tenacity of ponderosas is evident in their huge roots crawling fully exposed down the broken boulders. Look low for velvety purple **skullcap**, the earliest-blooming mint.

Where the trail enters a lower-than-typical-elevation stand of quaking aspen, look for more **star Solomon's seal** and waning **wild plum**. A nearby abandoned road hides petite, pink-veined **spring beauties**.

Well-placed stepping-stones accommodate a creek crossing rewarded by a few **shooting stars**. Traverse a grassy hillside past clusters of white **sand lilies** and **golden banner**. The decomposed granite trail continues along the south bank of the creek, where the fragrant stars of **Rocky Mountain phlox** rest on needle-leaved mats. Early-season hikers enjoyed **pasqueflowers**.

After another creek crossing, the trail winds into a drier habitat, where **Parry milkvetch, bladderpod,**

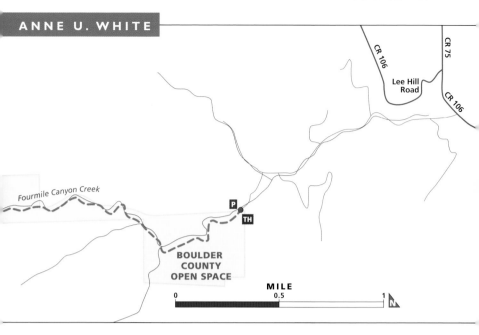

and vivid **Lambert's locoweed** bloom. Ahead, a sandstone bench beckons. Beyond it, look for **James starwort**, a chickweed, before again crossing the creek.

Evergreen shade nurtures **Canada violet** near the next few crossings. Watch the left side of the trail for an outcrop nurturing a sheet of moss pegged with **snowball saxifrage** and overarching **Solomon's plume**. The ardent searcher may spot the leathery, mauve sepals of **sugarbowls** here.

Where a brief rise brings on drier conditions again, look for **lanceleaf chiming bells**, each bud a cool pink, each dangling bell powder blue. More creek crossings ahead lead to an outcrop with a clinging garden featuring **bluemist penstemon** and **wild geranium**, as well as substantial **false Solomon's seal** and its quantity-not-quality cousin **star Solomon's seal**.

Pull up shortly onto an open bench that nurtures **sulphurflower**. In mid-May, look far off to the left for fluorescent pink **mountain ball cactus**. Look trailside in dry, lithic soil for **blue-eyed Mary**, a tiny annual, and showy, white **tufted evening primrose**.

A seasonal tributary flows down from the right to double the volume of Fourmile Creek. Follow the canal-like left fork to more crossings and great clumps of dark red-barked river birch.

Pass through a stand of aspens, keeping an eye out for deep twilight blue **early larkspur** and perhaps a few covert **shooting stars**. **Redtwig dogwood**, **wild rose**, and **meadow anemone** precede a small waterfall flowing over smooth bedrock. Carefully cross the creek along the waterfall lip formation on the right. **Northern bedstraw**'s froth of white alerts you to be on the lookout for **spotted coralroot orchid** on the right, just before the umpteenth and last creek crossing.

Wildflower Hike 12

Lichen Loop

This easy, low-elevation hike is perfect for the early season.

Trail Rating	easy
Trail Length	1.3-mile loop
Location	Heil Valley Ranch/Boulder
Elevation	5,900 to 6,280 feet
Bloom Season	May to October
Peak Bloom	mid-May to early June
Directions	From Boulder, head north on US 36. Travel 4.8 miles past the junction of US 36 and CO 7. Turn left onto Lefthand Canyon Dr. and continue for 0.7 mile. Bear right on Geer Canyon Dr. and follow it for 1.25 miles to the trailhead.

SITUATED IN THE NORTH FOOTHILLS OPEN SPACE, Heil Valley Ranch is another gem in the Boulder County's Parks and Open Space program. Though the area has seen use as ranching property, and quarries here are said to have supplied much of the handsome reddish sandstone used to build the University of Colorado at Boulder, it has remained relatively undeveloped since prehistoric times. This makes it an excellent habitat for wildlife.

The 1.3-mile hike around Lichen Loop is a tranquil and easy way to get into nature. Early-season hikers enjoy a head start on the Front Range wild-flower season at this plains-foothills life zone transition elevation. About 50 species—including cream tips and the delightfully soft downy painted cup—bloom along the trail in early June.

Park in designated, pine-shaded slots or in an overflow area.

Look for a trail map and information board marking the trailhead for Lichen Loop at the north end of the picnic grounds. Cross a sturdy bridge spanning a tiny seasonal creek where **watercress** sends up tiny white flowers in the typical four-petaled cross of the mustard family, then follow the path north up a drainage valley.

Trailside, watch for paired swan-necked tubes of **skullcap**, a royal purple mint, the first of its kind to bloom. **Fleabane daisies** quietly dot the hillside, while **Lambert's** or **Colorado locoweed** grabs attention in vivid magenta. **Miner's candle** shoots up a spike of white forget-me-not-like flowers, the bristly grey skeletons of which once served to make tallow-dipped torches.

Curving somewhat to the east now, the track brings you to bits of bright **spiderwort** and umbels of white **sand onion**. Areas of open ground feature the pallid stars of **spike gilia**, spires of **plains larkspur**, aromatic **field mint**, and wide-petaled, white **prickly poppy**. The sloping, gravelly soil is just right for a plethora of **creamtips**—each golden head a close collection of disc flowers, not a ray to its name. The flower's stems grow up to 1.5 feet long and bear finely cut leaves softened by whitish hairs. Enjoy wide swaths of white **Rocky Mountain locoweed** in May.

As it continues to curving around on rocky soil, the trail encounters **wild blue flax**, most easily spotted in the cool hours before petal drop or on days of dense cloud. Bedded among rugged boulders, **prickly pear cactus** prepares its big, silky, yellow blossoms. Barely pastel **Great Plains paintbrush** or **downy painted-cup** grows along the gentle hillside. Found only at plains elevations, the deeply cut, down-covered modified leaves and bracts spout a single flower shaped like a hooded snake's tongue.

As you enter a stand of ponderosas, pause to sniff a tree's bark—its vanilla scent is most prevalent on warm days. Under one pine, **blue rock clematis** twirls its vining arms, waiting for the time to flower. The waving awns of needle-and-thread grass tower over other species in the sweep of grasses to the right.

Zigzag up, looking for **woolly mullein** along the trail's disturbed edges. Rocks displaying multicolored lichen provide the possibility for spotting fragrant **linear leaf blazing star**, a spindly plant that carries pointy creamy yellow petals. It is also known as **yellow evening star** or **stickleaf**, the latter name due to hooked leaf bristles.

GREAT PLAINS PAINTBRUSH
Castilleja sessiliflora

Great Plains paintbrush earns another common name, **downy painted-cup,** from its soft pink and green hues. Its bracts and modified leaves shelter a pale, yellow, arched flower with a lolling tongue of a pistil; the flower will darken with age. Pollinated by the super-tongued hawkmoth, this winsome member of the figwort family is hemi-parasitic, sending out tubes in search of a host from which to steal nutrients. Sage and certain bunch grasses are fair game.

The paintbrush clan is named for 18th-century Spanish botanist Domingo Castillejo. Cousins of the Great Plains paintbrush include the dazzling **orange paintbrush** (*Castilleja integra*), and **scarlet paintbrush** (*Castilleja miniata*).

Sedimentary rocks broken off from the nearby stretch of the Dakota Hogback stud a grassy meadow brightened by a smattering of **locoweed**. Nearby, stiff-haired clumps of **false gromwell** present clusters of terminal flowers, each tip tightly closed around a protruding style. A member of the borage family, this quick-growing plant is also called **marbleseed** due to its opaque white, stone-hard seeds.

Descending now via zigs and zags toward a log rail fence, the path aims the keen-eyed hiker toward **spotted coralroot orchid**. A hand-lens look at this saprophyte reveals a spotted white lip on each of its delicate blooms. Camouflaged by pine boughs, rockbound Plumely Canyon, home to majestic golden eagles, may be glimpsed to the west.

Head out of the forest and into the open, where a pool of early-blooming **bluemist penstemon** complements endemic **whiskbroom parsley** and **golden draba**. More ponderosa and **wild geranium** lead the way southwest along the rail fence.

Where it merges with an old ranch-quarry road, the loop turns south, down a valley. Young ponderosas gain a roothold on a stony cutbank backed by a vista of forested hills. In the ravine to the left, shrubs of **chokecherry, three-**

leaf sumac, **boulder raspberry**, and willow welcome pink **wild geranium**. Across the drainage, note manmade slides of rock—evidence that the area was once quarried.

Scattered among pasture grasses, lanky **lupine** sends up candelabra spires of ivory flowers that soon turn tan, not a hint of blue among them. Like a four-leaf clover, three-petaled **spiderwort** occasionally produces four satiny petals to a bloom. The nature of those fragile, purple-blue petals inspires other imaginative common names such as **widow's tears** and **cow slobbers**.

Cross the drainage, looking for snowy white **prickly poppy**, each red-pistiled, golden-stamened reproductive center surrounded by broad, crepe-paper petals. Stunted **hawthorn** and **creeping hollygrape** grow beside the level roadway, while along the cutbank, **copper mallow**, or **cowboy's delight**, offers orange sherbet flowers. This relative of okra and cotton likes xeric soil and was reportedly a source of crude chewing gum for early Americans.

Before reaching another gate, leave the roadway on a path leading back to the trail information board. Keep an eye out for the spidery blooms of **scarlet gaura**, a member of the evening primrose clan, whose flowers open white to attract night-flying moths before shading to salmon the following day.

Come to a brook that is a repository for nice specimens of **American brooklime**. Its sweet flowers are a muted blue and dot the succulent plant like scalloped sequins. Also called **water speedwell**, this wet-foot wildflower is, unbelievably, related to paintbrush. **Watercress** and **mint** keep it company along the Lilliputian waterway. Continue along until you reach the parking area.

Ponderosa parkland invites exploration.

Foothills/Hogback Ridge Loop

Widely spaced ponderosa pines shelter clumps of late-spring-blooming wild iris.

easy to moderate	**Trail Rating**
2.3-mile balloon loop	**Trail Length**
Boulder Open Space/Boulder	**Location**
5,550 to 6,400 feet	**Elevation**
May to October	**Bloom Season**
late May to early June	**Peak Bloom**
From Boulder, head north on Broadway. At the US 36 junction, head left. Continue for 0.4 mile. Turn right onto the access road. The parking lot is just ahead on your left.	**Directions**

CHOOSE THIS 2.3-MILE BALLOON LOOP through Boulder Open Space for its low elevation, diverse wildflower species, and views. Located in a plains-foothills transition zone, this loop exposes hikers to about six dozen wildflower species typical to elevations both below and above 6,000 feet.

Parking fills quickly on spring weekends, as several trailheads share the same lot.

Before leaving the parking lot, look west for a view of the Dakota Hogback, the goal of this hike. Head toward it on the multi-use Foothills Trail.

The meadow beyond the pedestrian underpass hosts **wild blue flax** and silky-haired **Drummond milkvetch**. **Two-grooved milkvetch**, extremely toxic due to concentrations of selenium in its tissues, is here too.

Early-blooming **musineon**, a member of the parsley family, hugs the trailside soil, while not far away **purple ground cherry** spreads low branching stems and wavy, matte leaves under star-centered rounds of flat flowers. A member of the nightshade tribe, this grape-juice-colored native is partial to disturbed soil. Farther ahead, peachy **copper mallow**, or **cowboy's delight**, displays its deep-lobed leaves.

The foot bed roughens as the trail drifts up to a bushy stand of erect **two-grooved milkvetch**, their plush inflorescences more angelskin-pink than white. **Spiderwort**, or **bluejackets**, presents its trios of fragile petals atop gangly green stems.

An area of cattails appears as the path narrows and comes upon a small pond. In May, a cacophony of chorus frogs may be heard here, their

PURPLE GROUND CHERRY
Quincula lobata

Also known as **Chinese Lantern of the Plains** for its inflated calyx, this low-growing, heat- and drought-resistant plant is a lover of disturbed soil and can often be found along roadsides. Deep-lobed leaves sport minute golden bubbles, giving them a rustic appearance. Its up-facing, royal purple corolla is embossed with a five-pointed star and a burst of purple filaments tipped with yellow anthers. **Purple ground cherry** produces a berry inside a plump, papery, five-paneled calyx. This plant is in the nightshade tribe, which is infamous for its toxic members.

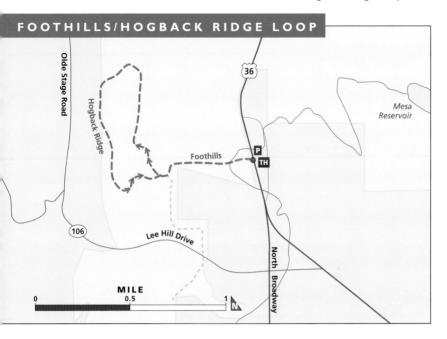

powerful voices belying their tiny size. The chorus stops at your arrival but resumes if you stand patiently silent.

As the trail continues, look right for a slope supporting **yucca**. Looking like giant asparagus spears shooting out of green dagger blades, **yucca's** bloom stalks little resemble their full bloom lily-like bells. The reddish or greenish-tinged buds open to succulent, creamy white tepals. Native Americans once made great use of yucca—eating its buds, pounding its root for shampoo, and using the tough fibers of its leaves to make sandals and thread.

Along the warm south slopes, look for radiant **orchid** or **sidebells penstemon**; its glaucous leaves have a waxy look. Avoid patches of glossy three-leaved poison ivy as you pass **wild blue flax** and pink clumps of **wild geranium**.

Continue straight through a rusty gate and head left (west). As the trail steepens, look for **Rocky Mountain locoweed**, golden **meadow arnica**, and toxic, creamy racemes of **death camas**. Look up a grassy ravine, past crawling **wire milkvetch** and sweetly tinted **chiming bells** to a stand of very purple **wild iris**. Waning **sand lilies** and **early pink milkvetch** hide in the lengthening grasses, while the exploring tendrils and bright magenta flowers of **American vetch** peek through.

Another intersection soon arrives. Bear right, following the **mouse-ear**–flanked trail west toward ponderosa pines. The rocky, narrowing trail soon leads to another junction and the beginning of the Hogback Ridge loop. Head left (west), past occasional **meadow arnica** and the fragrant, globular heads of **purple** or **field milkvetch**. No dogs, horses, or bicycles are allowed on this portion of the trail.

Before the trail steepens, pause near a mature ponderosa. To the south, the red sandstone slabs of the Flatirons can be seen jutting into the sky, and beyond them sits the I.M. Pei building housing the National Center for Atmospheric Research (NCAR).

Take a deep breath and start the climb. A golden trailside haze of **snakeweed** blooms here in late summer. For now, **spiderwort** perches on its angular foliage.

Upon reaching the top, pause for views of the red-roofed University of Colorado campus, then head north across a side slope. Travel past **bush sun-flower, wild blue flax, wild plum, wavyleaf flase dandelion**, and perfumed **wild rose**.

Lichen-shrouded outcrops and ponderosa pines stand over **whiskbroom parsley** and early **pink milkvetch** at the entrance to the secret glen of Hogback Ridge. In June, a hillside of the rose-relation **ninebark**, ambitiously named for its layers of shedding bark, amasses white blooms between rustic boulders. Other raw outcrops harbor **boulder raspberry**, another rose family member, while **wild iris** sentinels sing Mother Nature's praises in the shelter of this secluded dell.

The loop resumes upward toward the highest point of the hike. Along the way, look for low-growing **longleaf yellow evening primrose**. Off to the west, ranges of forest-cloaked hills create an undulating vista.

Rock steps lift the trail past **bluemist penstemon** to a more level stretch, where the keen eye might spot **blue-eyed grass**, an iris relation. In late summer and into fall, trailside fallen timber shields the bunched, faded purple bottles of **prairie gentian**, while in spring **many-flowered puccoon** dangles its golden bells. To the right, the rocky ridge of the hogback might serve as a perch to view the far plains.

Begin descending through ponderosa parkland, where purple-veined **wild iris** studs the north exposure, and **sand lily** flowers alongside long-blooming **mouse-ear**. Blushing **fleabane daisy** flanks the trail as it zigzags down to a level segment overlooking Boulder Valley. Dropping again, the loop snakes toward convenient viewing benches.

Cross a seasonal seep on stepping stones, keeping an eye out for **musineon**'s compact golden snowflakes. An easy descent rounds out the balloon portion of the hike; only the string is left to retrace.

Commence celebrating spring along the Dakota Hogback loop, a quick entry into a world of wildflowers and hidden treasures. This 2.3-mile hike is the perfect first step into a new bloom season.

Mesa/NCAR Loop

*A bounty of silvery lupine forms a floral blanket
in front of the Flatirons.*

moderate	**Trail Rating**
2.0-mile loop	**Trail Length**
NCAR (National Center for Atmospheric Research)/ Boulder Open Space/Boulder	**Location**
5,800 to 6,160 feet	**Elevation**
May to August	**Bloom Season**
late May to June	**Peak Bloom**
From central Boulder, head south on Broadway/CO 93. Turn right (west) down Table Mesa Dr. Continue for 2.4 miles, dead-ending at the NCAR parking lot.	**Directions**

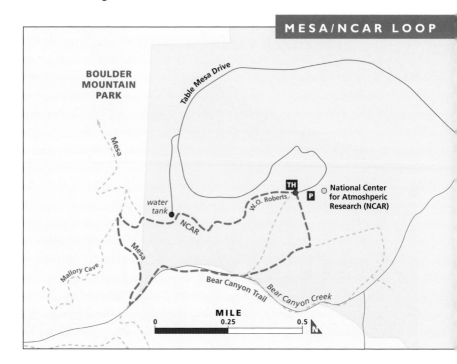

MESA/NCAR LOOP

BOULDER
MOUNTAIN
PARK

Table Mesa Drive

Mesa

water
tank

W.O. Roberts

TH

P

National Center
for Atmoshperic
Research (NCAR)

NCAR

Mesa

Mallory Cave

Bear Canyon Trail

Bear Canyon Creek

MILE

0   0.25   0.5

THE MESA TRAIL/NCAR LOOP takes in views, a hidden valley, and a
fine array of wildflowers.

In early spring, this loop invites discovery of about 50 plains and foothills
wildflower species. Summer produces a flood of purple and white lupines.

Parking is found in the extensive paved lot east of the NCAR building.

About two dozen types of wildflowers may be found on the way to the
NCAR/ Mesa trailhead along the 0.2-mile Walter Orr Roberts Weather
Trail. Follow the wide crusher fines pathway, staying left, until you reach a
sign that directs you left again, along the NCAR Trail. Travel down stone
steps, across a slope studded with ponderosa pines, and through a small
juniper wood.

This uneven section of the trail is the place to look for low-growing, yellow-
gold, umbellate **musineon**. This earth-hugging member of the parsley clan
has small, tight flowers as thick as dots of dried paint surrounded by leathery,
ferny leaves that appear to have been stamped from forest-green leather.
Musineon is its Latin genus name as well as its common name. In the same
area, look for more yellow bloomers such as **golden banner**, **leafy cinquefoil**,
early spring **senecio**, and **sulphurflower**, all complemented by **spiderwort**'s
brilliant yet ephemeral purple-blue petals.

Further along, the track bisects a small grove of junipers. This tree's shaggy bark is often burned with sage to provide aromatic smoke for Native American purification ceremonies.

Where the trail reaches a junction, stay to the right. A wing of fence overlooks the broad Boulder Valley, 600 feet below. Nearby, look for **spike gilia**'s tiny, milk-white, pointed trumpets. Crowding its lax stalk's fuzzy tip, the starry inflorescence recalls a nebulous Milky Way.

Perhaps the stateliest wildflower to bloom here in spring is elegant **wild iris**, patches of which flank the NCAR Trail. Native Americans once used this plant's tough leaf fibers to construct snares.

The trail rises along a grassy, east-facing slope, passing the white blooms of **sand lilies,** and later, **boulder raspberry**. A stretch of stone steps, broken up briefly by switchbacks, leads to an enclosed water tank. Immediately after, the path drops and levels out. Stay left along the NCAR Trail at the first Mesa Trail junction. Uphill on the right, a stand of pure white **wild iris** may be in bloom.

While the ubiquitous common dandelion is an import—with a whale of a marketing program around the world—the various species of dandelions indigenous to the Americas are ironically called false dandelions. One seen along this segment of the trail is **wavyleaf false dandelion**, whose long, wavy leaves are covered in pale, soft hairs. In early July, the dandelion's red-tinged blooms give way to **prairie coneflower**, **bush sunflower**, **prickly pear cactus**, and the wide, white daisies of **showy Townsendia**.

On the left, **wild roses** bring their pink blooms to a little meadow, which in spring sparkled with **wallflower**'s warm, sunny hues. A mustard tribesman, **wallflower** is long-blooming and may be maturing long, slim seedpods even while buds at its top are still opening. The seeds were once used to flavor food as well as cure dysentery; the healing juices were applied to blisters.

The NCAR Trail reaches the end of its 0.6 mile at a t-bone

SILVERY LUPINE
Lupinus argenteus

Silvery lupine grows up to 3 feet high. This prolific, bush-like member of the pea family sports palmate leaves and whorls of spiring blue flowers composed of banner, wings, and keel. Its seeds project forcibly from the mother plant to land some distance away. Scientists have found lupine seeds frozen since the last ice age that they believe to be viable. Poisonous alkaloids make this plant toxic. There are 500 species of lupine scattered about the globe; **white lupine** (*Lupinus argenteus ingratus*) is practically a twin of **silvery lupine**.

with the Mesa Trail. By the Fourth of July, the hideaway meadow here is full of cupped **sego lilies**, white **prairie clover**, **many-flowered puccoon**, white **plains larkspur**, **wild roses**, and great swaths of **silvery lupine**. Head left (south) along the Mesa Trail.

After passing through the south end of the small meadow where **irises** bloom, the path heads into ponderosa pines where **chiming bells** abound. Abundant **mahonia** or **creeping hollygrape** flanks the trail in broad swatches. This low-growing shrub produces fragrant, bright, yellow-belled clusters among holly-like leaves. Its berries are puckery-tart but edible.

Continue straight ahead, passing the turnoff for the Mallory Cave Trail. Follow the level footpath through conifers, watching for occasional clearings that may display **beebalm** or more **wild iris**.

As the **iris** wanes in mid-summer, **wild geranium** comes into bloom. Its five pink petals, lined with darker nectar guides, surround 10 stamens and a pistil that elongates into a slim seedpod. The emerging leaves of this hardy plant were once eaten by Native Americans, who also used the root to make a contraceptive tea.

Listen for the sound of Bear Canyon Creek as valley views materialize to the east. The path narrows, slanting down a hillside of stunted **wild plum** and **hawthorn** thickets. **Wild plum**'s delicate early-spring blossoms open while its gray branches are still bare. Its tart-skinned fruit ripens in fall, providing a valuable food source for wildlife.

Upon reaching a wide natural surface road, turn left onto Bear Canyon Trail, which follows Bear Canyon Creek through **smooth sumac**, **chokecherry**, and more **wild plum**. Look for a high outcrop and a gnarled, old ponderosa on your left. Soon after, the trail reaches a post-marked intersection. Turn left, off of Bear Canyon Trail and onto a steep casual trail.

The ascent begins up a grassy ravine, where an occasional **iris** blooms, as does uninhibited **American vetch**. Varying in color from pink-violet to blue-purple, this member of the pea family sends its tendrils waving about for a neighbor on which to sprawl.

The track curls up over peeled-log waterbars in pursuit of NCAR's pine-topped mesa. A lone juniper grows halfway up, providing meager shade for a rest. When the trail eases somewhat, a nice view to the east appears. The mechanical humming of I. M. Pei's soaring architectural statement, the NCAR building, broadcasts the closing of the loop.

Doudy Draw

*The Doudy Draw Trail offers spreading views
of the Flatirons and beyond.*

easy	***Trail Rating***
3.8 miles out and back	***Trail Length***
Boulder	***Location***
5,850 to 6,100 feet	***Elevation***
early May to October	***Bloom Season***
late May to early June	***Peak Bloom***
From Boulder, head south on CO 93. The Flatirons Vista Trailhead is 0.3 miles past the intersection of CO 128. Turn right into the fenced-in parking lot.	***Directions***

LOCATED JUST SOUTH OF BOULDER, the easy, scenic Doudy Draw Trail has a lot to offer. Attractions include ponderosa parkland, an interesting array of mesa-top flora, Flatirons views, and distant vignettes of the Indian Peaks.

Visit during spring, when 60 to 70 wildflower species put on an appearance. One caveat: Flowers can be sparse when cattle graze the tableland, but the gated draw makes up for it. Parking for cars and horse trailers is usually adequate.

From the Flatirons Vista Trailhead, aim right along a gravel road marked as the Doudy Ditch Trail. Be sure to close the trailhead gate behind you. Look for bright **orchid penstemon** and **spiderwort** as the trail curves. **Sandwort**'s delicate white stars swing on wiry stems above tough, grasslike leaves. Summer hikers will find lanky **chicory** offering up ragged, sky-blue flowers.

Peer off the trail for flesh-colored and textured stalks of **naked** or **clustered broomrape** ending in periscope-shaped tubes. Unable to produce chlorophyll, this sticky parasitic commonly taps into fringed sage for sustenance.

As the trail continues, look for **Great Plains paintbrush**, or **downy painted-cup**. This soft, graceful member of the figwort family produces ragged fountains of pastel bracts and modified leaves spouting flowers like pale yellow, hissing snakes.

Pastureland stretches before you, framing the distant Flatirons—grand, red sandstone slabs formed by the ancient Fountain Formation. Look in moist spots for the brazen gold heads and odorous foliage of **meadow arnica**. **Scarlet gaura** and white **sand onion** are satisfied with xeric conditions. Later in the bloom season, **nodding onion** bows cool pink umbels. Pioneers and Native Americans appreciated onion's vitamin and salt-rich contents. Its pungent bulbs also served them as insect repellent.

The track passes through an iron gate and heads west, rising on stony soil to meet **silvery lupine** and an occasional **blanketflower**. Sheltered

WHISKBROOM PARSLEY
Harbouria trachypleura

Whiskbroom parsley's bright yellow, snowflake heads bloom above thread-like leaves, creating the form that explains its common name. This endemic plant grows in a narrow belt along Colorado's eastern slope in the foothills and south-facing montane areas. It is the only species in its genus. The genus name honors J. P. Harbour, who, in the first part of the 1860s, combed South Park, Colorado, collecting plants.

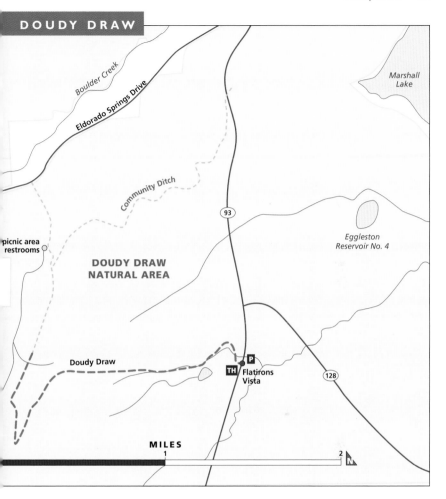

DOUDY DRAW

Boulder Creek

Eldorado Springs Drive

Community Ditch

Marshall Lake

93

Eggleston Reservoir No. 4

picnic area restrooms

DOUDY DRAW NATURAL AREA

Doudy Draw

TH / **Flatirons Vista**

P

128

MILES
1   2

by stout ponderosa pines, **bluemist** and **orchid penstemons** enjoy the company of **whiskbroom parsley**, **sulphurflower**, and **mouse-ear**. Keep an eye out for lax stalks of **spike gilia** pasted with washed-out stars.

In the distance, the Indian Peaks rise through a canyon gap. When snow-creased in early spring, this nearby mountain range is quite photogenic.

Check the stony ground for native false dandelions, such as **wavyleaf**. Many of the so-called false dandelions are early-spring bloomers.

Coast into a dip that, in years of sufficient moisture, sponsors a show of **golden meadow arnica**, **larkspur**, and **wild iris**. Sporadic but bold **blanketflower**, with its dark red disc surrounded by notched yellow rays, can also be seen.

Pass through another gate and continue up the flat, stony track, past **three-leaf sumac** shrubs, **leafy cinquefoil**, and **sulphurflower**. **Sandwort** joins at another well-sprung gate.

Early-season hikers and equestrians may find a muddy track where Doudy Draw itself opens below, but azure splotches of **bluemist penstemon** and gossiping groups of **naked broomrape** combined with the draw's scenery make progress worthwhile. Endemic **whiskbroom parsley**'s sunny snowflakes brighten ponderosa shade.

Looking into Doudy Draw reveals a steep hillside rife with **ninebark**'s white inflorescences that age to rusty coral. **Miner's candle** points to **prickly pear cactuses** setting bud. A pocket view of Indian Peaks snowfields pops out again, matching the pristine blooms of **boulder raspberry**, whose drupes are typically dry, seedy, and insipid.

Drifting down, the trail passes **white gilia**'s snowy fairy trumpets, as well as rubbery-looking **green gentian**, or **monument plant**. Farther along, lush vegetation hems in the track. **White-flowered peavine** winds laxly among **hawthorn** and **chokecherry**, while **limber milkvetch**, a pea-clan member, sends out little flowers of subdued pink.

A spot of seriously named **death camas** signals a wide view of Boulder Valley to the northeast. Dangling gold tubes of **many-flowered puccoon** grace both sides of the declining trail, along with **silvery lupine**, **white gilia**, and **false gromwell**. **Mouse-ear** looks up to an occasional **meadow arnica**. On the plush slope, two-toned **purple field milkvetch** presents scented globes where **chiming bells** once charmed early-season hikers.

A switchback continues the shrub-flanked drop into the draw. Morning sunlight opens the fragile, silken petals of **wild blue flax** growing trailside; its tough stem fibers were once sought for cordage and nets. The descent steepens over a rocky foot bed where little grassy pockets feature magenta **locoweed**, cool **lupine**, and pink **wild geranium**. Below, the sound of water beckons. The trail levels, taking you to a grassy seasonal creek where **golden banner** complements rich purple-blue **early larkspur**. Enjoy a contemplative pause, then turn around and retrace your steps.

Forgotten Valley

*Many species of wildflowers spatter the slopes
of Forgotten Valley.*

easy to moderate	*Trail Rating*
4.0 miles out and back with keyhole	*Trail Length*
Golden Gate Canyon State Park/Golden	*Location*
7,800 to 8,200 feet	*Elevation*
late May to September	*Bloom Season*
late June to mid-July	*Peak Bloom*
From Boulder, head south on CO 93. Just before you reach Golden, take a right onto Golden Gate Canyon Rd. Continue for 14 miles. At the Golden Gate Canyon State Park visitors' center, head right on County Road 57 and go 2.5 miles. Park at the Bridge Creek Trailhead. Fee required.	*Directions*

SURROUNDED BY 12,000 ACRES of great habitat diversity, fishing ponds, and picnic and campsites, the handsome visitors' center at Golden Gate Canyon State Park invites you to stop by. Many of the park's 35 miles of trail are rife with wildflowers. The route to Forgotten Valley not only offers over 80 species, but also allows a glimpse into the park's past at an old homestead overlooking a pond.

The 4.0-mile route rises steeply before evening out to travel through pine and then rise gently above an unseen creek. It then circles a keyhole loop beginning and ending at the homestead pond. All of Golden Gate Park's trails are named for native animals and each is conveniently marked with signposts featuring that animal's footprint.

Arrive early to get a coveted parking spot.

Follow Burro Trail under ponderosa pines to a map signboard, then over a bridge spanning Ralston Creek in view of **cow parsnip** and **bur avens**. Swing left along the stream, where a sign states: "Buffalo-Burro Trails to Forgotten Valley."

On the north side of the creek, an open hillside features **wild blue flax**, best seen in cool morning hours before daily petal shed. Joining it are **sulphurflower** and violet-pink **wand penstemon**. Closer at hand, **tall Jacob's ladder**, named for the arrangement of its leaves, pokes out of trailside grasses.

The posts featuring burro tracks indicate that you are on the right trail. Follow them up a south-facing slope to travel along a dry drainage of mixed conifer and quaking aspen. Rocky footing ensues as the trail becomes

BLANKETFLOWER
Gaillardia aristata

This showy member of the sunflower family is often called by its Latin genus name, *Gaillardia*. The tri-lobed ray flowers are yellow-gold; the center, composed of disc flowers, is a deep red. This summer-blooming perennial has rigid hairs on its largish, lance-shaped leaves, which are bristly to the touch. **Gaillardia** thrives in xeric foothills and montane zones and grows up to 30 inches tall, making it a great garden plant. The genus name commemorates amateur French botanist Gaillard de Charentonneau. **Showy Townsendia** (*Townsendia grandiflora*) is a cousin.

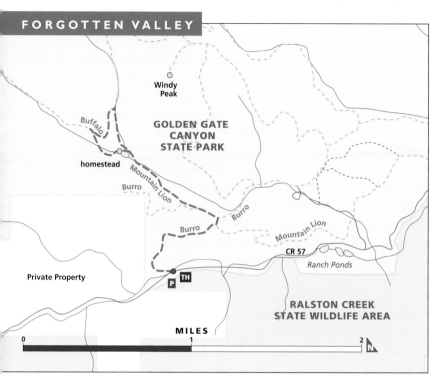

FORGOTTEN VALLEY

Windy Peak

Buffalo

GOLDEN GATE CANYON STATE PARK

homestead

Mountain Lion

Burro

Burro

Burro

Mountain Lion

CR 57

Ranch Ponds

Private Property

P TH

RALSTON CREEK STATE WILDLIFE AREA

MILES

0   1   2

more steep, passing **blanketflower, chokecherry**, and the dainty, blushed bells of **dogbane**.

Sandy and flat underfoot, the trail enters ponderosa pine parkland speckled with wildflowers such as pink **wild geranium** and vermilion **narrow-leaved paintbrush**. Presenting its gold tubes, **many-flowered puccoon** replaces endemic **whiskbroom parsley**'s sunny snowflakes and **wallflower**'s fading petals. **Fendler senecio, stonecrop**, and **silvery cinquefoil** are gearing up in yellow.

A junction sends our route left along Mountain Lion Trail. The surrounding lodgepole pine stand brings up intense, violet-throated **mountain penstemon** and **white gilia**. Back under ponderosas, frequent posts keep you on the correct track.

The wide, gentle trail eases down by aspens, accompanied by the pleasant sound of running water. Watch for **waxflower** shrubs' lovely waxy blossoms. Near a rocky cutbank on the old roadway, **ninebark** bushes appear. In the vicinity, **blue rock clematis** clambers among **boulder raspberry** shrubs.

After crossing a chatty little creek, admire **Lambert's locoweed, wild geranium**, and **leafy** and **silvery cinquefoil**. The track rises, passing **beebalm**, a bright summer bloomer. Add nearby sunny **blanketflower** and gripping blue **mountain penstemon** for a painterly palette.

As you pull up by an old dam face, the valley named Forgotten unfolds to reveal a serene pond and, on the far shore, an old homestead cabin. On the

left, **wallflower, lupine, black-eyed Susan,** and **aspen sunflower** accent the slope down to the water.

After absorbing the colorful scene to which you will return after completing a short keyhole loop, head north and continue following the mountain lion track, passing the trail to the homestead. **Bluemist penstemon** and evergreen **kinnikinnick** thrive along the road's cutbank. On the left, a meadow, fed by a willow-flanked brook, holds wildflowers such as **meadow anemone** and **meadow arnica.** Up to the right, dappled by aspen shade, burnt copper **wallflower** and **scarlet paintbrush** ask for notice.

Drawn to the lush riparian habitat again, look left to find **tall chiming bells, cow parsnip, meadow arnica,** and **tall false forget-me-not.** The latter is referred to more literally as **stickseed,** a name attributed to the charming, pale blue flower's maturation into barbed seeds which attach themselves to passing fur coats or sweaters. Press on past **wild rose** and **Geyer onion.**

A broad area, rather barren, signals a left turn onto the Buffalo Trail. Cross a tiny seasonal waterway where you may find **shooting stars** aiming black-tipped, hot pink darts. Later, **tall coneflower** or **goldenglow** will bloom here. Continue past more saturated blue **mountain penstemon,** in colorful competition here with **aspen sunflower, blanketflower,** and **locoweed.**

Within sight of the weathered homestead, the level trail crunches along on golden decomposed granite that suits tidy clumps of **cutleaf fleabane daisy.** Prepare to angle sharply left as Buffalo Trail wraps back around to the pond, passing a veritable **wild rose** garden. **Sulphurflower, leafy cinquefoil,** and a bit of **tall false forget-me-not** may put in appearances. As summer progresses, sandpaper-foliaged **bush sunflower,** a perennial, blooms along here.

The narrow trail saunters along a flowery, sloped meadow, winding down to the homestead pond's feeder inlet. Early hikers encountered **wintercress'** brassy inflorescences where the pathway comes upon the aging cabin. The historic old homestead, now restored, offers a shaded porch overlooking a stony slope spattered with **yarrow, wallflower, mountain penstemon, stonecrop,** and **locoweed.** Around the south side, picturesque with **wild rose** and overrun by **wild hops,** the inlet trickles into the pond.

Leaving the homestead porch, finish up the keyhole segment by passing a seep featuring **green bog orchid** and **wild mint.** On the periphery, **aspen sunflower, meadow arnica,** and **tall coneflower** sprout among rushes and sedges. **Aspen** or **showy daisy** blooms nearby. The trail rises gently to close the keyhole at a ponderosa pine.

Facing: Wildflowers bloom around a historic homestead pond.

Wildflower Hike 17

Raccoon Loop

View 100 miles of Continental Divide from Panoramic Point.

Trail Rating	easy to moderate
Trail Length	2.5-mile balloon loop
Location	Golden Gate Canyon State Park/Golden
Elevation	8,800 to 9,250 feet
Bloom Season	June to September
Peak Bloom	late June to mid-July
Directions	From Boulder, head south on CO 93. Just before you reach Golden, take a right onto Golden Gate Canyon Rd./CO 46 and go 14 miles to the Golden Gate Canyon State Park visitors' center. Travel 1 mile beyond the visitors' center and turn right on Mountain Base Rd. Continue 3 miles to the Reverend's Ridge Campground. Fee required.

WITH ABOUT 12,000 ACRES threaded by 35 miles of hiking trails, Golden Gate Canyon State Park is a great metro-close locale to bring joy to the wildflowerist's heart. Located about 15 miles northwest of Golden, this park offers varied terrain and activities, including fishing ponds, scenic picnic areas, campgrounds, and a handsome visitors' center. Diverse habitats offer a wide selection of wildflowers along Raccoon Trail, whose 2.5-mile loop accesses Reverend's Ridge Campground and Panorama Point, where a vista of Continental Divide peaks stretches over 100 miles.

In late June and early July, roughly 70 species of wildflowers, including plenty of Colorado blue columbine and possibly some uncommon spurless columbine, may be met along the mostly shaded trail.

The limited parking lot is shared with campers. An alternative is to park at Panorama Point and do the loop from there. Early-day hiking makes parking easier and optimizes chances of beating summer afternoon thunderstorms, which can brew up quickly. When paying the park entrance fee at the visitos' center, consider picking up a wildflower list.

Lodgepole pines flank the trail as it heads out from the northeast side of the Reverend's Ridge camper's facility building and amphitheater. The Raccoon loop follows posts imprinted with the pawprint of its namesake. At an intersection, head right along Raccoon Loop. Our route returns along the path to the left. Curve down through mixed woods, where you will encounter an occasional **blue columbine** or sunny **heartleaf arnica**. Keep left where an intersection sends Elk Trail straight ahead. Our trail bottoms out in a small drainage then ascends steadily, switchbacking through sparsely vegetated forest to reach the fabulous view at Panorama Point.

HEARTLEAF ARNICA
Arnica cordifolia

Bright gold ray florets and center disc florets of **heartleaf arnica** shine in dryish forests. Its sprawling, leafy colonies, spread by underground rootstalks, produce few flowers. Petioles support opposite lower leaves that are heart-shaped (hence the specie name) and furry. This member of the sunflower family grows from the foothills to the subalpine and from 10 to 18 inches high. Also called **leopard's bane,** it was once used to relieve abrasions and sore muscles; ingesting it may be toxic, though a drug extract is used to induce a mild fever.

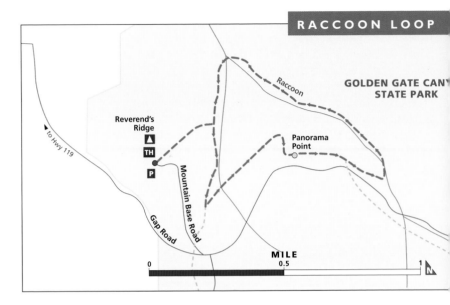

One hundred linear miles of Continental Divide are visible from the overlook deck here. The Indian Peaks range takes center stage with 13,397-foot South Arapaho, 13,502-foot North Arapaho, and 13,409-foot Navajo peaks. To the north, 14,259-foot Longs Peak finesses the commanding vista.

Raccoon Trail continues up to the right of the restrooms at the east parking area to travel through evergreens via an entrenched section, passing a close encounter with Gap Road as the route heads left. Ease along, searching for **spurless blue columbine**. A few of these uncommon specimens bloom on the left. The wide, open-faced blossoms honor a late 19th-century lady, Anna Dailey, who traipsed about in the Evergreen area. Her surname is part of the Latin species name of the spurless columbine, which is a form of the more familiar Colorado state flower.

Continue down to overhanging willows harboring **shooting stars** and bits of **brook saxifrage** near a seep. Look in the damp sands for the tiny faces, sketched with nectar guidelines but otherwise purest white, of **kidney-leaf violets**. Later, **monkshood** will line its tall stalk with hooded purple flowers.

On the left, a big conical blue spruce shelters a garden of coppery **wallflower, wild iris, blue columbine, tall chiming bells,** and **scarlet paintbrush.** Aspens shade rising stalks of **tall larkspur.** The path continues to a small footbridge framed by **tall chiming bells** and **shooting stars.**

The trail curves west into a dryish meadow, exposing **locoweed, mountain penstemon, gaillardia, scarlet paintbrush, lupine,** and subtle lavender-blue **tall Jacob's ladder.** In a good moisture year, also look for **blue columbine**, pink **wild geranium**, and orangey-gold **wallflower. Tall pussytoes** appreciate the filtered shade of occasional aspen trees. Snow-creased Indian Peaks peek teasingly through the trees.

The narrow, cruising path enters the aspen, which shelter frail **white geranium** and sturdy **cow parsnip**. As you approach a hairpin curve, look for fragrant wild **roses** growing side by side with snowy froths of **northern bed-straw**. On a declining gradient where small **ninebark** shrubs send out clusters of blushed white flowers, vegetation closes in and footing is less stable.

The surrounding aspens gain in girth, framing large-flowered clumps of **blue columbine**. On columbine's honeysuckle-scented heels, **fireweed** prepares magenta-rose spires.

An s-curve bends the narrowing trail down through smaller aspen and midnight blue **larkspur**. Drop through mixed forest to reach a wildflower slope where the Continental Divide again steals attention.

Leveling at last, the trail finds an aspen glade where water sound pricks up the ear and baby blue **tall false forget-me-not** perks up the scene. White spatters the next slope in the form of **mouse-ear**, **yarrow**, and, at the bottom, **meadow anemone**, its pristine cups rising long-necked from a dark green collar.

As the descent continues, conifers give way to robust aspens dancing over a wealth of **columbine** accented by **white geranium** and **mountain parsley**. Bridging the creek brings on **twistedstalk**, **cowbane**, **brook saxifrage**, and a host of **shooting stars**.

The path heads for a giant Colorado blue spruce where late-summer hikers will discover royal blue chalices of **Rocky Mountain gentian**. Also look for **northern paintbrush**'s cool yellow and **fireweed**'s hot pink. **Columbine**, that elegant wildling, invites you to linger and admire its splendid specimens.

Sail along through mixed forest to a small meadow where **tall chiming bells** produce pink buds and blue corollas. Where a private cabin appears, head around to the right and follow an old road designated with a white arrow. A raccoon pawprint sign sends the route left and uphill.

Golden banner and **heartleaf arnica** conspire to keep sunshine in the deepening shade. Thick bracts of rounded **northern paintbrush** signal a watch for green **bracted orchid** growing about a foot high, each of its flowers ending in a clefted waterfall lip. Aspens flatten the trail, revealing more pale **paintbrush**. At a four-way junction, the sound of running water cools the finish of the balloon portion of our loop. Head right along Raccoon Trail to complete our route's string and arrive, after an uphill trudge, back at Reverend's Ridge Campground.

Wildflower Hike 18

Loch Lomond

Wading through wildflowers in the subalpine life zone brings you to Loch Lomond.

Trail Rating	moderate
Trail Length	5.0 miles out and back
Location	St. Mary's Glacier/Idaho Springs
Elevation	10,360 to 11,200 feet
Bloom Season	July to August
Peak Bloom	late July to mid-August
Directions	From Denver, head west on I-70. Take exit 238 north on Fall River Rd./County Road 275. After 8.5 miles, turn left onto Alice Rd. Continue 0.9 mile until it becomes Steuart Rd. Travel another 1.5 mile to parking on the right side of the road. Respect private property.

LOCH LOMOND is a bonny lake just east of the Continental Divide, chaperoned by 13,250-foot Mount Bancroft and 13,294-foot James Peak. Weekends see increased off-road-vehicle traffic. One tricky stream crossing tests the mettle of boots and balance but is doable. Steadily rising and scenic, the rugged roadway arrives at a makeshift camping area among conifers. Another push up reveals the lake. Keep left on a trail above the west shore to end up near the scenic tributary cascade. The trail takes you into the subalpine life zone, offering about 75 wildflower species. The best display comes with the final objective, a flowery slope looking over the lacework stream feeding Loch Lomond. Because of late-lying snowbanks, some areas of flowers are at their best as summer advances.

Taking care to respect private property, park on the west alongside Steuart Road just before it comes to the Upper Forest Road intersection.

Passing lodgepole pine forest, set off west on Forest Service Road 701.2. Parry goldenweed, a late-bloomer in the boggling collection of ADYDs (another darn yellow daisy), complements purple tansy aster as the rough road begins its ascent. Early-season hikers find golden banner above a cutbank that suits bluemist penstemon. Up on the right, where talus courses down and limber pines grow, look for radiantly blue mountain penstemon, annual golden smoke, or scrambled eggs, and the suspended stars of Fendler sandwort. Down to the left, clustered orange berries adorn a mountain ash tree.

Stony underfoot now, the track leads to wild rose for a celestial sniff. Prickly common juniper bushes herald tall scarlet paintbrush, many-rayed goldenrod, harebells, and golden aster. Along the way, compare limber pine and bristlecone pine by examining the cones. Limber's are elongated with smooth-ended and rounded scales, while one touch of a bristlecone gives away its prickly nature—that and its resin-flecked needle bundles.

Increased gradient discloses the southeast skyline, lifted by fourteener Mount Evans. Rockier, but more level, the trail passes a tailing pile. Spruce and fir replace lodgepoles as shrubby cinquefoil bedecks its bushes with gold. Just after a sign reading "FS 701.2," look for unusual moonwort, more descriptively named grapefern, tucked in among wild strawberry.

From a hidden damp zone, boulders coax forth tall chiming bells. Shrinking aspens and flagged spruce reveal prevailing wind directions as purple fringe and mats of dotted or moss saxifrage enter the picture. Tall scarlet paintbrush and substantial clumps of rubbery-looking black-tipped senecio inhabit the same vicinity, as do wild raspberry and Colorado black currant.

Fireweed accompanies an ascent where jumbled granite exhibits the exerted golden stamens of purple fringe. American bistort waves white wands over queen's crown and arrowleaf senecio. Early on, Parry primrose reigned by the tumbling rush of a Fall River fork down below the trail.

Quartz intrusions swirl and layer granite boulders in view of Mt. Eva and Parry Peak, both thirteeners. Paralleling the creek brings on off-green spherical bursts of **Grays angelica**, showy **subalpine daisy**, and more **fireweed** and **arrowleaf senecio**. **Subalpine arnica** and **beauty cinquefoil** go for the gold while **bistort** settles for white.

Cobbles underfoot require careful boot placement. A tricky choice ensues as you approach a broad ford: crossing upstream or downstream. After crossing, keep right on the main trail. Look for **queen's crown** and early-blooming **marsh marigold**. **Harebells** create a soft purple pool on bare soil to the left. On the right, among the conical spruces, primitive campsites abound.

The trail is level now. Pass a verdant meadow nurturing **little pink elephants** and **monkshood**. Soon, another herd of **elephants** joins up with **subalpine arnica** and **subalpine daisy** as well as **rosy paintbrush**. Spruce shade suits both **bracted** and **sickletop lousewort** as well as **broadleaf arnica** and **slender hawkweed**.

Curve up to the west to reach a color-splashed hillside meadow. Cross the creek, which passes under the road. **Queen's crown**, **arnica**, **subalpine daisy**, **senecio**, **elephants**, **Porter's lovage**, and **bistort** create a pastel flowerscape. The winding road climbs past boulder-studded meadows flashing **tall scarlet paintbrush**. Here, the flower-lined tumbling creek presents vivid pink **Parry primrose**.

Stunted and contorted by prevailing winds, the spruce have shrunk into walls of krummholz. Look for **little rose gentian**—a few may be white "sports," or mutants. Cousin

WHIPPLE PENSTEMON
Penstemon whippleanus

Dusky penstemon is an alternate name for this dusty wine-hued member of the snapdragon family. Two-lipped tubes, the upper two-lobed, the lower three-lobed, pout over a plump throat where the fifth—and sterile—stamen boasts a tuft of hairs. **Whipple penstemon** also blooms off-white, decorated with muted purple lines. About 280 penstemon species are native to the western hemisphere. Explorer Captain A. W. Whipple commanded the Pacific Railroad Survey in the 1850s, surely meeting the mid-summer-blooming penstemon that would bear his name.

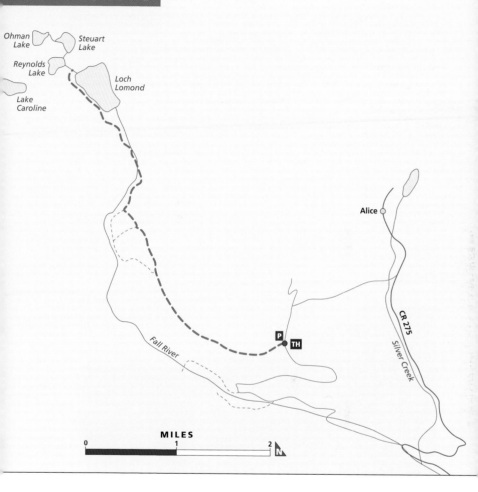

arctic gentian, that harbinger of summer's end, sends up pale chalices. **Blueleaf** and **beauty cinquefoil** cheer on brassy **alpine avens**. Sidehill rivulets support **tall chiming bells** where sweeps of big-leaved **Parry primrose** reigned earlier. Proceeding on, meet **yellow paintbrush** and **Parry lousewort**.

The roadway may harbor sassy pink **moss campion** and white **alpine sandwort**, creatively referred to as **sandywinks**. A barren expanse overlooking the lake and looking more parking lot than roadway harbors tidy clumps of **alpine dusty maiden**.

Rugged pewter rockscape and ragged peaks form Loch Lomond's granite basin as the route aims for Loch Lomond's west side, where the jeep road ends.

The trail continues through willow and spruce, exposing floriferous pocket meadows as it becomes hemmed in by vegetation and grows muddy underfoot.

Nearby **Whipple penstemon, tall chiming bells,** and **subalpine larkspur** will yield to the royal blue chalices of **Rocky Mountain gentian** in August.

Cross an old flanged iron pipe leading toward a rippling cascade and prismatic meadows, where wildflowers hold their bloom far into summer. Execute fancy footwork to cross seeps populated by airy **brook** and stolid **bog saxifrages** as well as **brookcress**. Willows shelter dusky purple **star gentian**. A golden flower-flow wends down to the sparkling lake.

Cross an outcrop to meet up with the pipe again. Stay to the right and outside of the krummholz, passing through grayed conifer trunks to navigate a section of poorly defined trail. An open overlook takes in the tributary cascade. Creeklets challenge your footing while flowers fill your eyes. Balance along a flattened pipe to meet compact **moss campion**.

Approach the towering granite wall at the lake's end, where late snowbanks allow late-summer hikers to still find **marsh marigold, subalpine buttercup,** and plenty of vivid **Parry primrose**. The thrusting cliff before you holds miniature rockeries full of vibrantly mixed bouquets. A flowery tapestry weaves down to the banks of bonny Loch Lomond. When you are ready, turn around and retrace your steps.

American bistort waves over Loch Lomond.

Apex/Pick 'n Sledge/ Sluicebox Loop

*Wildflowers
abound in Apex
Open Space.*

WHAT A FLORISTIC SURPRISE Apex Open Space is. With a humble beginning adjacent to Heritage Square Amusement Park/ Shopping Center, Apex Trail quickly leads to a ravine with a small creek. Before entering the ravine, foothills life zone flowerage begins, with the hillside offering a dozen or two wildflower species. An ancient Native American village was once located here. Much later, a toll road to Gregory Diggings, now known as Central City, passed through the area.

Find the trailhead kiosk on the northwest edge of the lower parking lot, then head west under elms and turn right to cross an intentionally

moderate	*Trail Rating*
4.5-mile balloon loop	*Trail Length*
Apex Open Space/Golden	*Location*
6,150 to 7,150 feet	*Elevation*
May to July	*Bloom Season*
June	*Peak Bloom*
From Denver, head west on I-70. Head west on US 40. Turn left onto Heritage Rd. and continue to the trailhead, which is adjacent to Heritage Square. Park by the northeast corner of the paved area.	*Directions*

rusted bridge. Take the first dirt path on the left, which bears a small sign reading "Apex Trail." The 4.5-mile balloon loop pushes into a ravine before a right turn sends it climbing to level out, then drop over switchbacks to complete the balloon portion before rejoining the string.

The metro-close loop boasts over 80 wildflower species in mid-spring.

Parking is easy, but summer afternoon thunderstorms are not. Stay alert for weather changes.

In spring, **orchid penstemon, scarlet gaura, locoweed,** and **chiming bells** color the grassland as the trail heads up Apex Gulch. A bit later in the season, fragrant **wild rose** blooms in both pink and white beside pastel-orange **copper mallow,** or **cowboy's delight,** and pink **wild geranium.**

Spanning both bloom times, **tall butter 'n eggs,** or **Dalmatian toadflax,** spikes the hillside with light yellow spires. Not only does this alien seed about freely, it also expands underground rather rapidly. The greedy habits of this plant—which displaces native wildflower species—have earned it a place on the Native Plant Society's "Most Unwanted" list.

Near where the trail meets a little creek, **orange paintbrush** approaches fire-engine red, demonstrating the color variation within the species. Following the sound of running water, look for pristine white **boulder raspberry** and purple **western spiderwort**—both common along this loop. White blossoms of rose family members **wild plum, chokecherry,** and **hawthorn** mature into fall fruits, providing food for wildlife. The track ascends past the polished leaves of poison ivy, summed up by the old saw: "Leaves of three, leave them be, berries white, a poisonous sight."

An interesting outcrop fronts a big trail map sign. Note the Apex/Pick 'n Sledge/Sluicebox loop. Just beyond the sign, **yellow stonecrop** thrives in shallow soil pockets on or next to rocks. With its succulent leaves and brassy stars, this plant adapts to foothills, fourteeners, and all elevations in between.

After briefly meeting the creek, Apex Trail rises over rocky ground until it comes to a junction where it heads right on Pick 'n Sledge Trail. Not far up the track, **prickly poppy**'s milky-blue-accented foliage appears, growing stubbornly in the rocky soil. Native Americans once used this plant's orangey-yellow, acrid juices to combat skin diseases. In the same locale, look for spires of white **plains larkspur**.

Where the trail climbs quickly across a dry south-facing slope, **spiderwort** reigns. Some interesting names attached to this plant are **bluejackets**, **widow's tears**, and **cow slobbers**—the latter probably refers to the ooze **spiderwort** flowers become at day's end.

At last, the trail levels a bit, reaching a panoramic view of the Denver metro area. Growing abundantly on the slopes nearby, prickly-leaved, early-blooming **creeping hollygrape**, or **mahonia**, flaunts brassy flower clusters. Great patches of little bluestem bunchgrass anchor the stony soil, turning salmon in autumn. The trail switchbacks toward the west again, flanked by big bluestem.

Grassy wildflower gardens of **wallflower**, **mouse-ear**, and **white gilia** grow in open spaces between stands of smooth sumac and mountain mahogany. Look for hemi-parasitic **orange paintbrush** growing in close proximity to the sage or bunch grasses plants from which it steals sustenance.

The trail continues its ascent, becoming rockier as it follows a switchback. Scattered ponderosa pines are preceded by **bastard toadflax**, or more genteelly, **pale**

BOULDER RASPBERRY
Oreobatus deliciosus

Found in the foothills and montane life zones, this rose family member floats wide, white blossoms on lanky bushes sporting currant-like dark leaves. Older bark shreds on drought-tolerant **boulder raspberry,** which does indeed usually grow in the company of boulders. The fruit is an insipid drupe that is seedy, dry, and disappointing, belying the species name *deliciosus*. Wildlife finds the fruits just fine. Related shrubs include **wild rose** (*rosa woodsii*) and **ninebark** (*Physocarpus monogynus*).

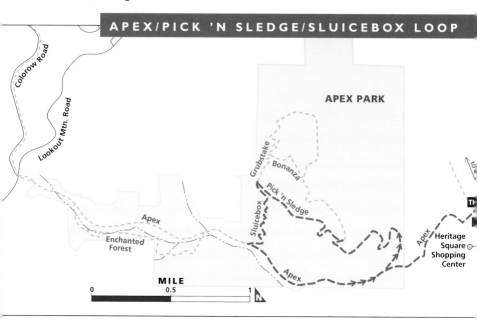

APEX/PICK 'N SLEDGE/SLUICEBOX LOOP

APEX PARK

Grubstake

Bonanza

Pick 'n Sledge

Sluicebox

Apex

Enchanted Forest

Apex

Apex

Heritage Square Shopping Center

MILE

0   0.5   1

comandra. This sole local member of the sandalwood family is common along Pick 'n Sledge Trail.

Where the trail turns a corner to view the city and the plains beyond, note a long, white shape on the horizon looking like a solitary range of permanently snowcapped peaks: the Denver International Airport.

Moving on, **scorpionweed** unfurls washed-out white inflorescences as coiled as the tail of a scorpion. This borage clansman is fond of disturbed places. Also partial to disturbed earth, nearby **cutleaf evening primrose** displays fine, pale, deeply cut foliage that bends under silver dollar-sized blooms.

The track eases a bit alongside shrubs sheltering **wallflower** ranging in color from lemon yellow to burnt orange to coppery red. This fragrant mustard family member's juices were once used to heal blisters. Sounds of civilization disappear as the route continues past a few lonely ponderosa pines, then turns up a switch-back onto a southwest-facing slope.

Soon, a junction sends Grubstake Trail right while this loop continues left on Pick 'n Sledge Trail. Rocky and rising, the trail heads up past low-profile swarms of **buckbrush**.

After the next switchback comes into view and the footpath levels, Douglas firs, which prefer north slopes, shelter **Rocky Mountain phlox**. The trail crosses a sunny slope where ivory wands of **death camas** poke above the grasses. In August, bright batons of rosy-purple **gayfeather** perk up the fading vegetation.

The shaded trail broadens as it starts down, passing colonies of **bluemist penstemon**. An occasional ladder-leafed tuft of **Parry milkvetch** blooms in off-white accented with purple-tipped keels.

Another junction soon arrives where the loop angles left onto Sluicebox Trail. A number of zigzags take the track through more **boulder raspberry**. As the track switchbacks under pines, a variety of wildflowers such as **early larkspur, yellow violet**, and more **wallflower** color the spring earth.

Sluicebox Trail drops quickly below the ponderosa pine belt to rejoin Apex Trail where the loop heads downstream. Legions of butterflies enjoy the creek, including little blue melissas, who "puddle" at every damp spot to quench their thirst for moisture and minerals.

Apex Trail touches the creek under narrow-leaved cottonwood. A grassy glade in deep shade presents **starwort**, a dainty chickweed family member with opposite lance-shaped leaves on thready stems, and five-petaled starry white flowers. Also edging the trail is abundant poison ivy. At the foot of a fern-draped northern bank where the route once again dips to meet the creek, search for hot pink **shooting stars** during their brief bloom season.

The trail passes to the right of a large outcrop and travels through extensive thickets of white-blooming **hawthorn, chokecherry**, and **wild plum**. The latter supports draping vines of **western virgin's bower**. Follow Apex Trail back to the parking area.

Creeping hollygrape blooms early.

Wildflower Hike 20

Rawhide /Longhorn / Maverick / Sawmill / Mustang /Belcher Hill Loop

Rugged outcrops and rampant wildflowers make this loop a must-do.

Trail Rating	moderate
Trail Length	3.8-mile loop
Location	White Ranch/Golden
Elevation	7,500 to 7,800 feet
Bloom Season	June to September
Peak Bloom	June
Directions	From Golden, head north on CO 93. Turn left down County Road 46/Golden Gate Canyon Rd. and continue 3.9 miles to take a right onto Crawford Gulch Rd. Travel 4.0 more miles, then turn right down Belcher Hill Rd. and continue 1.8 miles to the White Ranch Park's main parking area.

TUCKED INTO ROLLING PONDEROSA PARKLAND in the foothills west of Golden, White Ranch is an archetype of Jefferson County's Open Space array. Once a cattle ranch operated by the White family, this land is now a 4,207-acre open space park, providing nearly 20 miles of scenic trails. This 3.8-mile loop samples Rawhide, Longhorn, Maverick, Sawmill, Mustang, and Belcher Hill trails. Fine scenery complements the six dozen wildflower species along the loop. Hike in mid-June to catch both spring and summer species in bloom. Ample parking is available. Be alert for mountain bikers.

From the main parking lot, head left (northeast) on Rawhide Trail. Travel through level grassland, passing antique ranch equipment. About two dozen species of wildflowers bloom here, including **orange paintbrush**, **early larkspur**, **chiming bells**, **sulphurflower**, **orange agoseris**, and **locoweed**. As you pass the restrooms, look for **wallflower** blooming in showy gold and burnt orange beside complementary **bluemist penstemon** and **purple field milkvetch**. In late summer, spikes of vivid **gayfeather** brighten the tawny grass where the trail heads down between the comfort station and picnic area.

Continue east, following signs that direct you right on Longhorn Trail. Accompanied by hot **paintbrush** swabs, curve around to another Longhorn sign and descend through a sloping meadow, where **leafy cinquefoil** and its comrades **orange agoseris** and **wallflower** attract nectaring Aphrodite fritillary butterflies.

Narrowing through a rough little switchback, the trail reaches for a view of the Denver metro area and the vast plains beyond. Continuing down the slope through pines, noting **cinquefoil**, **paintbrush**, and **wallflower** by an outcrop. The eye soon encounters **buckbrush**. Here, as it is in so many Front Range parks, alien **tall butter 'n eggs**, or **Dalamatian toadflax**, is making aggressive inroads, to the detriment of native wildflowers.

Take an acute right turn, leaving Longhorn Trail to begin Maverick Trail. Up ahead, both **orchid** and **bluemist penstemons** decorate a pine-shaded outcrop. Also note **whiplash fleabane**, **spiderwort**, and flares of **paintbrush**.

Curve through a prize-winning rock garden decorated by Mother Nature with a palette of magenta **locoweed**, yellow **wallflower**, **bluemist** and **orchid penstemons**, **orange paintbrush**, and white **miner's candle**.

Dip into a ravine that nurtures **golden banner** and **false Solomon's seal**, then ascend log waterbars to travel the north bank of a seasonal creek. Along the creek, look for **few-flowered false Solomon's seal**; its sparse, tiny star flowers provide another common name, **star Solomon's seal**. Chunky, moss-cloaked granite favoring **waxflower** shrubs may also turn up a **blue columbine**.

A shady ascent brings on **spotted coralroot** before open terrain gives **skullcap** a chance to show off its purple velvet pairs. Spires of **silvery lupine** and **purple milkvetch**'s scented globes welcome a gentle trail segment that contours in sight of **boulder raspberry** and, in mid-summer, **beebalm**.

Back under open skies, log waterbars lead to lichened rocks overlooking **prickly pear cactus**. Nearby butter-yellow **tall false dandelion** or **pale agoseris** is a subtle native compared to that ubiquitous imported rogue of lawns, common dandelion. Late summer introduces **prairie gentian**.

A **bluemist penstemon** rock garden precedes an s-curve that further elevates the route. To the left, under an old ponderosa, a grand display of **spotted coralroot** pokes through a gray-green **pussytoes** carpet.

A distant view of red Ralston Buttes to the north rewards the next hill. Trailside **death camas**' creamy pyramids look pleasant but smell otherwise. The whole plant is toxic, as the name implies.

Drift along through **ninebark** shrubs displaying clusters of white flowers that age rusty-salmon to reach a junction where our loop turns right, heading briefly uphill along Belcher Hill Trail.

At a three-way intersection, turn left on Sawmill Trail, where a sign states: "hiker's camping area 0.6 miles." Check nearby for **Fendler sandwort**'s wee white stars suspended on wiry stems over grass-like leaves. In the vicinity, **mouse-ear** mix with **early blue daisy**.

As you wander along the old ranch road among soughing pines, look to the right for a quartz-laden outcrop that heralds an unusual wildflower: **false pimpernel**, also known as **blue toadflax**. Pause to enjoy the view from an exposed backcountry campsite.

Open-skied shrublands, composed mostly of **mountain mahogany**, begin where Sawmill Trail narrows to pass **kinnikinnick**. Partial to gravelly or lithic soil, this prostrate sub-shrub, also called **bearberry**, is a member of the heath clan and is related to manzanita. Where ragged granite breaks the skyline up ahead, a few scraggly aspens make way for lots of **bluemist penstemon** and a bit of purple **skullcap** and **blanketflower**.

One-third mile past the backpacker's camp, our loop takes a right on Mustang Trail. Lifted by log waterbars, the trail encounters lots of **few-flowered false Solomon's seal**. Resourceful Native Americans once ate the young shoots and leaves of this plant.

BLUE-EYED GRASS
Sisyrinchium monyanum

The only grass-like thing about this member of the iris family is the shape and clumping habit of the leaves. Its flower stalks grow up to about 18 inches tall, opening one bloom at a time. Six satiny, lavender-blue tepals enclose a pert yellow eye, later maturing into a ball-shaped seed capsule. Spreading from fibrous roots and preferring grassy places, **blue-eyed grass** thrives where there is spring moisture and summer dryness. Native Americans used the whole plant to make a tea for stomachaches and birth control; the roots were found useful as an anti-diarrheal.

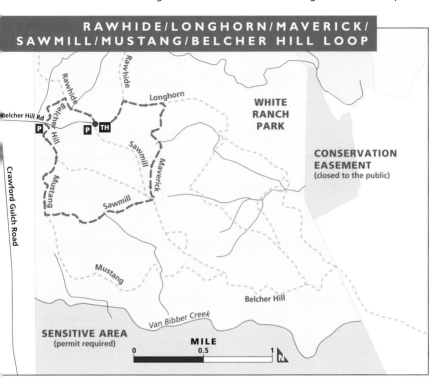

RAWHIDE/LONGHORN/MAVERICK/
SAWMILL/MUSTANG/BELCHER HILL LOOP

Pause at a lush little drainage on the left to observe hot pink **shooting stars**. The way they point indicates pollination success: up is fertilized; down is waiting for a pollinator. **Blue-eyed grass**, a starry iris relation, puts in a brief appearance nearby.

The trail steepens, switchbacking past rugged outcrops. Late-summer hikers will enjoy **goldenrod** blooming in disturbed trailside soils. After the last switchback, the trail flattens as it returns to the ponderosa belt.

A bench signals an upcoming fork where our route stays left, heading downhill on Belcher Hill Trail. **Tall pussytoes**, nearly 2 feet high, appear in clumped colonies; cousin common **pussytoes** spreads in creeping mats. Also look for an occasional **blue columbine** and plenty of six-petaled **blue-eyed grass**.

Continue downhill, crossing the wide entrance road to access a pleasant segment of the loop that continues downhill about two-thirds of the way into the parking area. Along this final stretch, **ninebark**, **chokecherry**, and **serviceberry** shrubs flank the trail along with Rocky Mountain maple. Ponderosas shelter the spurred flowers of **early larkspur** and sunny **heartleaf arnica**.

Pass aspens, heading out into open skies. A cool swatch of **wild iris** blooms to your left. In mid-summer, look for minty **beebalm**.

Bright wildflowers color a small rock garden where the trail reaches an old ranch road and heads right. Pass a big ponderosa cradling another swatch of **wild iris** in its shade. A wide-skied meadow returns you to your vehicle.

*Wildflower
Hike 21*

Red Rocks/Morrison Slide Loop

Chokecherry blooms near the red sandstone Fountain Formation visible along the Red Rocks/Morrison Slide Loop.

Trail Rating	easy to moderate
Trail Length	4.2-mile balloon loop
Location	Matthews/Winter Park/Golden
Elevation	6,200 to 6,730 feet
Bloom Season	May to October
Peak Bloom	mid-May to June
Directions	From Denver, take I-70 west to exit 259. Head south on County Road 93 under I-70. Take your first right onto Matthews/Winters Park access road. The trailhead is just past the footbridge.

This 4-mile loop is convenient to the Denver metro area and passes the historical 1859 Mt. Vernon townsite. About six dozen wildflower species pop up along the trail in the latter half of May. Early-season hikers may be rewarded with Easter daisies and sand lilies followed by blanketflower and orchid penstemon. Late summer exhibits rabbitbrush and gayfeather.

Mountain bikers share the busy trailhead parking lot, which often fills on fine weather weekends. Early arrival is recommended.

Check near the clear creek for potently sweet-smelling **wild plum** and colonizing **Macouns buttercup.** After crossing the footbridge, keep straight, passing through gray-green bushes of **rabbitbrush.** As the trail curves south, look for **sand lilies'** delicate white tubes nestled in dark linear leaves.

At a "T" intersection, where the spur to the Mt. Vernon cemetery heads west, continue south on Red Rocks Trail, passing a **wild plum** thicket. Note **milkvetches,** such as long-tubed and spreading **early pink,** milky-white and bushy **Drummond,** and white **Parry,** with its muted purple keel tip. **Spiderwort's** six neon stamens center its showy bloom that lasts but one day; however, plenty of drooping buds promise the next day's flowers.

Dipping briefly into a small, brush-choked ravine, the trail levels, passing **golden banner, puccoon** or **fringed gromwell,** and **lanceleaf chiming bells.** Nearby, prolific, alien **tall butter 'n eggs,** or **Dalmatian toadflax,** threatens native wildflowers. **Early pink milkvetch** leads to a red rock where yellow **bladderpod** puts in an appearance.

Changing from a north aspect to one facing south brings on luminescent **orchid penstemon**

GOLDEN CURRANT
Ribes aureum

This attractive shrub grows up to 6 feet tall. In early spring it sprouts smooth, green fans of lobed leaves; later in spring it dangles spicy-smelling, red-tipped, gold tubes; in summer it forms dark edible berries; and fall brings a lovely red tint to the leaves. The flowers' spicy aroma is that of cloves, initiating the name **clovebush;** another name is **buffalo currant.** The berries, used sparingly, were incorporated into pemmican—that compact paragon of nutrients and fat esteemed by resourceful Native Americans and later adopted by stalwart mountain men. A gooseberry clan relative is **wax currant** (*Ribes cerenum),* an unpalatable cousin.

in lavender-pink, **Lambert's locoweed** in loud magenta, and **Geyer larkspur** in electric blue.

The undulating track drifts into an arroyo where **copper mallow**, alternately called **cowboy's delight**, opens peachy-orange blossoms. Shaded by box elder trees, the seasonal trickle precedes a hillside of rich purple **early larkspur**. A lone Douglas fir nurtures **Canada violet** in its thick shade. **American vetch**'s arcing tendrils send this violet-pink pea family member scrambling over handy neighbors. Nearby **white-flowered peavine** is less unruly.

Pass outcrops featuring the paired, velvety blossoms of **skullcap**, the earliest bloomer in the mint family. **Bladderpod** and lustrous **orchid** or **sidebells penstemon** dwell here as well.

Cautiously s-curve down a loose segment, passing **wild plum** before crossing a drainage. Rocky Mountain maple and **chokecherry** signal a switchback ascent. At a junction, turn right on Morrison Slide Trail.

Easing upward, take a moment to study the Dakota Hogback ridge to the east—a locally renowned repository for dinosaur-era evidence. Another ascending switchback introduces **bluemist penstemon** and cream spikes of **death camas**, as poisonous as its name implies. Native Americans had an accurate name for it: poison onion. Today, **wand** or **lonely lily** are common names.

Punctuated by juniper, the steadily ascending trail enters a section of tumbled red sandstone boulders. Although **spring beauty** and **wild candytuft** often bloom in February, protected specimens under the oak scrub on this north-facing slope may still be in flower. Over to the left, watch for **golden currant**, or **clovebush**, dangling gold tubes redolent of spicy cloves.

Zigzag up on rockier footing to where the trail bisects an area of big boulders that harbor **boulder raspberry** shrubs. Here also is **waxflower**, a shrub of ancient lineage in the hydrangea clan with perfect, porcelain-looking flowers.

On a cupped shelf down a bit to the left, a specimen or two of **mountain ball cactus** flowers briefly in mid-May. Silky yellow **prickly pear cactus** blooms a bit later.

The ascent ends on an escarpment's flat bench, where a far-reaching panorama features Green Mountain in the foreground. Nearby, among the lichen-encrusted rocks, **orange paintbrush** flares up while yellow **wallflower** displays fragrant cruciform flowers. Also look for **mouse-ear**, **spike gilia**, **leafy cinquefoil**, and, in the early season, **Easter daisy**. **Meadow arnica**'s golden rays draw attention to damper zones.

Wend toward the bench's far side and drop via rugged switchbacks. Junipers stud the landscape clear to the Red Rocks Amphitheater to the south. Pause to view bright **spiderwort** and fevered bracts of **paintbrush**. About halfway down the descent, the crevices of an outcrop prow secret **boulder raspberry** and **bluemist penstemon**. In late summer, **snakeweed** adds touches of brassy yellow.

At a junction, a sign continues the loop straight ahead and up a short incline. Farther on, as the route heads north, trailsides nourish patches of

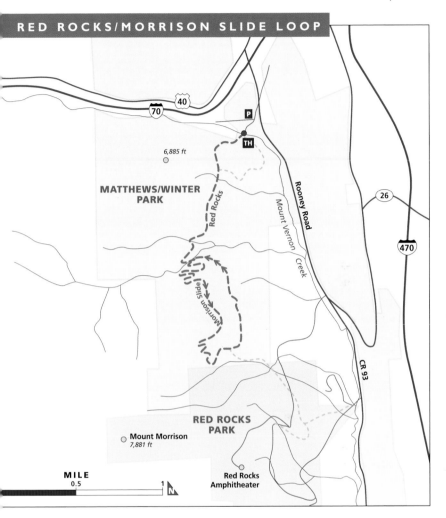

glossy-leaved poison ivy. Heed the old saw, "Leaves of three, leave them be . . ."

Perennial **bush sunflower** and **gumweed** brighten the loop's return along the escarpment's foot. **Skunkbrush, lemonadebush,** and **squawbush** are all meaningful common names for upcoming **threeleaf sumac.** The first realizes the crushed foliage's odor; the second, its sticky red berries as a refreshing drink ingredient; the third, its basket-weaving value.

Footing remains uneven as the trail cruises northwest. In mid-summer, swatches of minty **beebalm** present rosy-lilac fountains beloved of bees and butterflies. Check the stem's square shape, a characteristic of the mint family.

Arriving back at the creek drainage completes the balloon portion of the hike; only the string remains. At the rail fence triangle, stay left to travel down the zigzag. From there, return down the gentle slope through golden masses of late-blooming **rabbitbrush.**

Wildflower Hike 22

Beaver Brook West

Burbling Beaver Creek is Metro-close. In June, enjoy 70 species of wildflowers along this shady trail.

Trail Rating	moderate
Trail Length	3.0 miles out and back with reverse keyhole loop
Location	Genesee Park/Golden
Elevation	6,600 to 7,400 feet
Bloom Season	May to September
Peak Bloom	June
Directions	From Denver, take I-70 west to exit 253/Chief Hosa. Head right, then right again on Stapleton Dr. Continue 1.1 miles to the trailhead, located at a closed gate.

THIS SECTION of Denver Mountain Park's Beaver Brook Trail, quickly accessed from the Denver metro area via I-70, presents a worthy hike. June hikers may encounter over 70 species of wildflowers along the shady, 1.5-mile segment.

Begin at the Braille Trail parking area. From here, Beaver Brook Trail, sections of which were once used by Native Americans, shares its first 0.3 mile with Stapleton Nature Trail. It then crosses a footbridge and follows a conifer-shaded, east-facing path. Turn around when you reach lively Beaver Brook.

Parking on early summer weekends gets creative in the two small parking areas adjacent to the signed trailhead.

A sturdy cable leads our route off along a south-facing slope. This 0.3-mile segment, which is attended by a series of interpretive signs, leads to the Beaver Brook trailhead. Nearby, **bluemist penstemon**, **wild geranium**, and **lupine** enjoy the lithic soil. Joining them are **northern bedstraw**, **miner's candle**, and **whiskbroom parsley**. Look for both **loose-clustered** and **standing milkvetch**, which produce small, pea-type flowers. A bench follows on the right.

Edge down along the cable on uneven tread to a sign discussing juniper's soft, blue "berries"—actually, cones—which are used to flavor wild game and gin. Another relates the vanilla scent of ponderosa pine bark.

The cable is interrupted by an old stage road but resumes a couple of strides later, sending the trail into a pocket of aspen where **white geranium** and **cow parsnip** flourish near a seasonal waterway. The trail reaches a sign describing neighboring conifers: fir needles are friendly and flat, while those of spruce are spiky and square.

A couple of picnic tables precede a sign turning the route left, toward Beaver Brook Trail. Pick your way down uneven rock steps and across a footbridge. **Black-eyed Susans** and **bur avens**, both yellow, join the blues of **tall false forget-me-not** and **blue-eyed grass** blooming by the creeklet.

After the bridge, a turn to the right (north) puts you on the

WILD SARSAPARILLA
Aralia nudicaulis

This aromatic eastern plant shows up in shady spots, often near streams. It is in the herbally famous ginseng family, which, unexpectedly, includes **English Ivy**. Looking like a green Sputnik, the flowering head is shorter than the tri-leafed, 3–5 leafleted stalks. The spherically umbellate heads of nondescript flowers mature to green, then purple berries. **Wild sarsaparilla** roots constitute a beverage base. Native Americans considered the roots a survival food.

Beaver Brook Trail—to stay on course, watch for occasional tree-mounted, square-shaped trail markers lettered "BB." The evergreen shade here creates an environment conducive to **heartleaf arnica**'s sunbursts and **waxflower**'s porcelain-perfect stars. A plush collection of **ninebark, scarlet paintbrush, waterleaf, meadowrue**, and **tall false forget-me-not** also thrives here.

Leaving the lush, shaded vegetation, the track bursts upon plant life adapted to a dry habitat. Invasive and alien **tall butter 'n eggs**, or **Dalmatian toadflax**, competes with native perennials **bush sunflower** and **tall pussytoes** on this brushy, sunstruck slope.

The trail eases gently downhill, where more shade encourages dainty **blue clematis** to twine up and over trees, shrubs, rocks, and even itself. Its pale purple to nearly white sepals hide reproductive parts; its seedheads are showy platinum swirls.

Conifer shade and rocky soil create choice habitat for **waxflower**, a member of ancient lineage in the hydrangea family. The shrub's matte, light-green leaves, puckered by strong veins, sparingly clothe its rangy branches.

Pass through a nursery of Douglas firs sheltering **blue columbine** to reach a sunlit, rugged canyon hillside where **boulder raspberry** blooms whitely and red-centered **blanketflower**, or **gaillardia**, attracts butterflies that look like amber stained-glass windows. Nearby, look for the honey-scented dangling bells and lance-shaped leaves of **spreading dogbane**.

The gradient angles down stone steps to a small creek running over ribboned bedrock. Look for parsley clan members **cow parsnip** and **wild caraway** thriving under cottonwoods, aspens, and willow. A spruce with a BB sign on it invites you to pause by the clear brook and take a whiff of wild caraway's thready, bright green foliage. In the vicinity, **wild rose** overlooks the water, while **goldenglow**, or **tall coneflower**, shoots up for summer blooming and yellow **wintercress** fades.

Return to the descending trail, where decomposed granite soil proves ideal for strong-odored **canyon aletes**, another parsley tribesman. The plant's small, aromatic leaves, shaped like those of Italian flat parsley and redolent of citronella, support minuscule yellow flowers.

Pause to note a steep embankment where more **blue columbine** basks below oncoming **goldenglow**. Soon, sticky, alien **white bladder campion** pops up trailside. On a mossy north aspect leading to a descending set of stone stairs, Rocky Mountain maple provides shade for **Canada violet**. Down at creek level, narrow-leaf cottonwoods and **redtwig dogwood** shelter **cow parsnip**, **white geranium**, and primitive horsetails.

Undulating into an area of charcoal-gray rock to gain elevation above the waterway, the trail cruises by an outcrop perched on the left. A xeric slope on the left presents silky petals of **prickly pear cactus** in pale yellow, sandpaper-rough **bush sunflower**, and spiky **yucca**. Also look for soft violet **wand penstemon**,

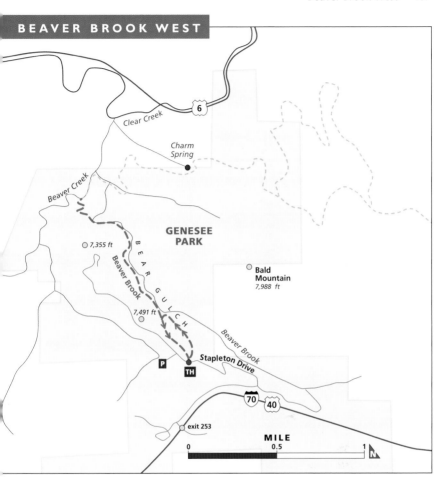

whose slender stalks grow up to 30 inches tall. Nearby **spiderwort**'s drooping buds open to three bluish-purple petals centered by neon yellow stamens.

The trail curves left (west) to begin a steeper descent into Bear Gulch. More sunny **aletes**, smelling like citrus-tinged celery, cling to the rugged canyonsides. The north-facing walls rising in close proximity to you are a favorite haunt of **waxflower**. Rocks and roots call for careful foot placement. Along the descent, **harebells** dance on wiry stems where earlier **cutleaf fleabane daisy**, a flea-bane, flowered in tidy clumps. Nearby, the deep-clefted leaflets of dainty **blue clematis** give a delicate look to its scrambling vines; its seed plumes flare into a rounded, platinum coif.

Gold and silvery gray lichen encrusts a sheer outcrop where the route takes a firm right—note the BB sign—and drops quickly on stone steps. The trail evens where outcrop ledges sustain early-blooming **snowball saxifrage**, identifi-able by its fine-toothed, rhomboid leaves. Moss-hung rock leads up to a couple of switchbacks where annual **golden smoke,** of the often-toxic fumitory clan, blooms.

A shelf of rock under a formidable cliff face becomes the foot bed for a brief bit of the trail before **spreading dogbane** and another "BB" sign arrive. Rocky tread brings you to **rock spirea,** an arching shrub also known as **mountain spray.**

You have now reached Beaver Brook. The joyful noise of it tumbling flow entices you to cool your feet in the clear water. After enjoying the creek—deeply shaded courtesy of maple, willow, and alder—retrace your steps to the trailhead. Be sure to drink plenty of water on the uphill return trip.

Once back to the footbridge and guiding cable, resume reading interpretive signs as you travel up the opposite (west) side of the Stapleton Nature Trail loop. Duff-padded tread ascends to the tiny spring-fed creeklet, which is spanned by a broad platform. Up on the left grows three-leaflet **wild sarsaparilla,** a member of the ginseng family. Nearby, **sweet cicely** sends its helicopter seedheads aloft where early-season hikers would have found **pasqueflowers.** The trail ends at the lower parking area with a last whisper of **wild rose** perfume.

Blanketflower is also known as gaillardia.

Meadow/Meadow View/Elkridge/ Sleepy "S" Loop

Wild iris grows where there is spring moisture and summer dryness—this loop through Elk Meadow Open Space provides just the right conditions.

easy	**Trail Rating**
2.6-mile balloon loop	**Trail Length**
Elk Meadow Park/Evergreen	**Location**
7,760 to 8,120 feet	**Elevation**
June to August	**Bloom Season**
late May to mid-June	**Peak Bloom**
From Denver, take I-70 west. Take exit 252 to merge onto CO 74 E/Evergreen Parkway and continue 6 miles. Turn right at Stagecoach Blvd. and continue 1.25 miles to the trailhead.	**Directions**

ELK MEADOW OPEN SPACE PARK, north of Evergreen, provides an island home for wildlife and wildflowers. About 12 miles of trail and a wildlife preserve, where elk can sometimes be seen, make this Jefferson County open space attractive. This 2.6-mile loop explores Meadow View, Elkridge, and Sleepy "S" trails. During late May to mid-June, you may encounter around 50 wildflower species typical to foothills-montane life zones.

The parking lot at the Meadow View trailhead fills quickly on weekends, so come early or, better yet, on a weekday. Wheelchair-accessible picnic tables and restrooms are a boon.

Follow well-graveled Meadow Trail past picnic sites and restrooms. **Mouse-ear, bluemist penstemon**, **Rocky Mountain phlox**, **chiming bells**, and **leafy cinquefoil** start the wildflower parade, soon joined by **skullcap**, the earliest of the mint family to bloom.

Shaded by big pines, the track levels toward vermilion **orange paintbrush**. In the same area, look for **early blue daisy**. This erect-stemmed fleabane has neatly clumped green basal leaves sporting stiff hairs on their margins and wider ray petals than many of its kin.

A junction soon appears where the loop leads left, on Meadow View Trail. Under a big ponderosa on the left, check for flat-inflorescenced **early spring senecio**, looking like disarrayed golden yellow daisies on a long stalk.

A meadow opens, featuring dusky-purple **sugarbowls**. This substantially-tepaled wildflower has earned labels such as **leatherflower** and **old maid's bonnet**. Resembling slightly bedraggled feathers, the pale green, soft-haired foliage acts as a foil for shining, pinwheel seedheads.

GOLDEN BANNER
Thermopsis divaricarpa

Golden banner is a lusty, colonizing plant, capable of spreading several feet a season. Banner, wings, and keel make up bright yellow corollas so tightly configured as to solicit fertilization by hefty, determined bumblebees. The plant grows from 12 to 24 inches tall and bears divided, three-segment leaves. This legume family member is very toxic, making alternate labels such as **yellow pea** or **spreading goldenbean** unfortunate.

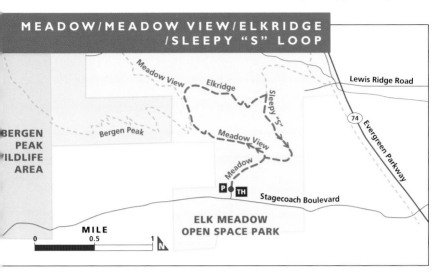

The trail enters coniferous forest where common juniper, a low, prickly shrub, is found. The cool environs also suit **spotted coralroot orchid**, whose bare, fleshy stalks rise out of the forest floor like reddish-brown asparagus. The exquisite design of each tiny orchid is best appreciated through a hand lens.

The narrowing path traverses deep shade, where it pays to keep an eye peeled for two small early bloomers: **golden draba** and **northern rock primrose**. Finding draba in low forest light requires a search. Look for a rich yellow pouf held high above a quarter-sized rosette of deep green, lance-shaped leaves. Northern **rock primrose**, an annual, is longer blooming and more common here, but even more visually elusive. Its minuscule stars perch on the ends of a wiry umbel hinting at the imaginative name **northern fairy candelabra**.

Continue along the level forest track, where **harebells** will eventually bloom. Openings of aspen, Rocky Mountain maple, and pink-budded **ninebark** frame brief views to the east. **Golden smoke**, also found here, tucks its yellow blooms into soft, California poppy like foliage. **Scrambled eggs** is a common alias fitting the odd flowers of this member of the often-toxic fumitory family.

Beneath the trees before the first switchback, evergreen mats of **kinnikinnick** line the trailsides. Scan the area for plumy seedheads of purple-chaliced, Easter-time-blooming **pasqueflowers**. **Wild geranium** and **lupine** bloom beyond a second switchback.

The trail eases as it passes some boulders, near which lush examples of **false Solomon's seal** prosper. This common member of the Mayflower clan sports 2- to 3-foot, arcing stems of large, shiny leaves and curved racemes of fragrant, creamy white flowers. **Few-flowered false Solomon's seal**, with narrow, lighter leaves and sparser flowering, grows nearby, offering a chance to distinguish between the two.

Pass the Bergen Peak turnoff and continue on Meadow View Trail as it swings east to traverse a southern exposure dotted with **boulder raspberry**. A little farther on, a spreading colony of **golden banner** lights the way.

Before long, a junction, anchored by a bench, heads our loop right along Elkridge Trail. On this open segment of the loop, **buckbrush** fills in the spaces between showings of **bladderpod**, **whiskbroom parsley**, **penstemon**, **senecio**, and more patches of **fleabane daisy**.

Level at first, then descending, the trail sparkles with mica. Here and there on both sides of the track are flat, white heads of **yarrow**. This gray-green, ferny-leafed composite was once used as a tonic, an insect repellent, a local anesthetic (chewing the leaves is supposed to numb the mouth), and a coagulant.

After a switchback, Elkridge Trail enters ponderosa parkland. Following a second gentle switchback, more plumed seedheads of **pasqueflowers** dot the grasses.

The next intersection turns the loop right on Sleepy "S" Trail. The track is even now as it heads southwest past a beckoning bench. Low-growing **silvery cinquefoil**, prolific in this locale, flanks the trail. Its summer-blooming yellow flowers are sparsely borne, and its sharp-toothed leaflets so dense with soft hair as to appear silver. Native Americans treated burns and sores with a powder derived from this plant.

Before the trail starts rising comfortably through large ponderosas, it passes some boulders, complete with the almost requisite **boulder raspberry**. In spring, just before the path makes its first sleepy s-curve, a nice stand of **wild iris** blooms on the left. Another bench soon appears on the left with a view of fiery **paintbrush** and a robust **cinquefoil**.

Just beyond this flowery open meadow, the loop rejoins Meadow View Trail, heading left back to the parking area.

If you'd like to spot some elk after your hike, drive up CO 74 along the east boundary of Elk Meadows Open Space, then turn west along the north boundary on Squaw Pass Road. Sight across a vast meadowed swale to aspen-edged forest for an elk-studded view. The elk are most likely to be here during fall rut. Binoculars assist immeasurably.

Grass Creek

*Fourteener Mount Evans rises over an emerald meadow along
the Grass Creek Trail.*

easy to moderate	**Trail Rating**
4.2 miles out and back	**Trail Length**
Evergreen/Mt. Evans Wildlife Management Area	**Location**
8,700 to 9,400 feet	**Elevation**
June to September	**Bloom Season**
June to July	**Peak Bloom**
From Denver, take I-70 west to exit 252 and merge onto CO 74 E/Evergreen Pkwy. Continue 7.4 miles toward Evergreen. Head right on Upper Bear Creek Rd. After about 6 miles, go right on Corral Creek Rd. for about 2 miles, then go left at a "Wildlife Area" sign. Continue approximately 1.5 miles to the trailhead and picnic area.	**Directions**

GRASS CREEK TRAIL, which follows an old road west of Evergreen, offers the majority of its wildflowers in the first half of the trek, before elevation gain gets aerobically demanding. Early in the hike, enjoy a wonderful walk along golden Bear Creek, peaceful in both sight and sound. Of the five dozen montane-zone wildflower species found in late June or early July, a full four dozen appear before the hike leaves Bear Creek to begin its relentless ascent.

Hikers beware: This well-managed area is open to hunting in the fall—check with the Colorado Division of Wildlife for dates before setting off.

While warnings are afoot, consider the strong possibility of summer afternoon thunderstorm activity; be prepared for them or, better yet, practice avoidance with an early hike.

Parking at the trailhead is usually adequate.

BLACK-EYED SUSAN
Rudbeckia hirta

Native Americans called this coarse-foliaged, hairy plant **deer-eye,** and valued it for its medicinal properties. Its roots were used to make a tea for colds and a wash for sores and snakebite. Growing up to 30 inches tall, **black-eyed Susan** features bright gold ray flowers centered by a cabochon of dark disc florets; each tubular disc flower produces a seed. The genus name honors Father Olaf Rudbeck and his son, both 17th-century Swedish botanists. The Latin species name, *hirta*, means "hairy."

A wide metal gate stands at the Grass Creek trailhead. Beyond the gate, wildflowers such as **black-eyed Susan, northern bedstraw,** and both pink **wild** and **white geranium** start things off. Golden granite cutbanks harbor drooping **dogbane** and **yellow stonecrop** stars before the trail/roadway heads up a long steady incline flanked by small quaking aspens. On the east-facing slope, **ninebark** bushes present blushed white blooms that age rusty-salmon.

As the route pushes for the crest, look for intensely blue **mountain penstemon.** Bright pink **wild rose** assists the quest with intoxicating perfume. **Scarlet paintbrush** and **tall Jacob's ladder** huddle in little hollows. Nearby **salsify**'s lofty yellow rays soon

GRASS CREEK

MT EVANS STATE WILDLIFE AREA

Bear Creek

P
TH gate

MILES
0   1   2

become baseball-sized puffs like dandelions on steroids. On the left, **blue columbine** decorates the understory of black-scarred aspens.

Drift down the hill's south side, passing carpets of **kinnikinnick** rooting along in ideally lithic soil. Snake past granite blisters poking up among stunted aspens and **black-eyed Susans**. Stalks of **yellow evening primrose** pop sporadically in disturbed roadside soil, as do **scorpionweed**, **dragonhead**, and **beauty cinquefoil**, whose cousins **silvery** and **leafy cinquefoil** also appear along the route.

Bear Creek sets the road off on a long level stretch. Colorado blue spruce spire into the mountain air. Along the road, gravelly earth supports abundant **wild rose** tall enough for a convenient whiff of heaven.

Creek sounds are life sounds to plants such as **green bog orchid**, **tall chiming bells**, and **shooting stars**. Great blocks of granite set the scene for roadside biennial **dusty maiden**, whose ashen-pink inflorescences rise above grayish foliage, making this rayless composite aptly named. South-facing cutbanks offer bright, peachy-pink **fairy trumpets**, or **pink gilia**. As the trail swings toward an open meadow, look on the left for a colony of white **meadow anemone**.

Look trailside for interpretive signs explaining the prescribed burns that took place in this small valley. Water sounds draw attention to the creek, where **cow parsnip** unfolds dinosaur-dinner-plate-sized leaves and broad white blooms. On the road's dry right side, **blanketflower**, or **gaillardia**, joins **lupine**. Hefty chunks of granite rear out of the hillsides where **beebalm** and **golden aster** will soon bloom.

On the left, willows stand guard over another gathering of pretty **meadow anemone**. On the xeric right, **tall false** or **stickseed forget-me-not** gains height before opening its baby-blue, five-lobed flowers.

Cross a sturdy plank bridge, leaving the golden stream to bright-winged Aphrodite fritillaries and tiger swallowtails. From here, it is a long aerobic climb to reach the emerald jewel of secretive Grass Creek. A majority of the resident wildflower species have already been sighted at this juncture, making the bridge a good turnaround point for those who don't wish to test their heart rate. Exercise and scenery enthusiasts should persevere on up to see a mass of gorgeous grass and a peek of Mount Evans' snowy folds.

Continuing up the wide, forest-flanked road brings you to sparse aspen, understoried by **golden banner** early in the season. **Tall pussytoes** take their blooming place, and a **dusty maiden** or two blooms in the roadway. As the trail rises, look for three craggy granite rocks on the right; behind them, a westward glimpse of 14,264-foot Mount Evans unfolds. Earlier, **bluemist penstemon** added to the view.

Drift down through soughing ponderosa pines to reach a small sign that says "Grass Creek." It fronts about 50 or 60 acres of green, green grass. A stone chimney is all that is left of a homesteader's cabin that once overlooked this meadow and was sadly set afire not so long ago. Entrenched Grass Creek curves in its iron-stained bed, nurturing **bur avens, rosy pussytoes, tall chiming bells,** and a few **shooting stars**. Waving above all is **American bistort**.

Lots of elk droppings in the vicinity attest to the fact that this is indeed a part of Mount Evans Wildlife Management Area. Before turning around, pause to enjoy meadow ambience and the snow-furrowed brows of high peaks to the west, such as Evans, Rogers, and Spalding. A wide view of Chief Mountain's ridge stretches to the south.

A tiger swallowtail butterfly at rest.

Tanglewood

Columbine prepares the way for a plethora of summer-blooming shooting stars along the Tanglewood Trail.

moderate	*Trail Rating*
4.4 miles out and back	*Trail Length*
Pike National Forest/Mount Evans Wilderness/Bailey	*Location*
9,250 to 10,440 feet	*Elevation*
June to September	*Bloom Season*
July	*Peak Bloom*
From Denver, take US 285 west. Head right on Deer Creek Rd./County Road 43. After 6.8 miles, bear left at the fork to stay on CR 43. Continue approximately 3 miles to Deer Creek campground. Head right at a creek crossing. The road dead-ends at the trailhead.	*Directions*

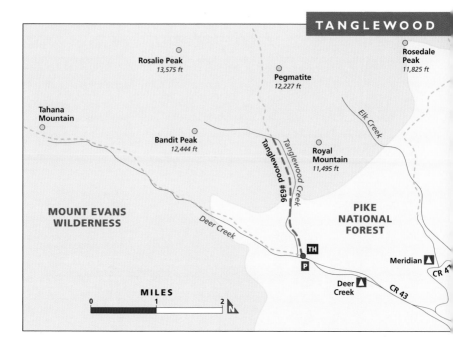

LIVELY TANGLEWOOD CREEK accompanies this great close-in hike through Mount Evans Wilderness and Pike National Forest. Follow the tight valley through alternating forest and flowery pocket meadows. A creekside meadow where a sawmill once operated is the turnaround point. Boots help mitigate the impact of wet or rocky trail stretches.

Pocket meadows of shooting stars and precious patches of calypso orchid highlight a hike that may count over 80 wildflower species in early July.

Sharing the parking area with horse trailers might mean a full house on weekends. Plan to arrive early, as those infamous thunder and lightning storms may brew up quickly on summer afternoons.

Lush pasture grasses surround the parking area, where a gap in a fence presents trailhead entry. Look for **wild caraway**, **blue columbine**, and **golden banner**. A sign announces that you are accessing Mount Evans Wilderness from the Deer Creek Trailhead.

With **wild strawberry** at your feet, look up the stony old roadbed for crisp pink **wild rose** among quaking aspens. Nearby saturated blue **mountain penstemon** is an outstanding example of the 160-some penstemon species in the Rockies.

A sign inscribed Tanglewood Trail # 636 sends you along on a level stretch into Colorado blue spruce shade. Streamside, **brookcress** gleams whitely, while **heartleaf arnica** and **few-flowered false Solomon's seal** grace the understory.

Tall chiming bells, lacy **cowbane**, **brookcress**, and **twistedstalk** rise near a split-log bridge spanning sparkling Tanglewood Creek. A mossy embankment on the left displays **green-flowered wintergreen** and spectacular **calypso orchids**. The far side highlights **blue columbine**, **cinquefoil**, and **boulder raspberry**.

Ferns flourish on a lichen-encrusted outcrop, while vibrant **shooting stars** enjoy the moisture at its base. Nearby, cerise cups of **red globe anemone** precede off-white **candle anemone**. **Tall scarlet paintbrush** flares on the east side of the creek. Where path and water touch, **white geranium** and more **shooting stars** nestle among feathery green horsetails.

A plank bridge deposits you on the west side of the creek, where **American bistort** waves furled white flags over an army of hot pink **shooting stars**. **Wild rose** blooms nearby. A culvert funneling water under the trail oversees airy **brook saxifrage**. Not to be redundant, but can there ever be too many **shooting stars**?

The track passes yellow **wallflower**, **cinquefoil**, and **mountain parsley**, complemented by blue **columbine** and **tall false forget-me-not**. A little farther along, determined aspens show off magenta **locoweed**. Timeless bristlecone pine exhibits bottlebrush needle arrangement characteristically flecked with pungent resin, a deer deterrent.

Coppery **orange agoseris** points the narrowing trail into a mixed conifer-aspen wood. This damp environment supports **white geranium**, **blue columbine**, and more pink **shooting stars**. Crossing another split-log bridge sends you toward **green bog orchids** and, up ahead, a plethora of . . . yes . . . **shootin' stars**—or perhaps a name change to **Indian chiefs** or **roosterheads** is timely.

The next meadow rebels with **golden banner**, **parsley**, **cinquefoil**, and **mouse-ear** accented by **blue columbine**. **Fireweed** promises a magenta future. Look in moist areas for **tall chiming bells** and pink **Geyer onion**.

GREEN-FLOWERED WINTERGREEN
Pyrola chlorantha

Like many of its brethren, **green-flowered wintergreen** relies on soil fungi for survival. Pale and waxy, the five-petaled corollas hang like shallow bells on a straight stem rising from a small rosette of rounded leaves. The curved style, which straightens when mature, peeks out while the 10 stamens remain hidden. This wintergreen family member is fond of mesic conditions—those with balanced moisture and light—and found in higher montane and subalpine forests. Its leaves contain a natural anesthetic— Native Americans mashed them and applied the resulting salve to wounds. Cousin **pink pyrola** (*rotundiflolia ssp. asarifolia*) carries the common name **shinleaf**.

Brassy **wintercress** is just going by as alternating forest and meadow find **wallflower** taking on gold and copper tones.

A sign incised with the words "Mount Evans Wilderness" signals that you have traveled approximately 1 mile. A second sign anchors a junction and continues Tanglewood Trail straight ahead. Advance adjacent to the creek. Peeled logs carry the trail up steep sections while slabs of rock frame **wild rose**, dark-blue **mountain penstemon**, and **pink pussytoes**.

An easygoing segment beside the frolicking stream offers more flowery arenas before ascending on a rocky tread toward dry habitats suited to **Parry milkvetch**. Travel back into mixed forest, where a log bridges a side stream nourishing **green-flowered wintergreen**.

Tread over matched logs placed side by side—this "corduroy" road once facilitated wagons over boggy stretches. As you ascend, look for **brook saxifrage's** red and white blossoms dancing on long wiry stems. Search open spots for **wild strawberries** and **mountain blue** or **hooked violet**.

Ascend the rocky, rugged trail through foreshortened spruces sheltering **northern yellow** or **two-flower violet**, quite unusual a species at this elevation. **Shrubby cinquefoil** tosses gold coins toward . . . oh no, oh yes . . . more **shooting stars**. Peek through creekside willows and spruce to spy a late-blooming clump of brilliant pink **Parry primrose**.

If you missed the **northern yellow violets** earlier, more appear where a big old log spans the waterway. A lovely meadow features **tall chiming bells** and both wine and off-white **Whipple** or **dusky penstemon**; its odor is said to attract flies as pollinators. **Rocky Mountain** or **Parry gentian** opens royal blue chalices in August.

Another generous meadow arrives, introducing **mountain death camas**, each green-glanded white star attached to an erect stalk. **Twinberry honeysuckle** bushes dangle paired gold tubes cradled by red bracts; the ensuing black fruit is inedible. When summer is bursting at its botanical seams, along comes **fireweed**.

Reportedly, a sawmill once hummed in this pleasant meadow. Now, **yarrow** lifts flat heads of clustered flowers above ferny gray-green leaves. Relax in the company of lush **tall chiming bells** and let the creek soothe your cares away before turning around and heading back to the trailhead.

Geneva Knob

Mount Bierstadt, at 14,060 feet, dominates the trek to Geneva Knob.

easy to moderate	**Trail Rating**
4.0 miles out and back	**Trail Length**
Guanella Pass/Georgetown/Mount Evans Wilderness Area	**Location**
11,669 to 11,941 feet	**Elevation**
late June to September	**Bloom Season**
mid- to late July	**Peak Bloom**
From Denver, take I-70 west to Georgetown/exit 228. Follow signs for Guanella Pass. Trailhead is located at the pass.	**Directions**

THE 2-MILE TREK to "Geneva Knob"—a granite outcrop on Geneva Mountain granted a name for the purpose of this hike—offers magnificent scenery, plenty of alpine wildflowers, and a look at some fourteeners. The trailhead is easily accessed on the south side of Guanella Pass.

The route follows the Rosalie Trail for the first mile, then diverges along an old wagon road to a saddle. It then aims southwest toward 11,941-foot Geneva Knob and circles it counterclockwise. The route earns a moderate rating because high elevation significantly decreases available oxygen: There is approximately 35% less at 12,000 feet than at sea level.

MOSS GENTIAN
Chondrophylla prostata

Also called **Siberian gentian,** this tiny tundra star is clear lavender-blue. Short stems support a four-petaled, tubular corolla pleated with small points. It is said that persistently cloudy days cause moss gentian to self-fertilize. A third moniker, **compass gentian,** comes from its resemblance to the compass rose imprinted on old mariner's maps. **Rocky Mountain** or **Parry gentian** (*Pneumonanthe parryi*) is a king-sized sapphire cousin.

About five dozen different kinds of wildflowers grace this above-treeline trail—some, such as scarlet paintbrush and its hybrids, in quantity. Boulders near Geneva Knob harbor uncommon dwarf columbine.

Parking at the pass is generous but may fill up with hikers heading out to bag fourteener Mount Bierstadt. This is thunderstorm-incubating country, so begin hiking early to avoid being caught out on the treeless tundra.

Dominating the trailhead scene is Mount Bierstadt and its notorious willow thicket, once a challenging maze-slog but now tamed into a single route by the Fourteener Initiatives Group. At the trailhead, look low for **little rose gentian, king's crown,** and **Parry louse-wort**. It takes a keen eye to spot **Lappland gentian**. Later-blooming **arctic gentian**'s chalices are translucent white.

Travel south along Rosalie Trail #603 to meet dark blue **littleflower penstemon.** Keep an eye out for **blueleaf cinquefoil** and **alpine avens,** the latter being the predominant yellow on the tundra. **Avens'** ferny foliage will stain vast reaches of the tundra wine-red in autumn. For more yellow, look for **yellow paintbrush** and shorter, ragged-bracted **alpine paintbrush.**

Rising evenly, the trail passes **American bistort** waving over its scrubby little brother **alpine bistort**. Glued to lithic

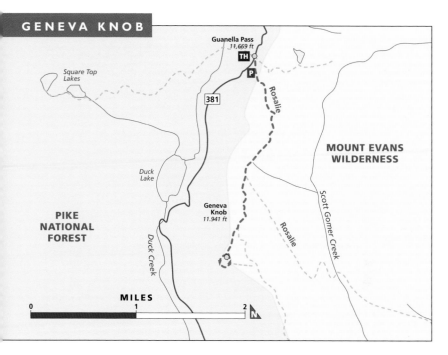

soil and rock, tight mounds of **alpine sandwort** keep white flowers coming for most of the growing season. Tundra flora miraculously perform emergence, flowering, fertilizing, and seeding in what may be a six to eight week summer window.

A sign continues you along trail #603 toward a krummholz patch introducing lavender **cutleaf fleabane daisy**. Snow willow crawls over surface rock, its glistening leaves intricately veined. Farther on, its larger relatives shelter **Whipple** or **dusky penstemon** and **king's crown**. Bi-colored **whiproot clover** knits the loose tundra soil nearby, while **one-headed daisy** adds a touch of purple to the flowerscape.

Walk in the lee of a north-facing hill, noting **Parry lousewort** and cool pink **subalpine daisy**, a fleabane often mistaken for an aster because of its wide petals. Here, cheerful **rosy paintbrush** hybridizes with **tall scarlet paintbrush**.

To the east, The Sawtooth, a rugged ridge connecting fourteeners Mount Evans and Mount Bierstadt, serves as background for fragrant globes of **Parry clover**. Fond of churned-up areas, this rosy clover attracts bumblebees, who exchange sweet nectar for pollination. A herd of **little pink elephants** trumpet the beautiful environs.

Farther along, **Whipple penstemon**, **rosy paintbrush**, and **American bistort** accent willows where the white-crowned sparrow may be nesting. **Orange agoseris** or **burnt-orange false dandelion** grows tall and tangerine in the foothills life zone; here, in the alpine zone, it is low and coppery. Hundreds of feet below, Scott Gomer Creek bisects a valley along Mount Bierstadt's broad base.

Rounded granite boulders anchor hillsides. Approach a ridge studded with clump grasses interspersed with dusky-pink **Hall's catchfly** and vividly rosy-purple **Hall's penstemon**. Both honor the same 19th-century botanist, Elihu Hall. **Snowball saxifrage** blooms early here.

After cresting the ridge to sight Square Top Mountain, descend a bit to find more sticky **Hall's catchfly**. Nearby **sky pilot** is only slightly less sticky and has foliage smelly enough to earn the nickname **skunkbrush**. **Alpine harebell** hides among the tufted tundra grasses here, as does demure and light-sensitive **moss** or **compass gentian**.

Continue along the fast-fading old road, crossing a meadowed saddle that introduces bright pink whorls of **alpine lousewort**. Where grasses obscure the roadway, **greenleaf chiming bells** contrast with vibrant **Hall's penstemon**. Nearby **alpine sandwort** hugs petite white blossoms to its dense, dark mat. Compare it with neighboring **Fendler sandwort**, which holds wiry-stemmed stars high above grass-like leaves.

At the meadow's south end, a sign turns trail #603 left, while our Geneva Knob loop continues straight ahead along the path of an old wagon road. Geneva Mountain rises to the south. Look among the buns and cushions for the sassy pink **moss campion**, a tundra pioneer plant that may be 10 years old before it blooms. Early in the season, furry gray-green, hairy-leaved patches regaled fragrant electric blue blossoms of **alpine forget-me-not**. Nearby **yellow stonecrop** is at home from the plains to the tundra.

Undulating somewhat, the trail passes compact **alpine cinquefoil**. Plenty of both **arctic** and **alpine sage** bloom in the vicinity. Another chance to admire tiny **moss gentian** arrives. The trail etches a vague turn to the right.

As Square Top Mountain's summit rises in the distance, the bright, 2-inch-high heads of **alpine sulphurflower** appear trailside. Pull up to a seasonal little pond for a look at high-country denizen **different-leaved senecio**, or **groundsel**.

Bend around toward an outcrop island decorated with **moss campion** and gold **pygmy tonestus**. Barely discernible in increasingly thick ground vegetation, a track forks right, on a saddle between two outcrops, heading out and around to the west of the bigger outcrop. A pause takes in Square Top, Revenue, and Silver Mountains.

Make your way counterclockwise around to the highest outcrop to find snatches of **purple fringe**, **mountain death camas**, and **frosty ball**, or **woolly thistle**—soft-looking, but thoroughly thistle. Crevices may reveal the little spikes of **alpine kittentails**. Look for uncommon **dwarf columbine** secreted among the massive lower boulders on the outcrop's west side. The south side shelters a bit of krummholz, **shrubby cinquefoil**, and **gooseberry**.

Continue around the bold granite outcrop, herein called Geneva Knob, and return to the old wagon road again.

Coyote Song/Lyons Back/Pass/Columbine/ Cathy Johnson Loop

A wide meadow accented by red Fountain Formation sandstone opens this route.

JUST WEST OF LITTLETON, this loop passes through a unique Jefferson County Open Space called South Valley Park as well as land administered by the Ken Caryl Ranch Foundation. Late May to early June brings out about six dozen wildflower species representing the plains-foothills transition life zone. Additional draws include prows of red Fountain Formation sandstone, extensive scrub oak copses, and open meadows.

easy to moderate	*Trail Rating*
4.0-mile balloon loop	*Trail Length*
South Valley Park/Ken Caryl Ranch Foundation	*Location*
5,850 to 6,070 feet	*Elevation*
May to October	*Bloom Season*
late May to June	*Peak Bloom*
From the Denver metro area, travel south on CO 470. Exit westbound onto West Ken Caryl Ave., then turn left onto South Valley Rd. The parking area is to your left.	*Directions*

The 4-mile balloon loop saunters down a grassy, oak-anchored valley on Coyote Song Trail before turning east on Lyons Back Trail to mount a ridge saddle. It then rounds north on commemorative Columbine Trail through oak and rock formation, before reversing south along the Cathy Johnson Trail. It then rejoins the Columbine Trail, angling north again to rejoin the string of the balloon loop at the saddle. Repeated elevation gains and losses add up to the moderate trail rating.

Parking is adequate in the paved lot. A weekday jaunt sees fewer mountain bikers and hikers.

Check the trail map and information board before heading out along Coyote Song Trail into a wide grassy meadow, where decomposing red sandstone formations create lithic soil for **bluemist** and upcoming **orchid penstemon**. Look among the grasses for **Drummond** and **limber milkvetch**.

As the trail rises slightly, look for **early Easter daisy** opening wide ray and disc flowers to the sky. Nearby, **purple field milkvetch** rounds out its scented globes. If you are a late-season hiker, look for abundant **gayfeather**, whose neon spikes define rosy-purple.

Farther along, juts and bubbles of sandstone rusted red with iron oxide contrast with emerald Gambel or scrub oak. **Lanceleaf chiming bells** shelter under rapier-bladed **yucca** while up on the left, sandpaper-foliaged **bush** or **perennial sunflower** ready their golden faces. Watch for rich purple **skullcap**, the earliest-flowering mint, and bright magenta **spiderwort**, whose three-petaled flowers melt into goo at day's end. Lustrous **orchid penstemon** and brash **locoweed** make themselves obvious, while a search through the lengthening grasses might be necessary to spot globes of **mesa nipple cactus**.

As the trail continues, get ready to hit cobalt blue on the pigment scale with **Geyer larkspur**. Appearing trailside are both robust **false gromwell** and

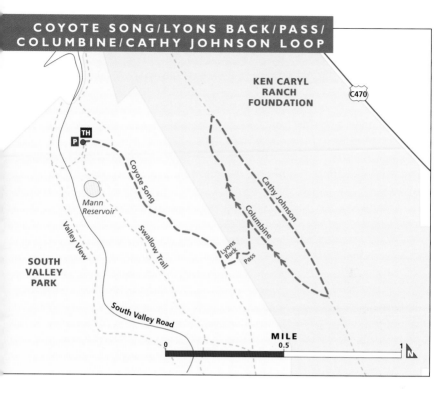

COYOTE SONG/LYONS BACK/PASS/ COLUMBINE/CATHY JOHNSON LOOP

more delicate **fringed gromwell**. The latter, also called **narrowleaf puccoon**, has butter yellow, up-facing, scalloped trumpets. Where the track undulates, **chiming bells**, **early larkspur**, and **early spring senecio** hold on in the refuge of oak shade. Leaf-wrapped stems of **miner's lettuce** shelter here as well.

A junction featuring early-morning-loving **wild blue flax** sends the loop left (east) along Lyons Back Trail. Ascending more, the route reveals white umbellate **sand onion** and snowy **boulder raspberry**. The warm exposure and raw red soil here encourage the growth of hot blue **Geyer larkspur**. Peek under trailside scrub oak to find **creeping hollygrape**, delicate-looking but tenacious **harebells**, and a few early **yellow violets**.

A prominent outcrop on the right signals a great view of Ken Caryl Valley and the forested foothills beyond. Look nearby for **fiddleleaf**, or **double bladderpod**. Juniper-flanked rock stairs lead to woody **ninebark**.

As the trail crosses bedrock, look to the south-facing slope for the queen of xerics, **prickly pear cactus**. **Easter daisy**, **sulphurflower**, and **death camas** also bloom here. The trail continues past a small drainage decorated with white and lavender-pink **standing milkvetch** and toward a crop of bright **yellow stonecrop** and luminous lavender-pink **orchid** or **one-sided penstemon**.

At the saddle where Lyons Back Trail becomes Pass Trail, a sign designates the jurisdiction change from Jefferson County Open Space to Ken Caryl

Ranch Open Space. A little farther along, a view to the Dakota Hogback opens east, and the loop heads left (north) along the Columbine Trail.

As the trail levels, look for glowing **orange paintbrush**, sharp **yucca**, and perennial **bush sunflower**. Lots of **Drummond milkvetch** also grows here, sporting hairy, gray-green foliage and thick, off-white racemes. A rocky spine to the right of the inclining path supports fevered **paintbrush** and **pale agoseris**, or **tall false dandelion**. Where the path levels amidst mountain mahogany and scrub oak, watch for the last vestiges of **early pink milkvetch's** long rosy tubes.

Open skies and a gentle rise precede an oak-flanked, winding decline sequined with spring wildflowers. Pass through a grass-dominated valley flanked by the Lyons formation and the Dakota Hogback.

At an intersection, head right (south) along the roadway that the Cathy Johnson Trail follows. A steep rock face over to the east may resound with the distinctive descending crescendo of the canyon wren. Along the gently declining trail, **wild blue flax** and **wallflower** grapple for a roothold in competing grasses. **Rocky Mountain locoweed** manages to secure scattered niches here, as do **copper mallow** and **prickly poppy**, the latter two fond of disturbed soil. Vibrant **gayfeather** or **liatris** revs up the late-season scene.

Cruise south until a sign directs you to turn right onto the Columbine Trail. Look up to the ridge you came down earlier for **orange paintbrush** and **limber milkvetch**. **Skullcap** and **creamtips** escort you toward a white limestone outcrop.

When you reencounter the junction for Pass Trail, head left (west) to retrace the string portion of this balloon loop.

GEYER LARKSPUR
Delphinium geyeri

The tufted clumps of **Geyer larkspur** blooms are neon sapphire. Deeply divided woolly leaves emerge in a congested mass, preparing the way for spires of five-sepaled flowers with the characteristic spur formed by the uppermost sepal. Four crinkled petals nest within the showy sepals. Due to alkaloids, this bright native bloomer is toxic to livestock, making it a bane to ranchers. The genus name *Delphinium* is derived from the Latin for "dolphin" and refers to the shape of the buds. The species name *geyeri* honors Carl A. Geyer, a plant collector who traveled the Oregon Trail with the Nicolett Expedition in 1844. Cousins found in the same territory include **plains larkspur** (*Delphinium carolinianum ssp. virescens)* and **early larkspur** (*Delphinium nutallianum*).

Castle/Tower/ Meadow Loop

Wildflower Hike 28

Conifers and wildflowers stud broad meadows along this pleasant loop through Mount Falcon, a popular Jefferson County Open Space park.

easy	*Trail Rating*
3.7-mile loop	*Trail Length*
Mount Falcon Park West/Conifer	*Location*
7,700 to 7,850 feet	*Elevation*
late May to September	*Bloom Season*
June	*Peak Bloom*

Directions

From Denver, head south on US 285. Turn right onto S Parmalee Gulch Rd. and continue for 2.7 miles. Turn right at Picutis Rd. and continue for 125 feet, then turn left onto Comanche Rd. for 0.1 mile. Make a slight right at Oh-Kay Rd for 0.1 mile, and another slight right at Picutis Rd. for 0.4 mile, then a slight left at Nambe Rd. for 0.6 mile. Make a slight right at Cameyo Rd. W for 203 feet, then continue straight on Mt Falcon Rd. until it ends at the trailhead.

THIS JEFFERSON COUNTY OPEN SPACE PARK is a justifiably popular destination close to the Denver metroplex. A highlight of this hike is the ruins of structures built by John Brisben Walker in the early 1900s. Walker envisioned building a summer home for United States presidents on his property; alas, his own elaborate home went up in flames in 1918, and his dream of a summer White House burned with it.

In the first half of June, expect to encounter about five dozen wildflower species.

Parking, shared by picnic facility users, can be tight on summer weekend afternoons. Come early, late, or on a weekday, keeping in mind that oft-occurring thunderstorms brew on summer afternoons.

SUGARBOWLS
Coriflora hirsutissima

Sugarbowls grow 1 to 2 feet high. Long hairs lend a silvered sheen to their gray-green foliage. **Sugarbowls** lay claim to imaginative names such as **vaseflower**, **old maid's bonnet**, and **leatherflower**. The latter describes the texture of their four pointed sepals. Once its glossy platinum seed plumes dry, they can serve as tinder. This member of the buttercup clan is related to clematis.

From the parking lot, head east on Castle Trail. Expect to see lots of **bluemist penstemon**, **whiskbroom parsley**, and **lanceleaf chiming bells** along this road-wide trail in early summer. Near the trailhead, big ponderosa pines shade **boulder raspberry**, **mouse-ear**, **pussytoes**, and **wild geranium**. Check the trailhead information board for a map and a bit of history.

The trail heads off into ponderosa parkland where a smattering of fragrant **wild rose** and **buckbrush** precedes early bloomers **golden banner** and **wintercress**. Yellow annual **golden smoke,** more imaginatively called **scrambled eggs**, likes disturbed trailside soil. Nearby **sulphurflower** is still budding but will soon produce flowers worthy of its mineral name. Keep an eye out for spreading colonies of **bluemist penstemon**.

Follow gently rising Castle Trail through a fire-ravaged area where stubs of granite outcrops support **yellow stonecrop** and more **bluemist**. A pocket wildflower

CASTLE/TOWER/MEADOW LOOP

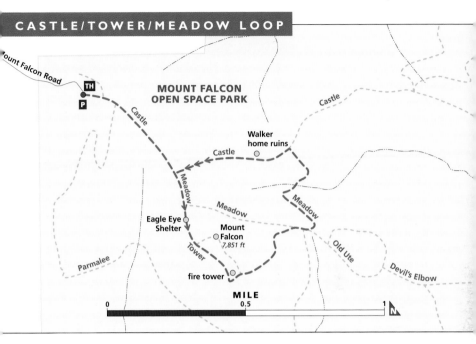

garden to your left precedes **chokecherry**, **wax currant**, **boulder raspberry**, and creeping mats of subshrub **kinnikinnick**.

Where our loop goes right on Meadow Trail, a double-sided bench faces westward for a view of Mount Evans. A reddish haze along the ground here denotes import **sheep sorrel**.

Continue through ponderosa, watching for frail-looking **James starwort**, a mouse-ear relation in the chickweed family. Where Meadow Trail makes a firm left, go straight on Tower Trail. You will soon reach the Eagle Eye Shelter, which boasts a view clear to the Continental Divide. **Spring beauty**, typically the first native wildflower of spring, may turn up here.

The trail rises on peeled log waterbars. An overhanging outcrop, home to **false Solomon's seal**, **waxflower**, and **creeping hollygrape**, looms trailside. Look for clustered golden bells among prickle-tipped leaves to identify **creeping grape holly**. Resourceful Native Americans sought its woody yellow roots for medicine and the blue-black fruits for puckery edibles.

The old fire watchtower for which this trail is named provides views to the east. Look for the stone ruins that you will encounter later on the loop.

Continue along the rounded ridge, watching for **scorpionweed**'s curled inflorescences, well-named for their profile and bristly nature. Dropping through scrub oak on a south-facing slope, search for the season's first mint family bloomer, royal-purple **skullcap**. **Prickly pear cactus** and **spiderwort** are also at home in this xeric habitat.

The route wraps around a crumbling outcrop accented by **boulder raspberry**, which indeed has a penchant for boulders. S-curve down into a conifer parkland understoried with **pussytoes**. Note the plumy seedheads of **pasqueflower**, that soft-purple harbinger of spring. Two other early-season flowers in the vicinity are **wild candytuft** and **snowball saxifrage**.

Thinning Douglas fir opens up to a wide meadow where **sugarbowls** bend on silky-haired foliage. In the buttercup family and related to clematis, this fascinating plant sports monikers such as **leatherflower** and **old maid's bonnet**. The same area is a repository for **beebalm**, a mid-summer bloomer.

Where Tower Trail intersects Meadow Trail, look left for **spotted coralroot**, an orchid unable to produce chlorophyll and dependent on decaying organic matter. A bench with a meadow view offers respite. Head right (north) on Meadow Trail. Look for **death camas**' creamy racemes where the trail curves left.

Continue through young Douglas fir and ponderosa, interspersed with lots of **sugarbowls** and **pasqueflower** plumes. Nearby **green gentian** spends years gathering energy before shooting up a substantial stalk, validating its alternate name, **monument plant**. **Golden banner** lights up the sloping meadow. Add **mouse-ear** and luminous **orchid penstemon** and you have a pleasing flowerscape.

A tiny creeklet, crossed by a footbridge, supports rushes, sedges, and a bit of **pink willowherb**. Farther along, a south-facing hillside nurtures **sulphurflower**, **yarrow**, and **golden aster**. Patches of **fleabane daisies** dot the grasses, as does the occasional **orange agoseris**, sometimes breathlessly called **burnt-orange false dandelion**.

The path enters pines; a breeze may strum their needles to create a soothing soughing. If you are observant and lucky, you might spot a yellow and black bird with a bright red head: the male western tanager.

The trail leaves the forest just before reaching Walker's shattered dream. Fireplace stones jut into the sky. Stems of rich **early larkspur** and arches of glossy green **false Solomon's seal** fill in the empty spaces of John Walker's castrated castle.

Turn left (west) to rejoin Castle Trail. The road-wide, gently ascending trail travels a ridge between low shrubs of **buckbrush**. **Wild rose** is next, followed by **leafy cinquefoil**, **green gentian**, and soft-foliaged **wild geranium**. Coming alongside a bench, Castle Trail brightens with the yellows of **stonecrop**, **whisk-broom parsley**, and **golden banner**.

When the route flattens, look for the bristled, congested stalks of **miner's candle**. Reportedly, miners dipped this plant's old gray skeletons in tallow to create torches. Short **bluemist penstemon** and taller **orchid penstemon** escort you in retracing the loop's "string" back to the parking area.

Hummingbird/ Songbird Loop

Wildflower Hike 29

Views of famous 14,110-foot Pikes Peak are a highlight of this foothills life zone hike.

moderate	*Trail Rating*
1.8-mile loop	*Trail Length*
Reynolds Park/Conifer	*Location*
7,200 to 7,400 feet	*Elevation*
May to September	*Bloom Season*
June	*Peak Bloom*
From Denver, head west on US 285. Pass through the town of Conifer and head left on County Road 97/S Foxton Rd. Drive for 5.1 miles to reach Reynolds Park. Parking is on your right.	*Directions*

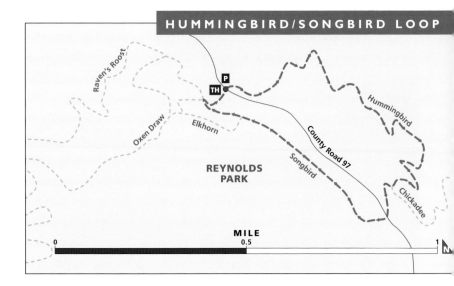

HUMMINGBIRD/SONGBIRD LOOP

REYNOLDS PARK is another jewel in the Jefferson County Open Space crown. A wide variety of habitats, ranging from riparian areas to grassy meadows and from warm, dry south-facing slopes to protected north faces, occur along the park's trails. Hummingbird and Songbird trails lie within the foothills life zone and get lots of southern exposure, making for a good early-season hike. Rewards along this 1.8-mile hike include an unexpected view of Pikes Peak framed by a canyon gap and, in June, around 50 wildflower species representing a number of habitats.

Parking is adequate.

Cross County Road 97 to where Hummingbird Trail takes off, heading to an abandoned road. Before beginning the steady climb, look for annual **golden smoke**. Also called **scrambled eggs**, this lover of disturbed soil is part of the fumitory family, which is rife with toxic members.

Along this uphill portion grows another plant of waste places, **houndstongue**, a prolific European import. A stout, rough plant with big hairy leaves, it boasts small five-petaled flowers the color of watered red wine.

At the top of the hill, the trail forks right, leaving the road and easing out across a foothills ecosystem. The southwest exposure supports shrubs such as **mountain mahogany**, whose nondescript flowers belie membership in the rose family. The furred, corkscrew seedheads show especially well when backlit by low-angle sun. Also called ironwood, mountain mahogany was once used for fuel and weapons by Native Americans.

Wax currant also flourishes in this xeric habitat, dangling blushing tubes that become puckery orangey-red fruits. Nearby junipers produce strong-tasting, bloom-coated bluish berries—actually cones—used to flavor wild game and gin.

A few Douglas firs, seldom found on hot south-facing exposures such as this, stand sentinel along the steep rocky slope. Sheltered by these "firs" (Douglas firs are not true firs), saucy **yellow violets** flourish. This drought-tolerant violet is common along this trail. Look also for intensely midnight-blue **early larkspur** and waxy, opaque-white **sand lily**.

Where the trail becomes fairly level, two early-blooming **penstemons**, **orchid** and **bluemist**, line up to be admired. **Orange paintbrush**, yellow **tall false dandelion**, and blue **lanceleaf chiming bells**, also known as **languid ladies**, add color to the gaunt scrubland.

On the trail's right edge marches a medieval army in royal purple dress and velvet hoods: **skullcap**, the earliest native mint to bloom. Almost level now, the trail allows a scan of the steep, dry hillside for low-growing, long-tubed **early pink milkvetch**.

Interspersed among upright shrubs are spiny spheres of **mountain ball cactus**, each sporting a green-tipped pistil (female) and a galaxy of yellow-anthered stamens (male). Satiny petals the color of an old-fashioned cabbage rose surround these reproductive parts.

The trail turns a sharp corner, revealing an abbreviated jut of serious xeriscape on the right. This area is paved with stones and partially buried **cacti** reminiscent of softballs. A view of the westside trails at Reynolds Park can be enjoyed from here.

Cross a scrub oak saddle, where pristine-white blooms of **boulder raspberry** preen. Look also for the flat, bright yellow parasols of endemic **whiskbroom parsley** and the hot magenta pea-type flowers of **Lambert's loco-weed**. Then look straight ahead to a uniquely framed view of Pikes Peak. The massive fourteener, as seen from this particular spot, is stunning when snowcapped.

Gentle switchbacks descend the north side of the saddle into the welcome shade of big Douglas firs and scrub oak. A seasonal

MOUNTAIN BALL CACTUS
Pediocactus simpsonii v. minor

Softball-sized **mountain ball cactus** erupts in silky pink flowers, each composed of myriad petals and stamens gathering around a green-tipped pistil. The partially buried base, having plumped up from winter's flaccid state, rises above ground, its tubercles displaying spines in spiral rows. The species name recognizes army engineer J. H. Simpson, who assisted Missouri Botanical Garden founder Dr. George Engelmann in the field in the 1800s.

creek may be heard. In this secluded dell, rambling vines of **blue rock clematis** may be blooming. **Few-flowered false** or **star Solomon's seal** colonize under the oak.

Moving out into the open again, descend a dry slope sprinkled abundantly with sunny **yellow violets**. Fleshy **naked broomrape** deriving sustenance from fringed sage may catch your discerning eye. The red ranch buildings to the south are part of an old dude ranch.

Cross County Road 97 to begin the Songbird Trail portion of the loop; it is only 0.5 mile back to the parking area on a cool riparian trail. Pass a few picnic tables perched in a field of rich blue **early larkspur** and white **pennycress**. A wooden bridge spans a creek, leading to a level, shady path. In sheltered moist spots along the route, look for lush clumps of **hooked violet**, also called **western** or **mountain blue violet**. This plant presents sweet flowers and leaves that are a good source of vitamin C.

When hiking the Hummingbird/Songbird Loop in June, stop to picnic in a field of blue and white.

The sound of running water and the cool hues of graceful **blue columbine**, **violets**, and **tall Jacob's ladder** make this shady portion of the loop a pleasure of blues. **Leafy polemonium**, another common name for tall Jacob's ladder, is a member of the phlox family. When bruised, the foliage is redolent of skunk.

Serene Songbird Trail, with its northern exposure, nurtures plush clumps of Colorado's state flower, **blue columbine**. Five gracefully pointed, lavender-blue sepals flare outward, cradling an equal number of white petals centered with playful yellow stamens and pistils. The cupped petals fuse into swept-back blue spurs, ending in tiny nectar-filled bulbs. The long spurs present no problem for hummingbirds, but frustrated bees have been known to nip holes in them to get at the liquid treasure. Another fine hike at Reynolds Park, Oxen Draw Trail, may yield the uncommon purplish-blue spurless columbine; there are blue and white spurless specimens there as well.

At the finish of the loop, rehydrate with pure mountain water drawn from an old-fashioned pump.

Elk Valley/ Carpenter Peak Loop

Wildflower Hike 30

Elk Valley's Carpenter Peak Trail shows off mountain penstemon and scarlet gilia.

easy to moderate	**Trail Rating**
7.2-mile balloon loop	**Trail Length**
Roxborough State Park/Littleton	**Location**
6,100 to 7,205 feet	**Elevation**
May to September	**Bloom Season**
late May to June	**Peak Bloom**
From I-25, head west on CO 470. Exit onto CO 121/South Wadsworth Blvd. Turn left onto Waterton Rd., then right onto North Rampart Range Rd. Turn left at North Roxborough Park Rd., then right onto Roxborough Dr. Fee required.	**Directions**

ALL OF ROXBOROUGH STATE PARK is stunning, but views of its distinctive red sandstone formations make this diverse balloon loop especially so. Several ecosystems are explored along the 7 miles, including a seasonal riparian zone along tiny Mill Creek, where shooting stars appear in late spring and early summer.

Parking in Roxborough State Park is fairly generous, but early arrival, especially on pleasant weekends, is wise.

Begin this loop at the Willow Creek trailhead, where stepping stones imprinted with local animal tracks anchor a map kiosk. Follow the trail through scrub oak, where **harebells** dangle their light purple bells.

On the left by a pole fence barrier is a sign to heed: "Leaves of three . . . leave them be." **Poison ivy** is rank along the first half of Willow Creek Trail.

Pass by **wand penstemon**, **sulphurflower**, and **leafy cinquefoil**. Further travel brings on **silvery lupine**, more **harebells**, and **alumroot**, whose long, bare wands are tipped with tiny greenish-yellow inflorescence. In the vicinity, check waist-high for **bunny-in-the-grass**, a whimsically named figwort sporting perky-eared brown bunny faces.

As Willow Creek Trail continues to wind through scrub oak, look for a tad of **yellow stonecrop**, and then **skullcap**, the earliest mint to bloom. Pass through an open meadow, where trailsides present **golden aster**, which is not an aster.

Pass white-petaled **cutleaf evening primrose** as the trail heads for shrubby confines providing shelter for white **Canada violet**, **white-flowered peavine**, and **northern bedstraw**. Sweet-scented and compression-resistant, **bedstraw** was utilized as mattress stuffing by early settlers.

Enter a glade where early bloomer **lanceleaf chiming bells** still dangles a few blue corollas and **collomia**, or **tiny trumpets**, pops its wee, pink flowers terminally. The trail lifts slightly, approaching an opening where **yellow stonecrop** stars shine. The view east features the red Fountain Formation, the pale Lyons Formation, and the aptly named Dakota Hogback beyond. In the foreground, **bluemist penstemon** rises from shiny-leafed mats, and a bit of **golden banner** hangs on. To your right, look for **sulphurflower** and spreading **fleabane daisy**.

Continue past **spiderwort**, **salsify**, and **mouse-ear**, a chickweed whose cleft petals do resemble their namesake. Curve around on decomposed red sandstone to a **mountain mahogany**–studded spot where luminous **orchid penstemon** thrives.

When you reach a junction, keep right, transferring to the South Rim Trail. As it heads toward a giant red sandstone fist on the right, the trail passes **scarlet gilia**, **silvery lupine**, **wand penstemon**, and, perhaps, coppery **orange agoseris**, or **burnt-orange false dandelion**.

Search trailside on the left under scrub oak for an ephemeral anomaly: yellow-stained **albino spotted coralroot orchid**; the lower lips of its blooms are white.

Enter a wide, **lupine**-spattered meadow where, later in the season, summer-blooming **monarda**, or **beebalm**, forms lapped buds that will open to fountains of rosy purple. When you reach a junction, keep right to join the Carpenter Peak Trail. Cross a footbridge, then a dirt road. Take a moment to read a sign informing hikers about mountain lions. The trail steepens, passing **orchid penstemon**, **spiderwort**, and sunshiny **bush sunflower**, a perennial with sandpapery foliage.

Curve around into an oak glade to spot white heads of medicinal-smelling **yarrow**, sweet-smelling **northern bedstraw**, and **orange agoseris**. After a brief pitch, the trail flattens. An optional spur to the east leads to a bench with great red-rock views. The loop continues on the scrub-oak-flanked main trail through more **yarrow**. Early-season hikers enjoyed an open slope of **golden banner,** while summer hikers will delight in rosy **beebalm**.

Where the trail levels briefly, look for complementary **bluemist penstemon** and **meadow arnica**. **Harebells** ring and **northern bedstraw** scents the air as the route climbs again. Some flowers already gone by at lower elevations bloom here, such as **early** or **Nelson larkspur**. Openings in the scrub oak allow observation of the Sundance Ranch house, which was built with locally manufactured yellow Silica brick.

The Fountain Formation is prominent as the trail switchbacks, coming upon wee, blushed bells of **spreading dogbane**, an oleander relation. Little pocket gardens may display **bluemist penstemon**, **stonecrop**, **wallflower**, and **mouse-ear**.

Where the incline eases, look for a Douglas fir–sheltered bench. The understory shrub, **ninebark**, presents tidy clusters of white that will age to salmon. Farther on, with the angled sandstone fins commanding the view, the wildflower parade continues with **Colorado** or **Lambert's locoweed**, **orange agoseris**, **bluemist**, and **gumweed**, a golden summer-bloomer.

WHITE-FLOWERED PEAVINE
Lathyrus leucanthus

White-flowered peavine's flowers display typical pea-family structure of wings, banner, and keel and are marked with reddish-purple nectar guidelines. The blossoms age to tan. This very common denizen of foothills and montane zones sprawls and crawls rather than climbs, as its tendrils are underdeveloped. Another moniker is **white vetchling.** The genus half of **white-flowered peavine's** scientific name comes from the Greek *la* meaning "very," and *thyros,* meaning "passionate." The initial species was once considered to be aphrodisiacal. A cousin is **golden banner** (*Thermopsis divaricarpa*).

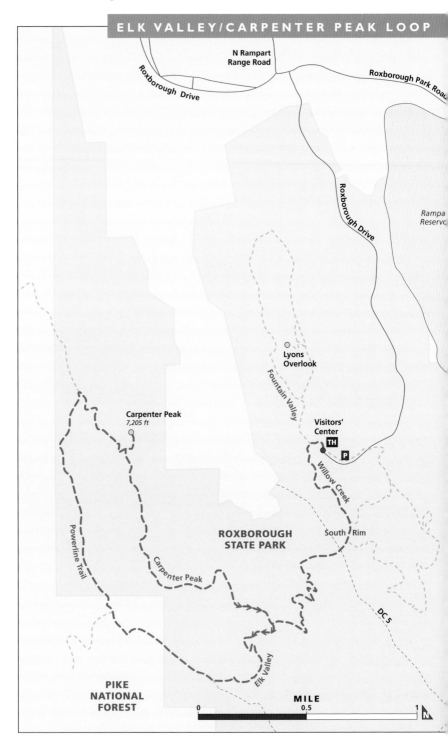

ELK VALLEY/CARPENTER PEAK LOOP

Stone steps lift you to a juniper-anchored switchback where **wild blue flax** blooms, its silky azure petals most easily seen in the cool hours. A Douglas fir shelters **early larkspur** on the way to a view of Denver. Ponderosa pine's long needles sough in the breeze.

Continue along and let color be your guide as zowie ultramarine blue **mountain penstemon** proceeds to take your breath away. On the calm side, budded **spreading dogbane** prepares to droop dainty blushed bells.

Hike along beneath shady conifers until you reach a junction. Head left on Elk Valley Trail. Ascending through woods leads to more **dogbane** and striking **mountain penstemon**. Coiled inflorescences of **scorpionweed** appear as the trail levels. On the way to a little drainage, check to see if a fritillary butterfly is nectaring on color-matched **orange agoseris**. Luminous **orchid penstemon** announces a wonderful ponderosa-shaded bench overlooking Elk Valley and the weathered bones of an old homestead. The trail continues through **scarlet gilia**, yellow **wallflower**, showy **mountain penstemon**, and **skullcap**.

Flanked by scrub oak and attendant wildflowers, the route descends into the valley, then levels to find **wire milkvetch**, **cutleaf evening primrose**, pink **wild** or **Fremont's geranium**, and **wild plum** thickets draped with sporadic unripe fruit. The uneven trail comes upon a big meadow with **bracken fern** and, up to the right, by weathered fence posts, **boulder raspberry**. Watch for a sign with trail mileages.

As the trail passes briefly through million-acre Pike National Forest, look for **sheep sorrel** amongst the scattered ponderosa pines. Enter scrub oak, passing **golden banner** and **wintercress**.

In the dappled shade, **meadowrue** grows lush, male and female reproductive organs on separate plants. The male boasts pendant fringe while the female is less showy, its tiny flowers tucked in its axils. **Meadow rue** is also called **false columbine**, because of leaf similarity. The real **blue columbine** blooms just a tad later at this elevation.

Old berms create undulating topography as the trail passes into quiet pine and oak shade where **white-flowered peavine** and **larkspur** bloom. Where the trail reenters Roxborough State Park, check the sign post's base for **chiming bells**.

Meet massive power lines as you transfer onto the Powerline Trail sector of our loop. Finding the gravelly soil accommodating, mats of evergreen **kinnikinnick**, or **bearberry**, crawl under ponderosa. Their tiny bells, having sparsely bloomed earlier, are now becoming minuscule berries more suitable for chipmunks than bears. **Canada violet** flourishes in the dancing shade of quaking aspen.

The trail eases gently toward a trickle of water euphemistically called Mill Creek, where a grassy slope harbors **golden banner**, **wintercress**, and **chiming bells**. Tranquility reigns where the little waterway flows past **few-flowered false Solomon's seal** to proudly offer a moist habitat for beautiful pink **shooting stars**. Flowers awaiting pollination point down, whereas those already fertilized point up.

Descend to where the seasonal waterway touches the trail to find **mountain blue violets**. Continue past a sign stating the distance to the Colorado Trail and other destinations, including our loop's Carpenter Peak Trail.

Easygoing for a bit, then gaining elevation by zigzags, the trail pushes through encroaching scrub oak, which serve as understory for Douglas firs and pines. Early-season hikers would have been enchanted by **pasqueflower**'s furry purple cups.

Easing past **spreading dogbane** and **boulder raspberry**, the trail s-curves back into brushy scrub oak and evens on approach to another junction, where our loop turns right to head downhill on the Carpenter Peak Trail. The left fork is a 0.1-mile spur to the summit of 7,205-foot Carpenter Peak, where a scramble through and up onto granite boulders provides hikers with sweeping vistas. The 3.2-mile descent to the visitors' center offers a collection of stunning views.

Having already met many a wildflower along the way, those on the descent, including **orange agoseris**, **scarlet gilia**, ultramarine **mountain penstemon**, and perhaps a late-blooming **wild candytuft**, may now be familiar. How does one learn a wildflower's name? Try a takeoff on realtors' litany: repetition, repetition, repetition.

Mesa Rim Loop

Prickly Pear cacti blossom along the Mesa Rim Loop.

easy	***Trail Rating***
2.6-mile balloon loop	***Trail Length***
Hidden Mesa Open Space/Castle Rock	***Location***
6,400 to 6,500 feet	***Elevation***
mid-May to September	***Bloom Season***
early June	***Peak Bloom***
From Denver, take I-25 south to exit 184/Founders Pkwy. Go left (east) for 2.9 miles. Go left on Copper Cloud Dr. and continue to a roundabout. Go right on Autumn Sage Dr. to reach Castle Oaks Dr. Continue for 2.5 miles, then go right at S Pleasant View Dr. The marked trailhead is to your right on a sharp curve.	***Directions***

LOCATED EAST OF CASTLE ROCK and just west of Franktown, the casual Mesa Rim Loop features views, rimrock, and plenty of spring wildflowers. Even Pleasant Valley Road leading to this west-side access point is a tucked-away, bucolic vale.

While the main trailhead, which accommodates horse trailers, is found off Highway 83/Parker Road, the east access off Pleasant View Drive is more obscure, being just a casual pull-off at a curve for a car or two; here, a step-over gap in a fence line offers hikers a much shorter loop access. Hidden Mesa Open Space signage, including mileage, follows immediately. Hidden Mesa trail maps are available behind the green metal gate.

Even though horse trailers are not permitted at the Pleasant View Drive entrance, parking is still very limited. Please be respectful of private property when parking.

Right off the bat, whitish wildflowers such as **sand onion, yucca,** and **Drummond milkvetch** act as foils for more exciting color schemes. Ahead, intense **orange paintbrush, standing milkvetch,** and **orchid penstemon** fill the color bill.

The level, two-track trail follows an old ranch road past **low daisy, wallflower, golden aster,** and **cowboy's delight,** or **copper mallow.**

A denizen of the plains, **white penstemon** grows alongside **senecio,** one of its many cousin species calling Colorado home. By the time summer is over, it's tempting to refer to them as ADYD: another darn yellow daisy.

Gambel or scrub oak dominates the woody scene. Under its fringes, look for **sulphurflower. Wire milkvetch** blooms shyly in pink alongside alien **salsify** or **goatsbeard.**

Some years, **yucca** puts on a show along Mesa Rim loop, looking like an army of fat candles. Also known as **Spanish bayonet,** yucca served as a super-market for resourceful Native Americans, providing everything from shampoo to sandal fiber, from netting twine to edible flower stalks and petals.

Ahead is another penstemon, **bluemist.** More **white penstemon** dots the flat mesa top, each tube consisting of two upper lobes and three lower, the throat displaying reddish nectar guidelines responsible for another moniker: **redline penstemon.**

While enthralled by incandescent **paintbrush,** which is hemi-parasitic—in other words, an opportunist—don't forget to look for subtle plants, such as **lanceleaf chiming bells** and parasitic **clustered broomrape.**

Off to the right, 14,110-foot Pikes Peak defines the skyline. **Cutleaf evening primrose** may present its four white petals, which will wither to pink with the morrow. Among many species of grasses, look for umbels of largish seeds on a bare stalk; this is very early blooming **biscuitroot,** or **salt and pepper,** a parsley family member that served as food for indigenous people. Pioneers later compared the taste to stale biscuits. **Orange paintbrush** and **prickly pear cactus** grow nearby.

Where the road curves slightly, a rock anchors **bluemist penstemon** and **pussytoes** in the shortgrass prairie. Look for **yellow stonecrop** and **sulphurflower** amid the bedrock as the trail passes **sand onion** and **standing milkvetch**.

With sandstone underfoot, the trail heads between mountain mahogany and scrub oak, also known as Gambel oak, to arrive at a signed junction. Here, a bench sits near a puddle of a pond edged with **cattails** and the floating leaves of **smartweed**. Take a moment to look back to the Front Range stretching across the western skyline.

Head right (south) to encounter bright magenta **Colorado locoweed** and equally bright **sulphurflower**. **Spiderwort** grows nearby. Passing between junipers brings you to rimrock in the determined grip of stunted ponderosa pines. Exposed sandstone tread makes **scarlet gilia** easy to see, its elongated trumpets perfect for the bill of a broad-tailed hummingbird, which you may hear trilling overhead.

Look for **leafy cinquefoil** sheltering under oak and pine. Weathered sandstone's hard surface is interlaced with soil patches supporting **stonecrop** and **prickly pear**. Winding on, be alert for the paired royal purple hoods of **skullcap**.

Boulders and small sandstone outcrops nurture **bluemist penstemon** and **leafy cinquefoil**. Follow stone cairn stacks across and between rocks. A view southwest presents the massive rock outcrop called Devils Head, atop of which, at an elevation of 9,748 feet, is a historic fire lookout.

Appearing sporadically by—surprise—boulders is **boulder raspberry**, whose showy white blooms belie its seedy, insipid, dry drupes. The trail crosses eroded bedrock, where the keen eye might spot **blue toadflax**, or **false pimpernel**.

Where a scraggly juniper rises, look under the low scrub oak on the right for **mountain ball cactus** and **chiming bells**. Continue along the bedrock path, keeping rattlesnakes in mind, as they are fond of rocky places. Sandy soil nurtures **stonecrop** where the trail passes into the shade of a picturesque ponderosa.

BLUE TOADFLAX OR FALSE PIMPERNEL

Linaria canadensis var. texana

False pimpernel's smooth, wiry, erect stems sport small, spurred, pale lavender-blue blossoms. This uncommon native wildflower, with its modest, open faces, takes a keen eye to spot. It is the only species in its genus. The genus name is derived from *linus*, referring to its leaves' resemblance to those of flax. A cousin is common **butter 'n eggs** (*Linaria vulgaris*), an invasive but attractive alien.

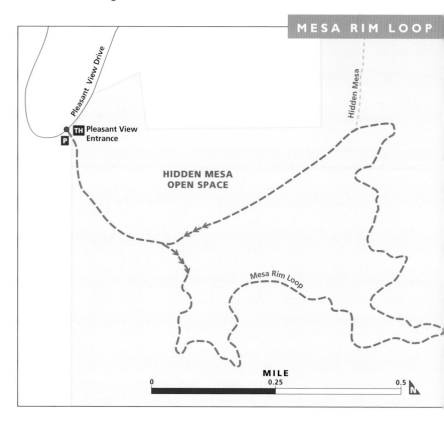

Pleasant View Drive

Hidden Mesa

TH Pleasant View
P Entrance

**HIDDEN MESA
OPEN SPACE**

Mesa Rim Loop

MILE
0   0.25   0.5

    Back in the open, the appealing combination of blue and yellow appears in **bluemist**, **stonecrop**, and **sulphurflower**. A Pikes Peak view leads a curve around the rocky mesa rim. **Sand onion** and **spiderwort** reside in the puzzle-piece bedrock.

    The mesa due south has Douglas firs growing on its north face. Next up, **prickly pear** on the right and a venerable ponderosa on the left introduce a table rock with toadstool legs. Bend low to see through this balanced act. **Pussytoes** elongate with the season where the trail steps down. A bit farther along, follow more steps up through a patch of scrub oak, where **scarlet gilia**, aptly called **sky rocket** as well, waves over **spiderwort**.

    Grasses dominate the next sector, where some **Drummond milkvetch** and lots of sentinel **yucca** stand guard over hemi-parasitic **paintbrush**. The paintbrush hue comes from modified leaves or bracts; its true flowers are skinny green toothpicks poking out from the colorful wraps.

    The trail grows sandy as it proceeds. Note the Black Forest to the east, but keep an eye peeled for delicate **false pimpernel**'s innocent wee blossoms. **Spreading fleabane daisy** dots the grasses. On the left, with **Indian paintbrush** torches in front, the Front Range panorama extends for at least 100 miles.

Broad leaves of meadow sage may harbor **clustered broomrape** when conditions and season are right.

Level and sandy, the trail curves around to pass clumps of **white penstemon** and **purple field milkvetch** and arrive at a bench. Keep watch for horned larks and bluebirds.

Wending toward the east, the trail finds **scarlet gaura,** which is typically more peach-colored than scarlet. Bedrock shares billing with grasses and familiar wildflowers as the trail continues around the mesa top. Before turning, the route again views distant Pikes Peak. **Winged buckwheat** thinks about producing its plain inflorescences, while **scarlet gilia** steals the limelight as does ardent **cowboy's delight. American vetch** utilizes support, via tendrils, from neighboring vegetation.

Another limelight stealer, as least as far as color goes, is hot magenta **Colorado** or **Lambert's locoweed.** Farther on, in a wet spring, **meadow arnica** tosses golden daisy heads on long stems. Another sturdy log bench appears, making for a nice contemplation seat.

Scrub oak and mountain mahogany flank the way past a repeat of wildflowers already encountered. Round the mesa edge, past **prickly pear** and a juniper-shaded bench. **Silvery cinquefoil** can be found on the way to yet another log bench, this one facing east to view Walker's Pit pond below and the Black Forest beyond.

On the left, **boulder raspberry** spreads its snowy petals. **Scarlet gilia's** red trumpets and **sulphurflower's** brassy umbels announce **scorpionweed.** The route heads north toward a sign continuing the loop, before a sign at another junction turns it left, stating there is 0.7 mile to go. Most of that distance travels a gently rising stretch through a weedy disturbed area. Many of the forbs along here are aliens, but complementary golden **senecio** and violet purple **tansy aster** are natives. So are the curious prairie dogs popping out of their holes.

Straight ahead, the Front Range mountain profile rises. The trail resumes its two-track character as the balloon portion of the loop rejoins the 0.3-mile "string." A right turn returns you to your car.

Wildflower
Hike 32 # Indian Creek

White-barked aspens shelter myriad meadow anemones along
shady Indian Creek Trail.

Trail Rating	easy
Trail Length	4.0 miles out and back
Location	Pike National Forest/Denver
Elevation	7,480 to 6,800 feet
Bloom Season	late May to August
Peak Bloom	mid-June
Directions	From Denver, travel south on US 85. Head west on CO 67/ Jarre Canyon Rd. and continue for 10.3 miles. Take a left onto Rampart Range Rd. Trailhead parking is to the left.

NOT FAR FROM DENVER METROPLEX, Indian Creek Trail presents an opportunity for a shady wildflower jaunt in Pike National Forest. The pleasant, forest-dominated trail takes off adjacent to the Indian Creek campground and descends gently to parallel Bear Creek. An old mining site turns our route around.

This 2-mile segment takes in blue columbine, meadow anemone, and birdfoot violet, along with about five dozen other wildflower species.

Parking is plentiful, with lots of room for horse trailers.

Head west from the parking area down a gravel roadway to reach a meadow, which offers spring yellows of **golden banner**, **black-eyed Susan**, and **wintercress**. Pink **wild geranium**, **lupine**, and **bluemist penstemon** add pleasing accents. Conifers shade the pathway down to an equestrian camping area. Pass restrooms on your right. The trailhead is just beyond.

The trail leads through dancing quaking aspens sheltering a flurry of white **meadow anemone**. **Chokecherry** and **Canada violet** make their home on a rugged, lichen-scabbed outcrop. Bennett Mountain's 8,045-foot bulk intercedes between the trail and the highway, so traffic noise is happily replaced with birdsong and the sound of running water.

Descending, the track passes scrub oak sheltering winsome **birdfoot violet**. More of these locally uncommon lilac violets, dressed in larkspur-like leaves, flourish under aspens on the right. Nearby, colonies of **heartleaf arnica** shine. Typically sparse bloomers, this particular colony excels in producing floral sunshine. Look for **candle anemone**, or **thimbleweed**, whose off-white petals compare meagerly to the plusher ones of **meadow anemone.**

Where the trees thin a bit, **wild rose** buds tease hikers who know the lure of their intoxicating perfume. In the same area, more **meadow anemone** boasts white-sepaled blooms. As the shade thickens again, look for nosegays of purple-blue **mountain blue** or **hooked violet** nestled among deep green, heart-shaped leaves.

Dropping some, then leveling, the narrow path travels under evergreens where lovely **blue columbine**

BIRDFOOT VIOLET
Viola pedatifida

The first noticeable trait of **birdfoot violet** is its deeply divided, palmate leaves, responsible for such alternate monikers as **larkspur** and **crowfoot violet**. This delicate violet's lavender faces top long, leafless stems. They bloom from mid-May to mid-June.

CANADA VIOLET
Viola canadensis v. scopulorum

Canada violet grows abundantly in rich, shaded soil, forming colonies of five-petaled flowers varying from white to pinkish-lavender. Petal reverses tend toward a soft purple; the throats are tinted yellow, and lower petals have plum-colored nectar guidelines. **Canada violet's** heart-shaped leaves grow up to an inch wide.

MOUNTAIN BLUE VIOLET
Viola adunca

This flower is also called **hooked** or **western long-spurred violet**—both of these names refer to the blossom's lowest petals, which form spurred sacs. The five purple-blue petals look like they are swallowing white mustaches. Violet leaves were used in a vitamin C–rich tea, and its flowers were once eaten raw and used to thicken soups. Though this flower's roots and seedpods may contain toxins, ants relish its oily seeds, hauling them to their nests.

flourishes. In the vicinity, look for brownish-red **spotted coralroot orchid**, with its red-spattered white lips.

Thinning aspens and a bit of sunny sky herald the appearance of **golden banner, pussytoes, whiskbroom parsley**, and intense blue-purple **early larkspur**. Nearby **meadowrue**'s smallish, columbine-like leaves account for its other moniker, **false columbine**. Early-season hikers encountered **pasqueflower**, while later-season passersby will find **beebalm**.

Just after the sunny space, woods return and Indian Creek Trail undulates through alternating sun and shade, passing **scarlet paintbrush** and **loose-clustered milkvetch**. Keep an eye peeled for **albino spotted coralroot orchid** in the deep-shadowed duff on the left. Like its dark cousin seen earlier near the trail, this orchid is unable to produce chlorophyll and depends on soil organisms to nourish its yellow stalks. Its blossoms have no spots and its bib-shaped lips are white.

The path switchbacks down to a double-log bridge crossing Bear Creek. Hearty specimens of elegant **blue columbine** flourish among resident grasses. In the damp soil, alders and willows encourage huge-leaved **cow parsnip** and lush **tall chiming bells**.

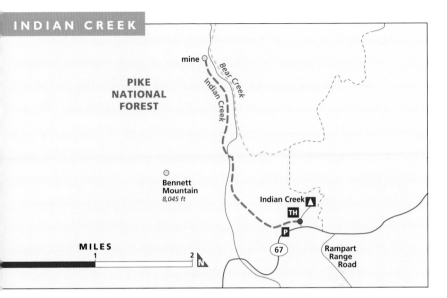

Cross the shallow creek, then continue north through a grassy meadow, where **wild blue flax** and **scarlet gilia** reach for the sun. The **meadow anemone**–flanked trail overlooks a streambank where horsetails put in an appearance.

The trail levels, once again entering forest shade, where more **Canada** and **mountain blue violets** bloom. Keep watch along the waterway for short-bloomed but striking **shooting stars**.

Scrub oak takes command as the creek drops over ledgy rock. In the neighborhood, light green, matte-leaved **few-flowered false Solomon's seal** contrasts with glossy emerald, heavier-leaved **false Solomon's seal** arcing over outcroppings on the left.

Return to creek level and follow the rocky trail up to a small pile of mine tailings and a short tunnel where man quested for mineral. For wildflowerists, this spot makes makes a good turnaround.

Wildflower
Hike 33

Spruce Mountain Loop

Enjoy expansive views and rugged rimrock outcrops along this 4.5-mile loop.

Trail Rating	moderate
Trail Length	4.5-mile balloon loop
Location	Douglas County Open Space/Larkspur/Palmer Lake
Elevation	7,100 to 7,605 feet
Bloom Season	late May to September
Peak Bloom	mid-June
Directions	From Denver, head south on I-25. Take exit 172 south on South Spruce Mountain Rd. Pass through the town of Larkspur and continue approximately 1.25 miles to reach the trailhead on the right side of the road.

THIS GEM in the Douglas County Open Space crown is easily accessed from I-25. In mid-June, expect to see spurred Colorado blue columbine on the lower loop and whorled Canada lousewort on the upper loop. Sweeping views and rugged rimrock outcrops capture visitors, as do the variety of wild-flowers and discretely positioned log benches.

Trailhead parking is adequate; those with horse trailers should park at the Noe Road trailhead for Spruce Meadows.

Begin by heading straight (west) on the lower loop of Spruce Mountain Trail as it gently ascends an old ranch road, passing scrub oak and yellow bits of **sulphurflower** and **stonecrop**. Nearby, budded **wild rose** awaits bloom time while **wild geranium** flares its pink flowers and **sheep sorrel** colors rusty red.

Mesas and buttes, such as Spruce Mountain and Eagle Mountain, punctuate the land-scape. Early-blooming **bladderpod**, a low, yellow mustard, wanes as **Fendler sandwort** lifts little white stars over thin, grass-like foliage. Also look for **wire milkvetch**, **leafy cinquefoil**, and **whiplash fleabane daisy**.

A trail mileage sign points our progress west, across rolling ranchland. Magenta **Colorado** or **Lambert's locoweed** may catch your eye, and tall, erect **wand penstemon** reveals violet pink buds. Note native **orange agoseris**, also known as **burnt-orange false dandelion**, and spires of **lupine**.

As you walk the two-track trail near ponderosa pines, look for complementary **bluemist penstemon** and brassy **wallflower**. The keen eye may catch **pale commandra**'s tiny, dull apricot stars. **Pussytoes** and oncoming **yarrow** prelude scrub oak–sheltered **purple field milkvetch**, a fragrant member of the pea family.

SULPHURFLOWER
Eriogonum umbellatum

Also called **sulphur buckwheat,** this bright yellow member of the knotweed family can be found from the foothills to the subalpine. This xeric plant's loose mats of gray-green leaf rosettes are evergreen; the leathery leaves are softly white-wooled underneath. Flowers as vivid as the mineral this plant is named for cluster in casually spherical umbels atop bare stems. The genus name means "wooly knees": Greek for *erion* meaning "wool," and *gonu* meaning "knees." Rodents eat the tri-angled seeds, and early peoples appreciated buck-wheats as good honey plants. A cousin is **subalpine** or **creamy buckwheat** (*Eriogonum subalpinum*).

Where a Douglas County Open Space sign assures your direction, observe some purple-blue **early** or **Nelson larkspur** and **wallflower** beneath scrub oak. Nearby **blanketflower** will soon open its robust heads above hairy, bristly foliage.

The trail curves into Gambel oak, where **early blue daisies** stare up at the sky and **lanceleaf chiming bells** droop earthward. A venerable ponderosa creates a shady glen where sweet pink **spring beauty** and more **larkspur** gain shelter.

The trail begins to steepen as you begin the 500-vertical-foot ascent to the mesa called Spruce Mountain. A series of overhauled switchbacks mitigates the grade.

Before pushing onward, enjoy the elegant company of **Colorado blue columbine**, the spurred wildflower that captured the state flower title in 1899. The blossoms, gently redolent of honeysuckle, are oversize here.

The route undulates, then pulls up to be flanked by **spotted coralroot orchid**, a plant boasting perfect, tiny orchids on its leafless stalk. Each blossom sports minuscule dots on its lower lip. This plant, which cannot produce chlorophyll, sends out coral-like roots dependent on forest duff.

At a curve in the trail, search for the tiniest of white stars on a wiry candelabra that defines **rock primrose**, an annual. Where and when spring moisture gathers, so may **meadow arnica**'s bright suns.

Bluemist penstemon anchors a trail junction, featuring a log bench, where our loop heads up and right; note Oak Shortcut, part of our return route, to the left. A switchback assists the ascent, passing **pinedrops**, another chlorophyll-challenged plant. Look trailside for annual **golden smoke**, or **scrambled eggs**, a member of the fumitory family fond of disturbed soil. Odd-looking **kitten-tails** follow another switchback.

Switchbacking continues to a view of Pikes Peak and the rock-rimmed top of Spruce Mountain mesa. Lichen-encrusted sandstone sculptures grip the mesa's ragged edge, and more **coralroot** stands soldier-straight amongst creeping mats of evergreen **kinnikinnick**. **Harebells** prepare to ring their nodding pale purple thimbles, while the occasional late purple **pasqueflower**'s seed plumes erupt like Albert Einstein's coiffure. Also look for **green gentian**, or **monument plant**.

Passing yellow **leafy cinquefoil** and **wallflower**, complemented by **bluemist penstemon**, the trail travels through open ponderosa pine parkland. Nearly prostrate **buckbrush** shrublets present creamy, scented clusters of minuscule flowers; the gray branches sport pointy branchlets of wannabe thorns.

Continue along under more open skies, where **scorpionweed** presents its coiled off-white inflorescences alongside those of **yarrow**; add saturated blue **early larkspur**, then red **scarlet gilia**, and you have a patriotic combination.

Reach a junction that signals the balloon portion of our loop, and take the left fork. Along a gritty road-cut on the right, watch keen-eyed for **sticky gilia**. Bright pink **wild geranium** and clumps of **early blue daisy** are much more noticeable.

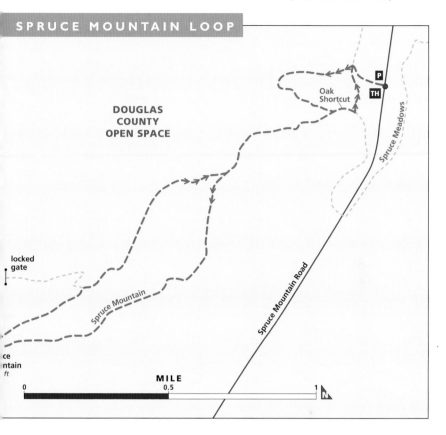

SPRUCE MOUNTAIN LOOP

DOUGLAS
COUNTY
OPEN SPACE

Oak
Shortcut

P
TH

Spruce Meadows

locked
gate

Spruce Mountain

Spruce Mountain Road

ce
ntain
ft

MILE
0   0.5   1

N

Drift down through grassy stretches into scrub oak to discover **Canada lousewort**. This member of the snapdragon family thrives here, near the northern extent of its range.

The trail levels, passing **larkspur** and **skullcap**. Ponderosa shade segues to grassy environs, signaling an embankment on the left yielding a whole sweep of **Canada lousewort**. Further travel brings on a wildflower-spattered meadow that leads to the rim's eroded formations and great valley views of Pikes Peak and the extensive open space of Greenland Ranch.

As you approach the loop's high point, meadow grasses on the right feature summer-blooming **beebalm**. Young Douglas firs lead the eye to the pale sandstone that delineates the 7,605-foot apex of Spruce Mountain, and the trail turns to show off intensely dark-blue **mountain penstemon**. Nearly all the world's penstemons—260 and counting—are in the western hemisphere.

Continuing views take you to more **skullcap**. Another handy log bench invites contemplation. Just ahead, spring moisture may nurture **meadow arnica**.

Ponderosa shade leads to sweet-scented **northern bedstraw**, with its froth of white flower clusters. **Tiny trumpets'** teeny pink tubes, tucked into a heavily bracted, terminal head, can be spotted by the observant wildflowerist.

Oversized Colorado blue columbine blossoms adorn the Spruce Mountain Loop with their graceful form and sweet scent.

As you continue along, look for early-blooming **few-flowered false Solomon's seal**, more simply named **star Solomon's seal** for the sparse, narrow-tepaled stars hanging on the ends of its dull-green zigzag stems. A bit farther on, compare the darker, larger, glossier leaves and fuller, terminal creamy racemes of **false Solomon's seal**. Both plants' flowers mature into reddish or greenish berries.

Look in sheltered places for **lanceleaf chiming bells** and **larkspur** complement **golden banner**. The latter boasts brassy blossoms configured in typical pea family parts of banner, wings, and keel; the keel secrets the reproductive parts tightly.

A couple of mushroom-shaped outcrops afford a Pikes Peak view again as the loop follows the rugged edge into ponderosas to find another bench. Look nearby for **boulder raspberry**, named not for the town but for its predilection for rocks. **Shrubby potentilla** or **cinquefoil** can also be found.

Continue straight through a junction. Nearby, a Boy Scout bench on a **kinnikinnick** carpet beckons.

Soon a turn to the right heads the trail up a brief incline to complete the loop's balloon portion. Continue straight through the intersection, and retrace the descending sector of the "string" back to Oak Shortcut Trail. Stay right on Oak Shortcut, passing a hefty, view-enhanced picnic table surrounded by bright wildflowers such as **orange paintbrush**, magenta **locoweed**, yellow **sulphur-flower**, **cinquefoil**, and **stonecrop**. A gentle, northward descent takes you back to your vehicle.

Puma Point Nature Loop

Stretch your legs and enjoy high-country views along the 0.8-mile Puma Point Nature Loop.

easy	*Trail Rating*
0.8-mile balloon loop	*Trail Length*
Wilkerson Pass/Pike National Forest/Lake George	*Location*
9,502 to 9,440 feet	*Elevation*
June to September	*Bloom Season*
late June to July	*Peak Bloom*
From Colorado Springs, head west on US 24. Continue through Woodland Park and Lake George to the Wilkerson Pass parking lot on your left. Trailhead is in the southwest corner of the lot.	*Directions*

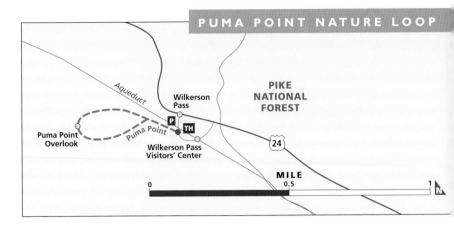

WILKERSON PASS IS A GREAT PLACE TO GET OUT, stretch your legs, and breathe mountain air. Brief Puma Point Nature Loop not only offers gentle exercise and a look at some regional wildflowers, but also culminates in a stunning view of immense South Park.

About four dozen wildflower species appear along this short, easygoing loop in mid-summer. From bushy white scorpionweed to pink gilia, from Bodin milkvetch to Rocky Mountain beeplant, Puma Point loop offers some different flora and a fine little walk. In dry years, Mother Nature may rein in her color parade.

Parking is ample and easy in the paved lot. On summer afternoons thunderstorms may move in.

Puma Point Trail leaves the parking area and heads west between a pair of posts. Nearby are **prairie cinquefoil**, **standing milkvetch**, and the graceful pink umbels of **nodding onion. Showy Rocky Mountain penstemon**'s intense blue-purple tubes attract attention and hummingbirds.

Nearby, in highway-disturbed soil, rosy-pink **Rocky Mountain beeplant** grows tall and somewhat spindly. This spidery-headed annual, spouting long-styled stamens, is a member of the caper clan. Seeding happily in disturbed places, it is also called **cleome** or **spiderflower**.

Arrow-straight **wand penstemon** also thrives in this shuffled earth, as does scrappy purple **tansy aster** and yellow **common evening primrose**. The same environs suit branchy **white scorpionweed** as well as **Colorado rubber plant**, with its perky gold daisies. Gold is also represented by **many-rayed goldenrod**.

Continuing to drift down, the trail exposes lots of **Bodin milkvetch**, endemic to the South Park region. Its decumbent reddish stems arc at the ends, displaying rosy-purple pea-type flowers that age steely blue. Spreading as wide as 2 feet, this milkvetch prefers gravelly soil. Nearby **little** or **bushy cryptantha** also likes coarse soil.

Quaking aspens appear and the loop evens out, leaving the string portion to start on the balloon part. Watch for blue melissa butterflies puddling for moisture and minerals in the path, especially after a rain. The dappled aspen shade suits cool-pink **nodding onion**, light purple **harebell**, and white **sego** or **mariposa lily**. This lily's three-petaled, three-sepaled cups are a highlight of summer.

Early-season visitors catch the **Rocky Mountain locoweed** pastel show; plump, up-pointing pods follow. Here too is perfumed pink **wild rose**; its powdered petals were once blown into sore throats. Not far east of here and just south of Highway 24, Florissant Fossil Beds National Monument informs visitors that roses' existence can be traced back about 40 million years.

To the north, Puma Hills' worn granite knobs preface 11,294-foot Badger Mountain. As summer progresses, look for **aspen daisy** and **asters** such as **tansy** and **leafy** decorating the grasses. Checking the phyllaries (bracts) under the flowers' heads reveals which is which; fleabane phyllary tiers line up like a row or two of picket fence slats, while those of asters are layered like shingles on a roof.

Look nearby for **many-rayed goldenrod**, **Colorado rubber plant**, and frisky-flowered **snakeweed**, once a source of treatment for snakebites.

Evergreens join aspens, and a late-summer yellow composite with lively green foliage, **Parry goldenweed**, shows up. Another later bloomer in the vicinity is arrayed with bright lime ferny foliage and impertinent lemon flowers: **yellow owl's clover**. Actually it is not a clover at all, but a figwort relation of paintbrush and penstemons.

Early-season hikers met **pasqueflower**, **leafy cinquefoil**, **whiskbroom parsley**, and **chiming bells**. In the same gritty soil, look for **kinnikinnick**, a woody, ground-hugging member of the heath family.

As the trees thin, spatters of daintily clustered trumpets of **pink**

ROCKY MOUNTAIN BEEPLANT
Cleome serrulata

Tall and rangy, with a branchy stem that bounces side to side in a wind, **Rocky Mountain beeplant** is an impressive annual. Rosy-pink to pink-lavender-hued spidery heads exhibit four-petaled flowers with seriously exerted stamens. Fond of disturbed sandy soil, it is a member of the caper clan and distantly related to the caper of culinary distinction. **Pink cleome** and **spiderflower** are other names of this mid- to late summer bloomer. Rocky Mountain beeplant's distinction lies in its greens, which Pueblo peoples boiled to black glop, dried, powdered, and later reconstituted in water to make a natural black pigment used in painting designs on traditional pottery.

gilia bloom, each tube perfectly suited for the rapier bills of hummingbirds. Along the way, early-season hikers may have encountered **three-nerved fleabane** sporting sturdy foliage and light purple daisy-like flowers. Blisters of granite poke up along the path as it exits the trees and reaches Puma Point Overlook.

A breathtaking vista of South Park stretches below, then progresses west to the Collegiate Peaks, a number of which are over 14,000 feet high. Facing south takes in the Sangre de Cristos, the Rocky Mountains' southern crest. To the northwest, the Mosquito Range lifts more fourteeners into the skyline.

When your spirit's quest for magnificent scenery and soul-stretching distances has been sated, check nearby granite nubs for **waxflower**, a relict in the hydrangea family that rivals the rose for ancientness. **Wax currant** and **boulder raspberry** shrubs bloom among the rough-textured boulders.

Continue around the loop through picturesque Pikes Peak granite rockeries, tinted pink like the airy **pink gilia** they frame. Under open skies, **golden aster**, **silvery cinquefoil**, **harebells**, and swabs of showy **orange paintbrush** adorn the native bunch grasses. Early-season hikers see **early blue daisy**, **wallflower**, and **few-flowered false Solomon's seal**. Overlooking a quiet meadow, **nodding onion** increases its pinkness, as do **wild rose** and **penstemon**. Gangly **winged buckwheat** struts height instead of color.

A bench offers another look at the westerly view. Then the balloon joins the string. Follow it back to the parking area.

Hornbek/Twin Rock

Wildflower Hike 35

Granite outcrops stud a meadow decorated with wild iris at floristic Florissant Fossil Beds National Monument.

easy	***Trail Rating***
6.0 miles out and back	***Trail Length***
Florissant Fossil Beds National Monument/Colorado Springs	***Location***
8,320 to 8,880 feet	***Elevation***
June to September	***Bloom Season***
early July	***Peak Bloom***
Take US 24 west from Colorado Springs for about 34 miles. When you reach Florissant, head south on County Road 1. Hornbek Homestead parking area will be on your right. Fee required.	***Directions***

FLORISSANT FOSSIL BEDS NATIONAL MONUMENT, located west of Colorado Springs, is a multifaceted park. From minutely detailed insect fossils to giant redwood trunks; from an 1878 log homestead to a rainbow of wildflowers; from sweeping scenery to diverse hiking trails; from ranger-led walks and talks to a helpful visitors' center staff, Florissant National Monument has it all.

Of course, for wildflower aficionados, the pièce de résistance is the abundance of wildflower species—90—to be sampled along the trail to Twin Rocks in early July. Indeed, *florissant* means "flowering" in French.

The generous parking lot at Hornbek Homestead is shared by those visiting the interesting pioneer log structures. An early start secures a parking space.

For the first 0.6 mile, follow the Hornbek Wildlife Loop as it passes in front of the restored Hornbek homestead's rail fence, ornamented by **silverweed**, a prostrate cinquefoil valued by Native Americans and pioneers. The wide meadow surrounding the log buildings features **wild blue flax**, best viewed in the early hours, before heat drops most of the day's petals, leaving numerous buds for the next morning's show.

Showy locoweed, defined by silvery foliage and erect stems topped with whorls of magenta beaks, blooms alongside bright magenta **Lambert's locoweed**. Nearby **yarrow** claims a rich history of medicinal use: ancient Grecians, Native Americans, and settlers have found a use for this plant.

Crossing the highway takes the trail by a smattering of **chiming bells**, **wild geranium**, **orange paintbrush**, and **narrowleaf puccoon** or **fringed gromwell**. Anchored by ponderosa pines, a gravelly knob exhibits **green gentian** standing sentinel over small, white **bushy** or **clustered cryptantha**, a member of the borage family. Hugging the earth, early-blooming **ground plum**, a milkvetch, now displays hyper-inflated reddish-green pods. Here too are tight buns of yellow **actinea** or **perky Sue**.

The trail lifts through a swale of **shrubby cinquefoil**, whose gold coins attract notice. Nodding dusty-pink corollas and wild-haired seedheads of **pink plumes** shelter in the bushes' lee; both are in the rose clan. Interspersed are stubs of oddly named **kittentails**, looking like scaled tails of green armadillos. Look trailside for the thready, if smelly, foliage and pert yellow daisies of **Colorado rubber plant**.

Gently ascending, the trail pushes into ponderosa pine and Douglas fir. Plush **Rocky Mountain locoweed** blooms here in ice-cream pastels, thanks to hybridization with Lambert's loco. Other bloomers in the vicinity include **whiskbroom parsley**, **northern bedstraw**, **alpine milkvetch**, and **mouse-ear**.

Wild rose signals a junction where a turn to the left takes you on Shootin' Star/Twin Rock Trail for 0.2 mile. A bit farther along, a view of triangular Signal Butte opens to the north. Elk-scarred aspens' leaves shimmy above **wild iris**, which colonizes by underground rhizomes. **Many-flowered puccoon** dangles gold tubes, joined by **candle anemone**, or **thimbleweed**, whose off-white cups surround an elongating cone, giving credence to the common names.

Immediately east of the aspen grove, a junction turns you left, onto an abandoned road bisecting ponderosa parkland. Early-season hikers would have admired soft purple **pasqueflowers** blooming in the gritty soil under the pines—airy seed plumes now identify their location. The broad meadows are spangled with **paintbrush**, **locoweed**, and small clumps of **wild iris**.

A bridge conveys you across a shallow drainage sparingly populated with **cow parsnip** and **tall chiming bells**. The banks are home to **tall false forget-me-not** in high-noon blue and that wildly prolific alien snapdragon family member, **common toadflax**, or **butter 'n eggs**.

Pulling up slightly, the trail passes thread-leafed, buttery-yellow **Colorado rubber plant**, as well as **ground plum** and purple **standing milkvetch**. Swabs of **orange paintbrush** and **blue flax** follow. Early-season hikers would have enjoyed tidy mats of **early blue daisy**. Pass by **silvery cinquefoil**, characterized by infrequent small, yellow flowers on branched stems with soft-haired, whitish foliage.

Riparian community wildflowers send the trail curving toward the base of a low dam. Look here for **skullcap's** velvety purple flowers. Stake a claim to a pine-shaded spot and watch huge blue dragonflies skim the pond's surface, while buttercup family member **water crowfoot** suspends its petite white flowers above the water.

Having spotted some **black-eyed Susans** shoreside, look on the trail's high and dry side among the **mountain mahogany** bushes for low-growing, lavender-tubed **Crandall penstemon**. Lobed gray leaves define **Fendler**

TALL FALSE OR STICKSEED FORGET-ME-NOT
Hackelia floribunda

This rangy, typically solitary-stemmed biennial grows to heights of 3 feet and displays pale blue, yellow-eyed, forget-me-not type flowers. Also called **many-flowered stickseed,** this borage family summer bloomer has seedpod nutlets with hooked bristles that are transported by people and animals, clinging to clothing, fur, and even feathers.

Cousin **alpine forget-me-not** (*Eritrichum aretioide*) is as short as **many-flowered stickweed** is tall.

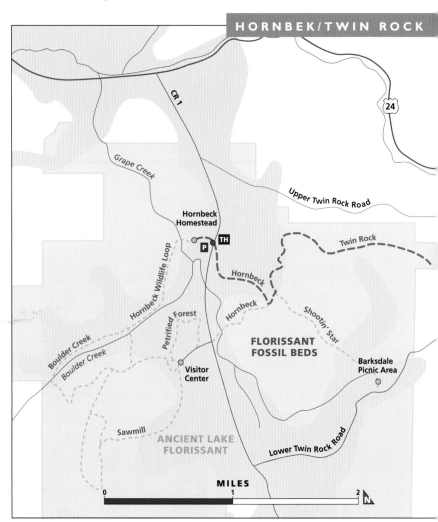

senecio—here this common yellow composite keeps company with columns of bristly **miner's candle** and rosy pink **wand penstemon**. An upcoming glen of grasses, sedges, and rushes provides fodder for an old rhyming saw that helps distinguish among them: "Sedges have edges and rushes are round, grasses have nodes from blades to ground."

On the way to Pikes Peak granite outcrops supporting **boulder raspberry** shrubs, pinnate-leaved **prairie cinquefoil** appears trailside. Where the path rises a bit and the pink granite erupts like inflated blisters, **tall chiming bells,** pale blue **tall false forget-me-not, shrubby cinquefoil,** and **silverweed** betray damp soil. Pink **shooting stars** also relish moist feet.

Where the valley highlights the sizable granite knobs of Twin Rock, waist-high **wand penstemon** greets you. Tread a grassy stretch before arriving at a short boardwalk, where rangy **bur avens** add a miserly touch of yellow. Right beside the trail, search for the open purple cups of **Parry harebell**.

Fond of cool wet roots, upcoming willows provide habitat for arrows of **shooting stars**, which pointed earthward before fertilization and skyward after. Along the narrow trail grow cousins **blue-eyed grass** and **wild iris**.

Painterly bubbles of pink granite encourage you toward the filtered shade of an aspen copse. Perch on a boulder and observe unruly **American vetch**, whose bright magenta flowers and tenacious tendrils scramble over neighboring wildlings such as **white geranium**, **pink plumes**, and **whiskbroom parsley**. Leaving dappled shade leads to a more xeric habitat, as well as the park boundary fence and the turnaround point.

*Wildflower
Hike 36*

Outlook Ridge/Geer and Lost Ponds Loop

Orange sneezeweed, an eastern slope anomaly, sprouts in a spruce-rimmed meadow along this Mueller State Park hike.

Trail Rating	easy to moderate
Trail Length	3.5-mile loop with spurs
Location	Divide/Mueller State Park
Elevation	9,280 to 9,680 feet
Bloom Season	June to September
Peak Bloom	July
Directions	From Denver, head south on I-25. In Colorado Springs, take exit 141 for US 24 W and travel 25 miles to the town of Divide. Head south on CO 67 and continue 3.5 miles to the Mueller State Park entrance on the right. Fee required.

LOCATED WEST OF COLORADO SPRINGS, expansive Mueller State
Park anchors about 15,000 acres of diverse terrain, from rolling meadow and
aspen copses to ancient granite outcrops. The park boasts about three dozen
trails, an extensive campground, and a handsome visitors' center. This fine,
3.5-mile hike offers diverse plants, views, and terrain.

The loop begins on a wide, easy gradient down Outlook Ridge Trail, then
takes a spur to an outlook featuring Pikes Peak's broad backside and distant
views to the Sangre de Cristo mountain range. A sudden turn sends a steep
section down to a junction for the Geer Pond Trail spur. Another brief, steep
pitch ascends to a cruising section accessing Lost Pond. The easy last 0.5 mile
returns you to the Outlook Ridge trailhead.

Celebrate America's beauty by hiking this loop around the Fourth of July,
when about six dozen wildflower species are in bloom.

Picnickers share trailhead parking, but there seems to room for all.
Summer afternoon thunderstorms are a possibility. Pets are prohibited.

Quaking aspen and conifer shade starts the trail down Outlook Ridge
toward **tall scarlet paintbrush**, **wild geranium**, **leafy cinquefoil**, and
Rocky Mountain locoweed. Early-
season hikers saw lots of **golden
banner** on the adjacent grassy
slopes.

Pass carpets of evergreen
kinnikinnick and prickly bushes
of common juniper—females
bear the signature blueberry-like
cones. With decomposed granite
underfoot, the trail comes alongside a little aspen copse sheltering
Canada lousewort on the right.
Crenellated basal leaves and glit-
tering hairs give a fresh look to
this lousewort, even after the swirl
of yellowed-ivory beaks fade.
Along the trail margins, a spindly
little plant with pointy-petaled
purple flowers and exerted stamens might draw the keen eye:
sticky or **pinnate-leaf gilia**.

A view opens up to granite
knobs and the occasional dark-
blue **mountain penstemon**.
Soon, a sign indicates a spur

CANADA LOUSEWORT
Pedicularis canadensis ssp. fluviatilis

This denizen of
the foothills sports
creamy-yellow,
hooded beaks,
consisting of
an upper lip—
a gently arced
beak or galea that
hides two pairs of
paired stamens—
and a lobed lower
lip. The whole
inflorescence swirls around a central stalk and
snuggles in a cobwebby cloud of glistening
hairs. Pinnately lobed leaves, structured somewhat fern-like, form a basal rosette. Some
species of lousewort once served as muscle
relaxants and sedatives. Cousins include **little
pink elephants** (*Pedicularis groenlandica*) and
Indian warriors (*Pedicularis procera*).

OUTLOOK RIDGE/GEER AND LOST PONDS LOOP

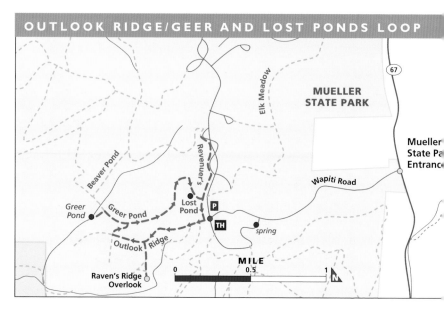

heading left (south) to Raven's Ridge Overlook. The spur takes you through
feathery **prairie cinquefoil** and whitish-leaved **silvery cinquefoil**.
Complementing the golden cinquefoils are **harebell**'s purple thimbles.

The vista from the spur trail exposes the broad backside of 14,110-foot
Pikes Peak, looking deceivingly low. Limber pines, whose bendable twigs account
for the name, appear along the way, each needle bundle a cluster of five. The
spur descends gently through sparse, mixed woods and dry grasses highlighted
by **pink gilia**'s long trumpets. **Miner's candle** spikes lead to knuckles of granite
for the scenic overview at Raven's Ridge Overlook, which includes a view of
little Brook Pond to the west.

Return to the main trail. Bypass the next two overlook spurs and prepare
for a hairpin curve that will send you down a steep pitch. Mind your footing,
as the decomposed granite can be a challenge.

The north-facing right bank favors masses of lichens and mosses, even
creeping mats of **twinflower**, its characteristic paired bells dangling daintily
from a forked stem. In the shady depths, wintergreen clansmen **one-sided**
and **green-flowered wintergreen** and cousin **pink pyrola** appear sporadically.

A sharp turn finishes the steep gradient. A touch of **dotted saxifrage**
clings to the embankment. Sweep into a damper zone, keeping an eye out for
sharpleaf valerian and **shy wood nymph**, also called **single delight** and **star-
flowered pyrola**. This diminutive member of the wintergreen clan bows five
waxy petals earthward, secreting a heady perfume.

A boggy spring, thick with lazy grass, promotes **shooting stars'** hot-pink darts. Also look for **tall chiming bells. Wild rose** oversees a junction. Head left down toward Geer Pond, a lovely little lake cupped in a verdant bowl.

Shooting stars, white geranium, and **cinquefoils** decorate the deeply shaded route. Conifers guard a trickle on the left. Skies widen and a standing army of **orange sneezeweed** dominates an upcoming meadow. Magenta **American vetch** clambers amongst tall sneezeweed, which typically grows west of the Continental Divide—the Pikes Peak region is an exception.

Just around a bend, past **blue columbine** and **Rocky mountain locoweed,** the soothing vision of Geer Pond appears. Relax on the grassy shores, knowing a herd of **little pink elephants** stands sentry at the pond's tributary.

Backtrack to the wild rose junction and head left on Geer Pond Trail up a stiff pitch, fortunately brief, which is followed by an easygoing segment, accompanied by fragrant white **northern bedstraw** and **harebells.** Lanky **winged buckwheat** makes up in height what it lacks in hue. **Tall scarlet paintbrush** does justice to the pigment department and aspens, scarred black by elk teeth, cool the way to mixed forest where a stand of young spruce shelters **Canada lousewort.**

Companionably wide, the trail saunters in pleasant shade to an obscure waterway supporting **little pink elephants.** Blue spruces lead up to diminutive Lost Pond, forlornly hemmed by dark forest. The pond introduces upfacing **Geyer onion, mountain penstemon,** and **green gentian.** Blooming a tad later near aspens, **nodding onion**'s bent umbels look like soft pink teardrops.

The gradient eases, following the ridge as several trail direction signs arrive; one indicates Outlook Ridge trailhead, our destination, at 0.5 mile. Take a right here, leaving the road to follow a narrow path that leads through pleasant, limber pine-inhabited forest.

*Wildflower
Hike 37*

Wildflower Path/ Stratton Springs/ Lower South Suburban/ Ridgeway Loop

Trail Rating	easy
Trail Length	2.8-mile loop
Location	Stratton Open Space/Colorado Springs
Elevation	6,240 to 6,480 feet
Bloom Season	May to September
Peak Bloom	early June
Directions	From Denver, take I-25 south to Colorado Springs. Take exit 140/Tejon St. south toward Nevada Ave./US 85. S Tejon St. becomes W Cheyenne Blvd. Turn right on Ridgeway Ave. Parking is immediately to your right.

STRATTON OPEN SPACE, in the western foothills of Colorado Springs, offers wide-sky wildflower meadows, pines and scrub oak, riparian vegetation, open scrubland, long views, and a musical interlude of carillon chimes at noon. This gem is not far from the Starsmore Discovery Center.

Paved parking off Ridgeway Avenue facilitates the 2.8-mile Wildflower/Stratton Springs/Ponderosa/Lower South Suburban/Ridgeway Loop. About half the loop is designated hikers-only. Elevation gain is gentle. About four dozen species are in bloom in early June, including several species of penstemon.

Parking is limited. A weekday hike is recommended, not only for a slot to park but also for less crowded trails.

From the trailhead information board, head right on Wildflower Path. The trail begins through a weedy meadow. Mustard family members **tansy mustard** and **false flax** bloom here. **American vetch** wraps around neighboring vegetation. Look for low-growing **wild rose**, which blooms in sun or filtered shade. Golden **senecio** rises above the thick grasses, while **spreading fleabane daisy** dots less competitive spaces.

After noting the pinnacle outcroppings on Cheyenne Mountain, from whence the carillon chimes emanate, check the base of a boulder on the left for wild asparagus, **wild rose**, and **American vetch**. Nearby, **yellow sweet clover** and **orange** or **broad-bracted paintbrush** bloom.

Glance uphill to scattered ponderosa pines and granite boulders, noting graceful **shrub rose** presenting cascades of pale pink blossoms. Ubiquitous **spreading fleabane** sprinkles the landscape around **paintbrush** and creamy, lily-like **yucca**. Less obvious are trailside specimens of delicate-flowered **scarlet gaura**, looking like frilly spiders. Off-white umbels of **sand onion** spatter the vicinity.

As the trail curves near a rough boulder, look for **prickly pear cactus**, **Colorado locoweed**, and **standing milkvetch**. Trailside, check for orange sherbet **cowboy's delight**, a mallow.

The occasional bushy **Drummond milkvetch**, its soft gray ladder leaflets growing in an arrangement typical of the pea or legume family, blooms eggshell-white. Blossoming shrub roses flank the pathway beyond a ponderosa, announcing a chance to observe spikes of **yucca** closely. Native Americans considered this plant invaluable, using it to make everything from sandals to sewing thread and from food to shampoo. Some traditional potters still use paintbrushes carefully chewed from its stiletto leaf points.

Demure blue corollas and pink buds help define **lanceleaf chiming bells**, an early-blooming member of the borage bunch that might be hanging on where a couple of birdhouses herald a social trail on the right. Our loop continues straight ahead. As you pass more purple **standing milkvetch**, note that it is without tendrils.

Arrive at a junction where a foray to the right, through ponderosa pines, leads to Stratton Open Space's La Veta trailhead, which, incidentally, has restrooms. Our loop goes left here, briefly joining Ponderosa Trail. In the vicinity, rampant **American vetch** introduces a less common cousin with larger blossoms, **wild sweetpea**.

As the path becomes more intimate, look left for fragrant heads of pastel purple **field milkvetch**. Dip into a pine-shaded drainage, then pop out in the company of white **cutleaf evening primrose** on the left.

At the next junction, turn left on hikers-only Stratton Springs Path, entering a more lush habitat influenced by a tiny trickle. Vegetation, including **chokecherry**, hems the route in. A word of caution on this section of the loop: watch for **poison ivy**, the leaves-of-three, leave-them-be plant of rash intentions.

MANY-FLOWERED PUCCOON
Lithospermum multiflorum

This member of the borage, or forget-me-not, family is partial to the ponderosa pine belt. Flowers on this hairy, branchy forb may sport either short styles or long ones, a cross-pollination contrivance. Some Native American tribes once cooked and ate this summer-bloomer's long taproot. They also used it to make a contraceptive tea and a reddish dye. The genus name is Greek, with *lithos* meaning "stone" and *sperma* meaning "seed." A cousin is **narrowleaf puccoon** (*Lithospermum incisum*), sometimes called **fringed gromwell**.

Inspect this fertile environment for **bunny-in-the-grass**, a square-stemmed relation of paintbrush and penstemons whose flowers resemble wee, perky-eared brown bunny heads. Gambel oak and a soft-needled white fir or two may be observed; pink **wild roses** grow tall in their shelter. Nearby, **wild plum** is in the process of fruit production.

Rising some, the trail approaches **many-flowered puccoon**, **wild geranium**, **spreading dogbane**, **chiming bells**, and **yarrow**. Look for elfin, light blue, four-lobed **American speedwell** dipping its roots in a rusty trickle. Upcoming is a nice patch of rushes interspersed with **star Solomon's seal**, or, for the agile of tongue, **few-flowered false Solomon's seal**. On the drier side of the trail, observe green **kittentails**, a curiosity in the paintbrush-penstemon snapdragon clan.

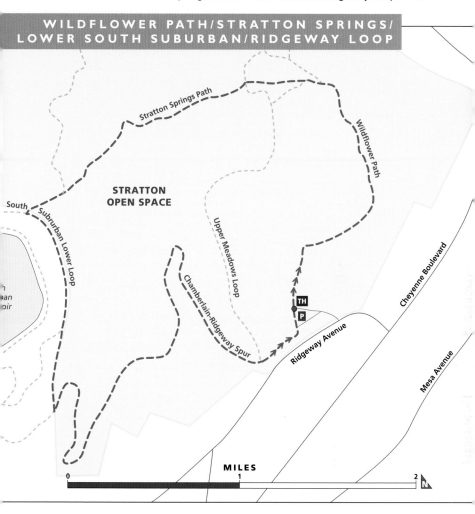

WILDFLOWER PATH/STRATTON SPRINGS/ LOWER SOUTH SUBURBAN/RIDGEWAY LOOP

Stratton Springs Path

Wildflower Path

STRATTON OPEN SPACE

South

Suburban Lower Loop

Upper Meadows Loop

Chamberlain-Ridgeway Spur

Cheyenne Boulevard

Mesa Avenue

TH

P

Ridgeway Avenue

an oir

MILES

0   1   2   N

Cross the little spring's flow for more wild roses and budded **showy milk-weed**, whose dusty pink globes produce a plethora of curious flowers with a unique pollination "trap." Trailside, look for more **many-flowered puccoon** and **kittentails**.

A brief hill brings on **pussytoes**, **rock spirea**, and **chokecherries**, whose fruit look like tiny bunches of hard green grapes; they ripen purple-black. Continue through the foothills "jungle," watching for more poison ivy before coming to boulders congesting the spring.

Pull up and out of the shade to find a patch of **bluemist penstemon** and more **rock spirea**. The open skies allow **mountain mahogany** shrubs to dominate. At the next junction, head left on multi-use Ponderosa Trail. Pass over a couple timber risers, watching for bright yellow **wallflower** and dull white **Drummond milkvetch**. A junction takes the loop right, toward fenced South Suburban Reservoir.

Along this sunny stretch, be on the lookout for star quality, clear blue **narrow-leaf penstemon**. **Standing milkvetch** is obvious, but a search amongst low grasses on the left may turn up the less obvious and rather uncommon pink-flowered **nipple ball cactus**, its name diagnostic.

The next junction brings on a broad trail called Lower South Suburban Loop. Head left (east) on a two-track, enjoying **Drummond milkvetch**, **cutleaf evening primrose**, hot **paintbrush**, and cool **milkvetch** spattered across a yucca-dominated flat.

At the next junction, keep left on Lower South Suburban Loop, the road now padded by crunchy, pink Pikes Peak granite. As you head downhill, look near budded **winged buckwheat** for stick-straight **wand penstemon**. Next up, more sky-blue **narrow-leaf penstemon** blooms near its buddy, rosy **orchid penstemon**. Also look for **violet tansy aster**.

Scrub oak shelters colonizing **bluemist penstemon** where the road joins a wider one billing itself as Ridgeway Parking Trail. A hairpin curve affords a great view of the Broadmoor Resort complex. Continue the easy descent, passing **sweet yellow clover**, **American vetch**, and yet another penstemon species, strongly hued **Rocky Mountain penstemon**.

The last hairpin turn boasts **wild blue flax**, a tough-stemmed but fragile-petaled wildflower whose silky, true-blue petals drop after a day; a succession of buds makes its bloom season fairly long. This plant's strong fibers provided snares, nets, and twine for resourceful Native Americans.

An escapee from cultivation in the legume family, **alfalfa**, rises on the left. Subtle **bluemist penstemon** and more blatantly showy **Rocky Mountain penstemon** announce a view not only of the city of Colorado Springs, but of the Ridgeway parking lot as well. Upon reaching a gate, head left to return to your vehicle.

American speedwell's dainty blossoms float serenely.

Meadow-Redrocks Loop

The Meadow-Redrocks Loop on the western edge of Colorado Springs offers foothills life zone flora.

easy to moderate	*Trail Rating*
2.0-mile balloon loop with spur	*Trail Length*
Section 16/Colorado Springs	*Location*
6,500 to 6,800 feet	*Elevation*
May to October	*Bloom Season*
June	*Peak Bloom*
From Denver, head south on I-25. Take exit 141 to US 24 W. Turn left down 26th St., then bear right on Lower Gold Camp Rd. Continue about 1.7 miles to the trailhead. Parking is on your right.	*Directions*

THIS SWEET LITTLE LOOP just west of Colorado Springs treads mostly on Section 16 Open Space. It encompasses grassland, scrub oak, and conifer-influenced communities and features a long ridge of worn red sandstone and varied views, including a distant one of Garden of the Gods. Upwards of 40 wildflower species line the 2.0-mile Meadow-Redrocks Loop in late spring and early summer.

Weekend parking may be challenging.

SPREADING DOGBANE
Apocynum androsaemifolium

Two-foot high **spreading dogbane** sports small, fragrant, pink bells with striped insides. Its droopy leaves, lighter underneath, turn clear yellow in fall. The plant's toxic milky sap can raise blisters. Woody rhizomes spread the species underground, while seed-pods up to 5 inches long disperse soft-tailed seeds. Native Americans used dogbane's strong fibers to make ropes. Dogbanes are relatives of such diverse plants as oleander, plumeria, vinca minor, and milkweed. Cousin **Indian hemp** (*Apocynum cannabinum*) grows up to 5 feet high; its leaves do not droop. **Indian hemp's** greenish-white bells are smaller and clustered.

Begin at the Palmer-Redrocks Trailhead. The trail rises immediately from the parking area, its edges rife with **Indian hemp**. Also called **dogbane hemp**, this oleander relation grows up to 5 feet tall and presents loose clusters of undersized whitish bells at its stem tips. Its milky sap is said to be toxic.

The path enters scrub oak and continues rising, passing glossy-leaved clumps of **bluemist penstemon** offering azure tubes. Also watch for **goldenrod** and **three-nerved fleabane**. Little, whitish, daisy-like flowers of **whiplash fleabane daisies** dot much of the route.

Interspersed amongst the dominant scrub oak are stands of **mountain mahogany** shrubs and **threeleaf sumac**. The trail eases past **prickly pear cactus** preparing its silky yellow blossoms, each centered with an emerald stigma. Bright **spiderwort** rests on lanky foliage while **wild buckwheat** readies for flowering on leathery evergreen mats and **tansy aster** scores in rosy purple rays.

Prolific and alien **sweet yellow clover** and purple-headed **alfalfa** thrive in the disturbed trailside soil. Continue along, looking for **Drummond milk-vetch** and **slender penstemon**. Early-season hikers enjoyed red flared tubes of radiant **orchid penstemon**. Here

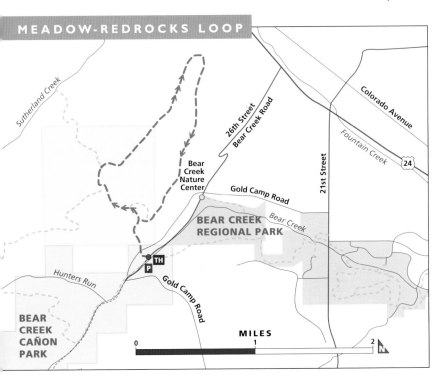

MEADOW-REDROCKS LOOP

and there, golden **actinea**, or **perky Sues**, cling to exposed earth in small clumps. The underbrush suits shocking swabs of **orange paintbrush**, whose bracts and modified leaves provide flaming color while protruding green toothpicks form the actual flowers.

Reach an open spot where the view to the northwest reveals a ridge of red sandstone. This area may harbor a bright pink **wild rose** or two. Soon after, look for a short post in the ground announcing the junction of Meadow-Redrocks Loop. Head right (east) to begin the balloon portion of the hike.

Along the easygoing path, lots of **prairie clover** present ruffs of tiny flowers spurting exerted stamens. **Slender penstemon** pokes up here and there in palest lavender.

Grassland opens to present **northern bedstraw**, which puts forth froths of minuscule white flowers. A member of the madder clan, which includes coffee, bedstraw once made a sweet-scented way to stuff mattresses or halt bleeding. Its tea reportedly assists weight loss.

Flames of **paintbrush** enliven the grasses as **golden aster** readies for its long bloom season. This meadow is also home to **candle anemone**, the cones of which elongate after petal drop. Nearby, **narrow-leaf penstemon**, **cutleaf evening primrose**, **showy milkweed**, and several kinds of **cinquefoil** bloom. Early-season hikers encountered lots of **blue-eyed grass**, an iris relation with seedpods like tiny green basketballs.

Above the meadow, the red ridge acts as a backdrop for **bluemist penstemon**, pink **wild geranium**, brilliant-rose **orchid penstemon**, and yellow **wallflower**. Mid-summer brings on rosy-purple fountains of **beebalm**, a mint tribesman. **Pasqueflowers** pleased early-season hikers, as did **lanceleaf chiming bells**.

Where gold-tubed **many-flowered puccoon** blooms, enter a ravine-like drainage shaded by ponderosa pines. Wiry-stemmed **sandwort** and perfumed **wild rose** sweeten the increasingly rocky foot bed. The trail detours around a fallen snag, where **meadowrue** and **dainty western clematis** enjoy the shady ravine.

Curving past a red sandstone knob, the track comes close enough to a ponderosa for you to sniff the crevices for that inviting vanilla aroma before coming to an intimate clump of purple **wild iris**. Nearby, **kittentails**, looking more like scaled armadillo tails, pop up greenly.

Rockier footing takes over and a sidehill opens the ravine to a pocket meadow where **golden banner** and **chokecherry** bloomed earlier. Now, tendrils of rosy-purple **American vetch** look for something to wrap around. Droopy-leaved **spreading dogbane** unveils dainty, delicate-scented pink bells with recurved petals. Also look for more clumps of **wild iris**, the only native iris in the region.

A treeless hill in the forefront signals a small post in the ground, turning our Meadow-Redrocks Loop left; the Innteman trail goes straight. Travel up sandstone bedrock and follow a great stretch of the iron oxide–stained Fountain Formation, keeping an eye out for **yellow stonecrop** joining white **mouse-ear** in pine-needle shade. Spires of rich rust **pinedrops** may shoot up nearby.

Continue to parallel the exposed rock ridge, passing shrubs of **mountain spray**, or **rock spirea,** draped in ivory clusters of minuscule flowers. The iron-hard wood of this member of the rose family once served for arrow shafts, digging sticks, and drum hoops. Another rose family shrub in the vicinity, **ninebark**, blooms in hemispheric white clusters that age to rusty salmon.

Protruding rocks and roots push the track up more seriously as the elevation lost during the first half of the loop is quickly regained. Before long, the main trail is intersected. Head left, back toward the parking area. Pass vivid magenta **locoweed**, brilliant **paintbrush**, and those pert **perky Sues**. Arrive back at the trail designation post to complete the balloon portion of the loop. From here, retrace the "string" back to the parking lot.

Zook/Sundance/ Talon Loop

Wildflower Hike 39

While hiking in Cheyenne Mountain Park, it is not uncommon to come across the mule deer (pictured here), elk, and wild turkeys that inhabit the area.

easy	**Trail Rating**
3.0-mile balloon loop	**Trail Length**
Cheyenne Mountain State Park/Colorado Springs	**Location**
6,200 to 6,400 feet	**Elevation**
May to September	**Bloom Season**
mid-June	**Peak Bloom**
From Colorado Springs, take I-25 south to exit 140/CO 115. Follow brown signs for Cheyenne Mountain State Park. Park at the day-use trailhead.	**Directions**

A PREMIUM PEARL in Colorado State Parks' treasure-house, Cheyenne Mountain State Park has everything: from camping to picnicking; from visitors' center to event center; from cabins to meeting facility; and, significantly, a 20-mile trail system. Formerly the JL Ranch, the land is now open to be enjoyed by hikers and bikers. Dogs and horses are not allowed on the trails. This nearly 1,700-acre park is conveniently located off Highway 115, just south of Colorado Springs.

Sixteen trail choices may be boggling, but for the wildflowerist the easy-going Zook/Sundance/Talon loop is an excellent selection. In June, especially mid-month, the diversity of wildflowers is as appealing as the diversity of landscape, which ranges from grassy meadow to pine parkland, affording flora of a transition zone between the plains and the foothills.

Check out the handsome visitors' center and "Trail's End," the gift and book store, before embarking on your hike.

The paved day-use parking lot is huge, and a restroom anchors the trailhead end of it. Summer thunderstorms may develop, so stay alert to changes in the sky. Adjacent Fort Carson Army Base uses a siren to warn soldiers in the field that heavy weather is imminent.

From the southwest corner of the day-use parking lot, Zook Trail begins by passing the north side of the restrooms. Watch for bluebirds dipping through the air in pursuit of insects. The route heads west through grasses where wide, white, crepe-paper petals of **prickly poppy**, an annual, stand out. Cloying and bright, prolific **yellow sweet clover** looms over whitish globes of **sand onion** and lavender **spreading fleabane daisy**, a ubiquitous fleabane whose thin rays awaken to the sun. **Wild rose** grows low here while brassy **wallflower** elongates with the season.

A junction sends Zook Trail straight ahead to meet spidery, peach-tinted **scarlet gaura** and observe the waving tendrils and purplish pea flowers of **American vetch** as it rambles over neighboring vegetation. A patch of **cutleaf evening primrose** heralds a sturdy bridge.

Check the map sign to locate your position, and take a grateful glance at the engraved stone acknowledging work done by Volunteers for Outdoor Colorado, a great group that is responsible for many a Colorado trail.

Winding along on crusher fines, find yourself in scrub oak recovering from extended drought by sprouting from the base. At a second junction our loop goes right, leaving the scrub oak. Among field grasses, look for the complements of orange sherbet **cowboy's delight**, a mallow, and dainty, powder-blue **chiming bells**. Upcoming ferny-leaved **yarrow** will open myriad white florets on each head.

Where an old corral from JL Ranch days sags into vegetation, look for **narrow-leaf penstemon**; it is also called **sky-blue penstemon**. Continue past

Gambel oak, including an old-timer in a drainage on the right that heralds **orchid penstemon.**

A couple of milkvetch cousins, purple **standing** and eggshell **Drummond,** arrive next, then lavender **white penstemon.** Look for buds of very hairy **false gromwell,** which retain their shape—like a double-ended cone—and pale mint color when fully mature; they never open, just display an exerted style like a thin, impudent tongue. **Pussytoes** and **American vetch** also grow nearby.

Rising slightly, Zook Trail passes a drainage on the left featuring **standing milkvetch** and **wallflower.** A few ponderosa pines and a white fir or two thrive in a scrub oak nursery.

A junction angles our loop left, onto Sundance Trail. Undulating some, the gravelly route greets **perky Sue** and **Colorado** or **Lambert's locoweed.** Granite boulders shelter deep pink **wild four o'clock** and clear pink **wild rose.** Check in the next oak copse for early-blooming **bladderpod,** a yellow mustard clan member.

The trail heads into the open, where grasses such as tall, thin needle-and-thread and blue gamma flourish. To the east is the U.S. Army's Fort Carson. In the foreground, look for **yucca, cutleaf evening primrose, orange paintbrush, orchid penstemon, perky Sues, wavyleaf thistle,** and **plains yellow evening primrose.**

The next junction sends Sundance Trail right (west), aiming toward Cheyenne Mountain itself. Future bloomers include lanky **winged buckwheat** and tall **common evening primrose.**

BRANDEGEE MOUNTAIN PENSTEMON
Penstemon brandegei

Snapdragon family member **brandegee mountain penstemon** is stunning in full bloom. It is substantial in foliage and flower, and the inflated tubes lining the sturdy stems may range from clear blue to lavender, both of which may be suffused with pink or violet. Found in Colorado's southern counties, this spectacular penstemon is one of about five dozen species native to Colorado. In this featured species the staminode—the non-working fifth stamen—is strongly notched. The leaves are, as typical, opposite on the stalk. The name honors Townshend Stith Brandegee, a botanist with the Hayden Surveys of the latter 1800s. A cousin is **slender penstemon** (*Penstemon gracilis*).

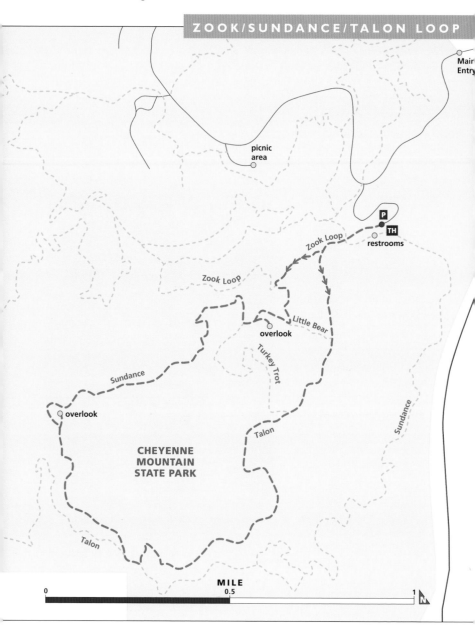

ZOOK/SUNDANCE/TALON LOOP

For now, enjoy **perky Sue, standing milkvetch,** and **evening primrose.** Mountain mahogany shrubs and oak flank the trail.

An optional spur called "Overlook" takes a brief jaunt left, revealing **whiplash fleabane daisy, paintbrush, perky Sues,** and, if you are lucky, the beautiful **sego** or **mariposa lily.** The short spur ends at a south-facing bench.

Return to the trail, passing a trail map and keeping right. Angle back through scrub oak and **snowberry** toward an interpretive sign describing Fort Carson's important role during World War II.

Keep a keen eye out for rangy **wild four o'clock**. A fine view of Cheyenne Mountain precedes more **prickly pear** where careful observance reveals alien-looking green **kittentails**. Mountain mahogany may shelter **skullcap**. Nearby, **three-nerved fleabane** prepares to cover its 18 to 24-inch form with pale purple daisies.

Enter ponderosa pines, which create shade for hikers as well as **many-flowered puccoon**. Look trailside for **spiderwort**. In the vicinity you may find not only the usual silky yellow blossoms of **prickly pear** but a sunrise apricot hue as well. Back out in the open, the trail crests for a long view to the Great Plains, and sun-loving lizards scurry about.

Where the trail travels along a south-facing dry aspect, late-afternoon hikers may find creamy bursts of branched **blazing star** opening. Nearby, note **cowboy's delight** and **scarlet gaura** growing together. **Brandegee mountain penstemon**, a first-rate bloomer that is jaw-droppingly beautiful, also grows in this area.

Passing a piñon pine, glance left, over waving meadow grasses, to enjoy spatters of kaleidoscope color among them, while keeping the uphill side scouted for more marvelous **mountain penstemons**, some in strong blue. **Prairie clover**, or **dalea**, prepares to dance in a magenta, or sometimes white, tutu.

Continue along past a trail marker labeled "Sundance," where a late-blooming, somewhat untidy buckwheat known loosely as **prairie baby's breath** grows. Nearby, **paintbrush**, **northern sweetvetch**, and **false alfalfa**, or **psoralea**, flourish.

Whiplash fleabane daisy reaches out across the trail to prepare the way for more afternoon-opening **blazing star**. On the right, as the trail heads for an uphill curve, **sego lilies** bloom from white to lavender, even a pale rose. Red is the eye-grabbing hue of a **prickly pear** blooming by a mountain mahogany bush, also on the right.

The route becomes more intimate as it wends through scrub oak to offer more rosy and sprightly **northern sweetvetch** and **perky Sue**. Prepare for a parade of a clematis called **Scott sugarbowl** or **leatherflower**. **Harebells'** delicate purple dangling bells appreciate the dappled shade of a mixed wood. Birdsong is a bonus.

Early-season hikers would have honed in on **pasqueflower** where the trail gets a real backcountry feel, with wild-looking Cheyenne Mountain looming over all. Descend now in pine shade, past **pussytoes**, budded **golden-rod**, and **skullcap**. Recurved tepals help identify more enchanting **Scott clematis**. Continue to descend under sizable ponderosas to a Pikes Peak pink granite boulder, and look around for **orchid penstemon** and **candle anemone**, or **thimbleweed**.

An inviting overlook spur angles back to a little-used bench, passing **Colorado locoweed**, **snowberry**, **perky Sue**, **false gromwell**, and **paintbrush**. Nearby **green gentian**, or **monument plant**, may be in mint-green bloom, its swan song after spending years gathering energy to push up an impressive but fatal flower stalk. **Sand onion**, **mountain penstemon**, and **wallflower** grace the space as well.

Perfumed **wild rose** gets you started back on the main trail. A little open-skied meadow flanks the wide trail as scattered ponderosas harbor **slender penstemon**, **candle anemone**, and **Scott clematis**. Stroll the wildflower-embellished parkland to interpretive signage about animal survival.

Descend through native needle-and-thread and Indian rice grass to view graceful **sego lilies** and a bit of **silky locoweed** in pale magenta, the color a hybridization trait. To the right, look for **sweetvetch**, **showy** or **big-flowered Townsendia**, **wavyleaf thistle**, **bluemist penstemon**, and **wallflower**.

Pass through white fir and Douglas fir, the latter not a true fir. A couple of junipers anticipate pointy stars of **yellow stonecrop**. As you proceed, look left to a wide meadow studded with **yucca** spires and, closer in, **perky Sue**, **scarlet gaura**, silvery-lavender **sego lilies**, and **spiderwort**.

At a junction, our loop turns left down Talon Trail. Perhaps a cluster of **mountain ball cactus** hides in the grass. The trail curves and drifts past **showy milkweed**'s dusty-rose globes. Drought-stressed scrub oak leads to a junction anchored by a map sign where purple **field milkvetch** grows, as well a rainbow of wildflowers already encountered. Continue along Talon Trail.

Sail along amongst smatterings of wildflowers, including **big-flowered Townsendia**, low-growing **stiff flax**, purple **field milkvetch**, **slender penstemon**, and its loud magenta cousin **orchid penstemon**. Look for pink **wild geranium** as you approach a Talon trail marker. Rejoining the penstemon parade, **narrow-leaf penstemon** blooms in sky-blue before a dip takes you to a colony of **bluemist penstemon**. Wide skies and expansive meadow lead to pockets of shattered rainbows representing wildflowers familiar by sight and, hopefully, by name.

Continue along, noting **chiming bells**, sometimes referred to as **mertensia**. Curve through scrub oak to find **spreading dogbane** and, perhaps, those odd **kittentails**. Drift down to another green and yellow Talon trail marker. A **Scott sugarbowl** sighting leads to another meadow and trail junction; turn right to stay on Talon Trail. The next interpretive sign talks about unseen 14,110-foot Pikes Peak. Saunter along for a color shock of magenta and orange in the guise of **locoweed** and **paintbrush** decorating a knob on the right. When you reach the Zook string, retrace it back to your car.

Canyon Loop at Aiken Canyon Preserve

Wildflower Hike 40

Scrub oak and paintbrush team up in a pocket meadow in this Nature Conservancy preserve.

easy to moderate	**Trail Rating**
4.0-mile balloon loop	**Trail Length**
Aiken Canyon Preserve/Colorado Springs	**Location**
6,432 to 6,880 feet	**Elevation**
May to September	**Bloom Season**
early to mid-June	**Peak Bloom**

Directions Head south through Colorado Springs on I-25. Take exit 140B south to CO 115. Continue for 15 miles to Turkey Canyon Ranch Rd. Turn right and drive 200 yards to the preserve parking area. The trailhead is behind the interpretive sign before the field station. Open dawn to dusk, Saturday, Sunday, and Monday. Fee for guided activities.

THE NATURE CONSERVANCY'S Aiken Canyon Preserve is unique in many ways. It contains a number of less common wildflower species, approaches the northern limits of one-seed juniper and firecracker penstemon, and tallies over 100 species of birds, including the greater roadrunner. In addition, a friendly, helpful research staff and volunteer naturalist cadre answer questions and lead hikes from an adobe field station.

It's a good idea to check on Aiken Canyon Preserve's regulations and limited opening times. All trails are foot traffic only, and pets are not permitted on the preserve. A fee may be imposed for guided activities.

Canyon Loop covers 4 miles of diverse habitats, ranging from piñon-juniper woodland to Gambel oak-mountain mahogany to tall prairie grass to seasonal riparian. The trail begins levelly along a drainage and then eases up, increasing in gradient to Bear Pass. It then dips down into a wide meadow before winding back through forest and grassland.

The loop introduces well over 50 wildflower species in early June, when there is an overlap between spring and summer flowering. Wildflowerists may want to pick up a list of Aiken Canyon's vascular plants at the field station.

Parking is generous.

Between the parking area and the field station, flowers such as **spreading fleabane, cutleaf evening primrose, greenthread** or **field coreopsis**, and **pinnate-leaf gaillardia** abound. **Scarlet gaura, narrowleaf puccoon, narrow-leaf penstemon,** and spatters of **orange** or **broad-bracted paintbrush** lead to the pueblo-style field station visitors' center.

Stone-outlined Canyon Loop Trail begins on the far side of an interpretive sign detailing the history of Aiken Canyon Preserve. Follow it down into an oak-juniper-piñon-mountain

NARROW-LEAF PENSTEMON
Penstemon angustifolius

Open-lipped, azure tubes of **narrow-leaf penstemon** call forth the moniker **sky-blue penstemon**. A denizen of mesas and lower foothills, this member of the figwort family is related to **paintbrush** and **lousewort**. It boasts soldier-straight stalks and bluish-green leaves covered with a fine white powder. The species name, *angustifolius,* meaning "narrow-leaved," is responsible for the common name. There are over 150 species of penstemon in the Rocky Mountains. Local cousins include **orchid penstemon** (*Penstemon secundiflorus*) and **bluemist penstemon** (*Penstemon virens*).

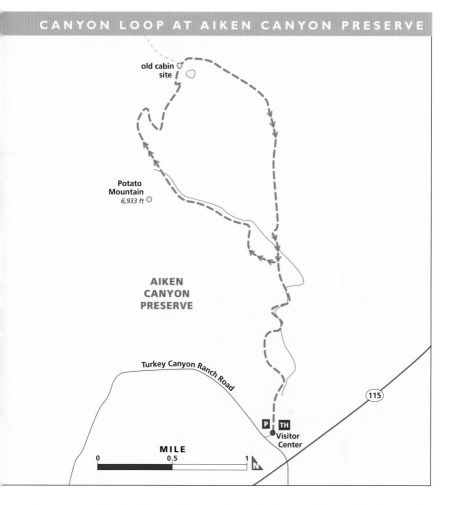

mahogany woodland, where a view to the north features the granite dome of Potato Mountain.

Narrowing, the "string" segment of the trail edges into a shallow draw, where **orchid penstemon** waves over matted **pussytoes**. Ponderosa pines flank the trail as it rises, passing into scrub oak, piñon, and grasses before dipping back into the sandy red draw, where **wild geranium** blooms beside odd-appearing **winged buckwheat**.

Leave the draw once again to find **orange paintbrush** and **greenthread coreopsis** dotting the needlegrass. Pass one-seeded juniper, which is at its northern limit here. Again, the trail crosses the rocky draw to attain the pine-shaded far side. **Limber milkvetch** sprawls where **wallflower** and **perky Sue** or **actinea** may be waning.

Canyon Trail's "string" ends at a junction where **narrow-leaf penstemon** blooms from pale lavender to bright blue. Head left, accompanied by open skies. Back along the draw, look for **wild rose, chokecherry, pasqueflower,** and **Scott clematis**, whose nodding purple tepals sweep into a graceful inverted vase. Nearby, **white-flowered peavine**'s reddish-veined flowers fade to tan, and **many-flowered puccoon** dangles gold tubes.

Keep an eye out for a few specimens of **hoptree**, at its northern limit here; this citrus family member may be identified by its citrus-scented, bright green, lance-shaped leaves. Tropical-looking leaf rosettes of **green gentian** pop up occasionally where the trail edges a **wild rose**-spattered ravine banked by the red sandstone Fountain Formation.

Fleabane daisies and **Indian wheatgrass**, which Native Americans called "white man's footsteps" due to its predilection for disturbed soil, dot the open slope where the trail pushes into scrub oak and begins climbing. **Tall pussytoes** and fading **bluemist penstemon** encourage the ascent.

Daisy-like **showy Townsendia** thrives in the lithic soil of a xeric slope where the canyon tightens and the track switchbacks. Also look for **prickly pear cactus**, whose myriad, tactile-sensitive stamens slowly curve their anthers inward when activated by a light touch, such as that of a pollinator. Nearby, a shark fin of red rock harbors **perky Sue** and **bluemist penstemon** around its base.

Potato Mountain comes into view as you crest Bear Pass, the high point of the hike. The trail then drops into a wide grassy meadow studded with young ponderosas.

A signed junction sends our Canyon Loop straight ahead, while a spur to the left aims toward an old cabin site. Continue across a flat meadow, where long-blooming **golden**

SCOTT CLEMATIS
Coriflora scottii

Recurved tepals tip inverted urns on Scott clematis. The hairy, crinkle-edged flower develops into a feathery plumed seed. Also called **Scott sugarbowl**, this southern Colorado member of the buttercup clan sometimes grows upright, but is often lax, even sprawling. Its bluish-green, compound leaf divisions are ovate (egg-shaped, with the broad end at the base). **Sugarbowl**, (*Coriflora hirsutissima*), is a cousin.

aster grows trailside. Check low-growing shrubs for **New Jersey tea** or **redroot**, a member of the buckthorn family displaying small, tight clusters of white flowers.

Enter a rocky draw flanked with lots of **Fendler senecio**, one of a confusing collection that goes under the adopted name of "senecio." Frustrated tries at putting "senecios" into genus and, worse yet, specie categories, may cause one to lump them into the ADYD—"Another Darn Yellow Daisy"—category.

In August, uncommon **dianthus-leaf dayflower** blooms along the draw. With three blue petals and a bright gold spathe, it looks like a skinny spiderwort, which it is.

Rock cairns mark the rugged trail as it curves south toward more open terrain, passing **tall** or **wand penstemon**. Scrub oak precedes level grassland where **yucca** shoots up thick stalks resembling giant asparagus. Fine-foliaged **creamtips** lean rayless heads over **showy Townsendia** and copper **mallow**, also cleverly monikered as **cowboy's delight**. Perhaps Native Americans told cowpokes about a sort of chewing gum derived from its stalks.

Head back to the parking area through the PJ (piñon-juniper) community to rejoin the loop's string.

Scrub oak, pines, and seneco lead toward red sandstone.

Wildflower Hike 41

Black Powder Pass

Subalpine daisy adorns this trail east of Breckenridge.

Trail Rating	moderate to strenuous
Trail Length	3.4 miles out and back
Location	Boreas Pass/Breckenridge/Como
Elevation	11,481 to 12,159 feet
Bloom Season	late June to August
Peak Bloom	mid-July to early August
Directions	From Denver, take I-70 west to CO 470. Continue 5.7 miles to US 285 S. Drive 57.8 miles to reach the town of Como. Turn right onto Boreas Pass Rd. and continue 8 miles to Boreas Pass. Trailhead is on the right, in front of the log section house.

IN THE LATE 1800s, Boreas Station was an active railroad stop. For a decade, windy 11,481-foot Boreas Pass even boasted its own post office. Today, the section house has been handsomely restored and is the takeoff point for this floriferous Black Powder Pass hike, along which you can expect to see nearly 100 wildflower species in mid-July. Both Boreas and Black Powder passes straddle the Continental Divide.

Approximately halfway between Boreas Pass Road and the section house lies a wide, stony trail that heads north to reach a water diversion ditch before aiming northeast up a very steep ravine to then emerge onto wide-open meadowland. The final pull is trailless but treeless, enabling hikers to sight in on the low, flat gap of Black Powder Pass.

Parking is limited at the pass, so arrive early to secure a parking space and avoid fast-forming summer afternoon thunderstorms.

Begin your hike by locating the vague scrape of road that becomes the trail in front of the section house. Aim northeast along the stony route, flanked by willows and sporadic wildflowers such as **beauty cinquefoil** and **Whipple** and **littleflower penstemons**. Reach a diversion ditch where waterflow is controlled by sluice gates. Follow the left side of the level ditch to observe masses of white **brookcress**, a mustard tribesman.

The downhill slope is rife with swabs of **sulphur paintbrush** and **pink-headed daisy**. Ladylike pale **pink willowherb** laces the manmade waterway near power-pink cousin **fireweed**. Also look for **purple fringe**, whose blowzy spikes darken as the season advances. To the northwest rises Breckenridge Ski Area and the imposing Tenmile Range.

Bordering willow thickets, indicative of moist soil, **tall chiming bells** present pink buds and blue bells while **arrowleaf senecio** flickers in bright gold, complemented by a stately spire or two of royal purple **monkshood**. **Tall scarlet paintbrush** joins yellow **paintbrush** and golden **arnicas** on a slope studded with conical spruce.

GLOBE GILIA
Ipomopsis globularis

Unforgettable in flower and fragrance, the spheres of tundra inhabitant **globe gilia** are to be found only in the Hoosier Pass region. This lovely endemic, partial to gravelly limestone soil, sports another amazing feature— azure anthers. Sometimes called **alpine gilia**, this member of the phlox family snuggles its pale stars in a soft bed of angelhair cobwebs. Cousins include **scarlet gilia** (*Ipomopsis aggregata*) and **sticky gilia** (*Gilia pinnatifida*).

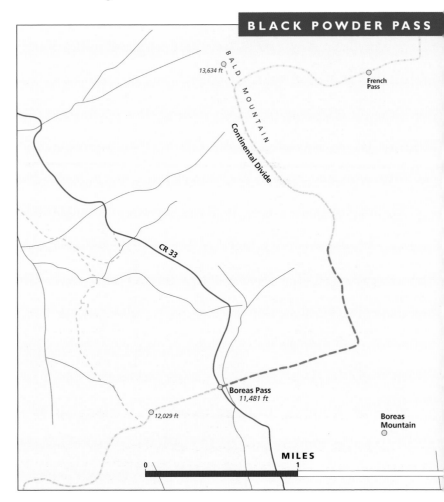

Along the ditch path, early-season hikers encountered bluish **drop-pod locoweed**. Advance to unusual-appearing **alpine dusty**. **Fireweed**, which Native Americans used as a vitamin C–charged potherb in summer, forms magenta patches near **pink-headed daisy**. The level track curves around to overlook purple **subalpine larkspur** and golden **arrowleaf senecio**. A bit farther on, look for **heartleaf arnica** and **rayless senecio**.

Cautiously edge onto a talus slope where lovely **blue columbine**, lavender **one-headed daisy**, sour **alpine sorrel**, and nodding **frosty ball thistle** grow. The rock supports tufts of **rock groundsel** and **Fremont** or **rock ragwort**—both plants are often tossed into the catchall of "senecio." Listen for sharp-voiced, rabbit-related pika.

A trickle heralds a minuscule pond garlanded by **pink-headed daisies** and bits of burnt-red **king's crown**, **alpine veronica**, and **homely buttercup**. The far verge highlights **yellow monkeyflower**.

At this point, the trail takes a sharp right, up a tight ravine populated by **nodding** or **daffodil senecio**, **delicate Jacob's ladder**, and both **subalpine** and **broadleaf arnicas**, plus a goodly sum of **blue columbine**. **Orange agoseris** leads to a well-watered display of airy **brook saxifrage**, snowy **brookcress**, plush **tall chiming bells**, and showy **subalpine larkspur**. Check out myriad tints of paintbrush, including rich **rosy paintbrush** exhibiting hybridization.

Cool pink **subalpine daisies** encourage you up an awkward yet brief pitch above a gurgling creek. The gradient eases midst a shattered rainbow of petals and perfumes luring pollinators. Time is short and competition high, which may explain why unpretentious heads of **Grays angelica** and unappealing-odored **Whipple penstemon** are fly-pollinated.

Continuing to pull up, the narrow track meets ivory **narcissus-flowered anemone**, scented **Parry clover**, and fringe-throated **little rose gentian**. **Little pink elephants** wave their trunks and **bistort** sways over paintbox **paintbrush**.

Skies widen as the path proceeds along a xeric bank on the other side of the creeklet. **Horned dandelion** presents golden discs and **harebells** dangle light purple corollas, while **dwarf goldenrod** and **alpine milkvetch** huddle in the tundra grasses above treeline. Over by the rock-paved, moss-mounded waterway, a few brilliant pink **Parry primrose** hang on, as does **marsh marigold**. Look nearby for **queen's crown**.

Blueleaf cinquefoil and low-growing **Patterson Colorado tansy aster** dot the steadily rising, fading trail as it pushes up a hump toward the willow patches that cap Black Powder Pass.

A troop of **little pink elephants** trumpets in a swale as you trek through lean, trailless terrain. Aim for the gap that accommodates Black Powder Pass, noting intense blue **greenleaf chiming bells**. Reach knee-high willows spattered with clear spaces that may shelter tiny gems such as soft blue **moss** or **compass gentian**. In some, creamy **Parry lousewort** bloomed early where less-common cousin **alpine lousewort** now swirls in rose-pink.

Southwest of the willows, a mosaic pavement of bare ground and broken rock supports clumps of **pinnate-leaved daisy** and the ragged gold heads and gray foliage of **hoary senecio**. **Whiproot clover** and endemic **Leadville milkvetch** knit the tundra. Endemic and deeply pigmented **dwarf alpine larkspur** is only ankle-high up on the flat saddle of the pass. Wide golden faces of **old man of the mountains**, sometimes referred to as **alpine sunflower**, watch over the tundra where **sky pilot** greeted early-season hikers.

A pervading fragrance entices you to locate **globe gilia**, another endemic. Examine the center of one of the clustered flowers in the glistening woolly head for aqua anthers. Specific to the alpine life zone of this area, this phlox family member is alternately named **alpine gilia**.

Before the return descent, take advantage of this moment astride the Continental Divide to look north into the French Creek drainage and the north end of South Park.

Kenosha Pass West/ Colorado Trail

*An aspen grove on the west side of Kenosha Pass
shelters masses of Columbine.*

Trail Rating	easy to moderate
Trail Length	5.8 miles out and back
Location	Pike National Forest/Grant/Kenosha Pass
Elevation	9,960 to 10,400 feet
Bloom Season	June to August
Peak Bloom	mid-July
Directions	From Denver, take CO 470 east. Exit onto US 285 S toward Fairplay. Continue to Kenosha Pass. Park before the Kenosha Pass campground gate, at Colorado Trail access parking.

JUST AN HOUR from the Denver metro area lies Kenosha Pass Trail, a delightful trail that conveniently starts adjacent to US 285. This trail to Guernsey Gulch shares a trailhead with the Colorado Trail. At one point along the rewarding trail, the Continental Divide forms the entire western skyline, and, in a good year, mid-July whips up a white froth of Rocky Mountain locoweed that covers acres of the foreground slope.

Though the trail is generally fairly easygoing, elevation gains and losses make for a good workout.

Over seven dozen wildflower species bloom here, representing habitats from high mesic meadow to aspen grove and from dry lithic to riparian.

Parking is limited in the small Colorado Trail access lot outside the Kenosha Pass campground gate. However, more parking lies just south, beside US 285.

Enter the campground gate, looking for plush, clumped masses of elegant **blue columbine** in the quaking aspen woods on the left. **Golden banner** and **northern paintbrush** also bloom here.

A sign at the campground pay station points the Colorado Trail and this hike's route left. Amongst aspens, **beauty cinquefoil** and darkest blue **mountain penstemon** admire **aspen sunflower** and **white geranium**. Soon, another sign directs the trail through aspen's rich understory, which boasts both **northern** and **tall scarlet paintbrush**. Stick to the main trail, ignoring cross-hatching social paths.

Before long, the trail drifts up through lodgepole pine and then into mixed woods of pine, spruce, and elk-scarred aspen. A break in the trees opens to a scene of snow-creased peaks framed by **Rocky Mountain** or **silky locoweed**. Nearby is shorter **showy loco**, each flower a magenta beak poking through soft, silvery hairs. Scattered in between are the graceful, angel-skin pink umbels of **nodding onion**.

The sky widens to include vistas of South Park's expansive pastures and rangeland. Far to the south, note the Sangre de Cristos, the southernmost range in the Rocky Mountain chain. Clumps of native grasses harbor **harebells** and **Rocky Mountain locoweed**. Though white in its pure form, **Rocky Mountain loco** cross-pollinates with magenta loco, resulting in unlimited pastels. Pink **wild geranium** joins slender-stalked **wand penstemon**, striking **sego lilies**, and butter-yellow **leafy cinquefoil**.

Taking in the Tarryall Range to the southeast, the trail coasts down to meet sprawling, endemic **Bodin milkvetch**; its violet-rose flowers age a steely blue. Surrounded by mountains, aspen-accented stretches of South Park backdrop **golden banner** and yellow **wallflower**.

Appearing on the right, an ancient bristlecone pine thrives in the lithic soil. Dark, stiff-needled bundles flecked with white resin are characteristic of the bristlecone. In the vicinity, **tall scarlet paintbrush** enlivens yellows of **beauty** cinquefoil and **whiskbroom parsley**. Trailside, **alpine milkvetch**'s little keeled flowers look up to **three-nerved fleabane**'s skinny lavender-pink rays.

Aspen, interspersed with bristlecone pines, flank a level section. Search for a creeping, woody **Crandalls penstemon** whose lilac tubes are tinged with tender blue. Heftier and more highly pigmented cousin **mountain penstemon** also blooms here.

Leading the eye to a distant peak, a painterly meadow calls hikers to carefully step in a few yards along an obscure old roadway to discover brisk blue **littleflower penstemon** sharing the flowerscape with gold **shrubby cinquefoil**, white **mouse-ear**, orangey-gold **meadow arnica**, and creamy whorls of **Parry lousewort**. **Pink plumes**, **Geyer onion**, **shooting stars**, and late-blooming **subalpine daisy** bring pink tints to this flowery meadow. Later-season hikers can expect royal blue chalices of **Rocky Mountain** or **Parry gentian**.

Return to the main track, passing early **blue daisy** and **yellow stonecrop** tucked in granite rock pockets along an easy ascent. Narrowing and leveling to overlook a pond, euphemistically called Baker Lake, the trail again encounters ground-hugging **Crandall penstemon** and sturdy **mountain penstemon**. Stunted aspens bring on **Indian warriors**, a stately fern-leafed lousewort whose hooded blooms suggest pointed helmets.

Descending now, watch for **tall larkspur** before coming to a south-facing hillside replete with **sandwort, nodding onion, sego lily**, and **standing milkvetch**. A switchback takes you past an outcrop featuring common **alumroot** and wonderfully fragrant **wild rose**.

Quaking aspen woods, understoried with **tall scarlet paintbrush, white geranium**, and an occasional **blue columbine** and its foliage-pretender **meadowrue**, shade the way. On the last curve before leaving the aspen, a damp habitat nourishes **wild iris, tall larkspur, shooting stars**, and rosy **shortstyle onion**.

RED GLOBE ANEMONE
Anemone multifida ssp. globosa

Red globe anemone opens tepals from soft pink to bright cerise. Variously named **Cliff, Cutleaf**, and **Pacific anemone**, as well as **red windflower**, this member of the buttercup family grows up to 18 inches tall. Deep cut, palmate leaves rise in silky-haired clumps from a woody taproot. *Anemone* is Greek for "wind," and legend claims that as Venus shed tears for her lost Adonis, an anemone—or windflower—sprang up where each tear touched the earth.

Narcissus-flowered anemone (*Anemonastrum narcissiflorum ssp. zephyrum)* is a high-country cousin.

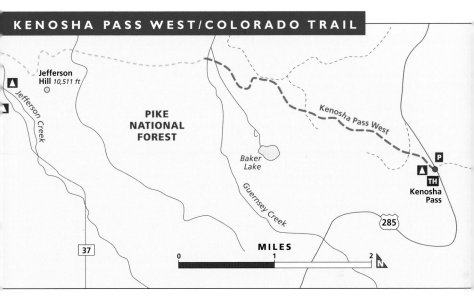

A slanted, mesic meadow filled with **shrubby cinquefoil, Geyer onion,** and **pink plumes** spreads out before you. **Wild irises** spangle the grasses, as do shell-pink specimens of **red globe anemone** and swaying heads of white **bistort.** Standing midst this floristic bounty backdropped by a procession of marching mountains conjures Emerson's remark "The earth laughs in flowers."

Ahead, **Rocky Mountain locoweed** blooms so thickly that fluffy white clouds seem to have settled directly on the earth. An occasional purple **standing milkvetch, orange paintbrush,** or bright, lazy **Bodin milkvetch** only accentuates the effect. Even a few **wand penstemon** take nothing from the snowy floral spectacle. Descending Kenosha West Trail bisects the floral fluff.

Undulating across the panoramic horizon, the Continental Divide is anchored by 12,853-foot Glacier Peak and 13,078-foot Whale Peak. The Divide's clinging patches of snow echo the blooming white slope sweeping across your vision.

An old irrigation ditch returns the trail to aspen woods and tête-à-tête meetings with **blue columbine.** Peeled logs hem in crusher fines, creating a solid foot bed over a damp pocket meadow of **shooting stars, mouse-ear,** and **pink plumes.** Nearby, **tall larkspur** and **iris** nestle midst **shrubby cinquefoil.**

Wend your way down toward Guernsey Gulch and the sound of running water. Guernsey Creek is crossed by a single massive log beam with lacy **cowbane** in sight. Sparse-flowered **bur avens, tall chiming bells,** and a bit of white **brookcress** accompany Guernsey Creek as it curves in its golden bed in dappled aspen shade. This is an excellent place to turn around.

Wildflower Hike 43

Peak 8 SuperChair Nature Walk

The ski slopes of winter give way to a wonderment of wildflowers in the summer.

Trail Rating	easy to moderate
Trail Length	2.0 miles out and back
Location	Breckenridge Ski Resort
Elevation	11,059 to 11,440 feet
Bloom Season	chairlift opening to closing; call resort for details
Peak Bloom	mid-July
Directions	From Denver, take I-70 west to exit 203 (Frisco). Head south on CO 9 and follow signs to Breckenridge Ski Resort Peak 8 parking lot. Take Colorado SuperChair. Unload at the top of the chairlift and turn right onto Nature Walk Trail. Chairlift fee required.

A UNIQUE AND EFFORTLESS WAY to ascend over 1,000 vertical feet to view high-country wildflowers is offered at Breckenridge Ski Area. Not only is Peak 8 Colorado SuperChair fast and fun, but quad seating makes it companionable. Interpretive signs along the Peak 8 Nature Walk Trail guide you past sloping meadows full of pretty wildflowers and grand scenery.

One caveat: when thunderstorms hit, the chairlift closes down until the lightning is no longer within 12 miles. Take the chairlift's first morning run to avoid fast-brewing afternoon thunderstorms. If you don't start out early, be sure to keep track of time so you don't miss the last chairlift down—it is a long hike back to the base.

Peak 8 Nature Walk Trail tallies an amazing 80 subalpine wildflower species in just 1 mile, many in the vicinity of the wetlands near the chairlift off-load point. Trail maps are available when you purchase a chairlift ticket.

Summer parking is free and plentiful in Peak 8 Base lots.

At the Peak 8 Colorado SuperChair offload point, the chair slows to a crawl. Unload, and walk a few yards to a map indicating the Nature Trail begins to the right. Then, fasten your sights on a spruce-rimmed glade on the left, where a trickling seep nurtures **scarlet** and **rosy paintbrush**, **Colorado thistle**, **yarrow**, and **marsh marigold**. **Little pink elephants** guard pink-globed **queen's crown** and delicate white doilies of **cowbane**. Also look for **white bog orchid**, **tall chiming bells**, **bog saxifrage**, and **globeflower**. Early-blooming **globeflower** often appears here with **marsh marigold**. In late July, look for dusky purple **star gentian**.

Head back toward open skies, where spruces shelter pale bluish **delicate Jacob's ladder**, white **parrot's beak lousewort**, and whorled **Parry lousewort**. Cool pink **subalpine daisy**, rosy **Parry clover**, and stamen-happy **purple fringe** show up nearby. Several

PATTERSON COLORADO TANSY ASTER
Machaeranthera pattersonii

The near neon-violet rays of **Patterson tansy aster** are yellow-centered. Toothed and dark, the leathery leaves act as a foil for the daisy-like flowers, whose phyllaries arc downward in thick tiers. Growing low in well-drained soil, this bright wildflower is a mid-summer eyeful. Harry Patterson, who collected plant species around the Grays Peak region, is honored by both the Latin specie and the common name.

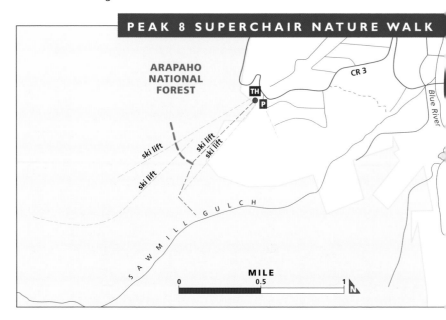

arnicas and senecios in the vicinity qualify for the ADYD category: Another Darn Yellow Daisy.

An interpretive sign welcomes you to the Nature Trail. Read it to learn about elevational ecosystems, such as tundra, which typically begins around 11,500 feet in this part of the Rockies. Spruce flanks the trail as it winds up to another interpretive sign.

Clumps of starry **Fendler sandwort** rise on wire-thin stems over grass-like leaves. Not far away, cousin **alpine sandwort** clings to dark green, hard-to-the-touch mats. In late July, vivid violet **Patterson Colorado tansy aster** zings up late summer flora.

The trail, garlanded by flowers, ascends to a bowl meadow featuring **rosy paintbrush**, **tall chiming bells**, and **narcissus-flowered anemone**. Continue along the leveling track to reach a slope colored like a calico quilt. **Subalpine daisy**'s rich pink petals flood the flowerscape while **Whipple penstemon** adds subtle wine hues. Identify resident **pink-headed daisies** by their seductively soft, pink-haired phyllary collar, most obvious on the nodding buds.

The gradient increases to reach another interpretive sign, this one revealing thistles as a food source for resourceful Native Americans and early explorers. Look for more jaunty **Indian paintbrush** as well as **bistort**, **mountain blue violets**, and **black-headed daisy**, a short, white fleabane with a fuzzy collar of black wool. Nearby, tiny pink **pygmy bitterroot** asks for recognition. Those ADYDs keep coming as the trail edges through conifers to greet a meadow spiked with **orange agoseris** and **Colorado thistle**.

A lush swale on the right supports **little pink elephants, blue columbine,** a bit of **subalpine larkspur,** and **Grays angelica.** Wildly pigmented **rosy paintbrush** declares color superiority.

Krummholz islands and boulders anchor **mountain prickly currant** with its tray-shaped flowers. Farther along the gentling trail, look upslope for **alpine avens** and clumps of elegant **Colorado blue columbine.** Look east for a view of the distant Continental Divide. Grays and Torreys Peaks, both fourteeners, are high points.

Pull up through spruce to reach a steep bank cloaked with a shattered rainbow of wildflowers. Don't miss subtle flowers such as **snowball saxifrage** and **mountain death camas.**

A gash filled with sharp rocks signals the start of a steeper gradient. Pause here to check the periphery of tumbled, lichen-encrusted rock for **rockbrake fern.** Eye the rocky slope for **alumroot, dotted saxifrage,** and **pinnate-leaved** and **one-headed daisies,** both in lavender.

Resume following the narrow, steepening track to reach **creamy** or **subalpine buckwheat** and **golden aster.** The trail weaves around rock and trees at close quarters, eventually coming upon a T-Bar lift dangling overhead. This is a good turnaround point. Retrace your steps through cheerful flowerscapes, and return to the chairlift for the scenic trip back to the base.

Walk through a bounty of wildflowers after a ride on the Breckenridge Peak 8 SuperChair.

Wildflower Hike 44

Dillon Peninsula

Curlyhead goldenweed blooms near the marina in Dillon Bay.

Trail Rating	easy
Trail Length	2.5 miles out and back
Location	Dillon Reservoir/Dillon
Elevation	9,070 to 9,230 feet
Bloom Season	June to August
Peak Bloom	July
Directions	From Denver, head west on I-70. Take exit 205 for US 6 east towards Dillon. Continue for about 3 miles. Park at the designated area on your right, just past a stop light.

WELCOME to one of the easiest hikes in the Dillon vicinity. Sandwiched between Dillon Bay and Snake River Arm, Dillon Peninsula offers lake and mountain views along with a wide variety of wildflowers. The nearly flat trail follows a well-packed service road that is closed to public vehicles.

Some six dozen wildflower species adorn the 1.25-mile trail to the West Portal of the Roberts Tunnel at the tip of the peninsula. A couple of less common species, such as creeping penstemon and dwarf lupine, make their rocky home here.

The parking lot above the highway holds a fair number of vehicles. Hike before noon to avoid summer afternoon thunderstorms. On some days, you may see the "Dillon doughnut," a phenomenon whereby the mountains encircling Dillon Reservoir are haloed in cloud while the lake basks in a sunny hole.

You are about to enter a high-country sagebrush ecosystem supporting a surprising variety of wildflowers. Pause to read a sign along the bike path announcing the Dillon Reservoir Recreation Area.

Before getting started, look in a pocket meadow to your right for spires of **fireweed**, gangly **saffron senecio**, white **northern bedstraw**, and pale blue **tall false forget-me-not**. Continue on past the intensely pigmented violet-blues of **Rocky Mountain penstemon** and soft-hued **wild iris**. In lithic soil nearby, bright lavender **Parry harebell** may be offering its open, tulip-like blossoms.

Start out along the broad expanse of dirt road beyond the gate, watching the sage-dominated hillside for towering **green gentian**, vivid **Rocky Mountain penstemon**, full-headed **creamy buckwheat**, and the magenta beaks and soft silvery foliage of **showy locoweed**, sometimes called **whorled loco**.

Disturbed road margins are perfect habitat for robust clumps of **curlyhead goldenweed**, while **yellow paintbrush** grows up to

CURLEYHEAD GOLDENWEED
Pyrrocoma crocea

This robust sunflower family member gets its common name from the flippant curls its yellow-gold rays acquire with age; its phyllaries are also curly. This mid-summer bloomer grows up to a yard tall. It has big, smooth, bluish-tinged basal leaves and is fond of disturbed soil, such as that alongside roads. Its genus name, *Pyrrocoma*, meaning "tawny mane," refers to its seed hairs, while its specific name, *crocea*, meaning "saffron-colored," refers to its lucent golden rays.

2 feet tall in the gray-green sagebrush above the road. Nearby, **littleflower penstemon** adds a touch of blue, and elegant **sego lily** opens generous three-petaled cups. That free spirit of flora, **American vetch**, twirls around them all.

A quilt of many colors, banded by **wild rose** and accented by **Rocky Mountain penstemon**, leads the eye down to Dillon Bay, where borage family cousins **stickseed** and **tall false forget-me-not** spatter the scene like bits of calico. Watch for mountain bluebirds dipping to land at one of the bluebird boxes attached to nearby utility poles.

The sage community brightens with **wild blue flax**—especially appealing in the cool hours before the sky-blue petals drop in the heat of day. Its stems are as tough as its petals are ephemeral—Native Americans once used them to make nets and cordage.

As you proceed, lavender **showy** or **aspen daisy** vies for attention with **scarlet gilia**, dangling **harebells**, and poised **aspen** or **nodding sunflower**. On the cutbanks to your left, sprawling **pink milkvetch** colorfully makes up for its unassuming cousins, **miser** and **standing milkvetch**. More **wild rose** blooms trailside, joined by **scarlet gilia** and a variety of penstemons.

Evergreens increase on the left, as do plush swabs of **Rocky Mountain locoweed** and luminous **sego lilies**. Early-season hikers enjoyed stars of **Rocky Mountain phlox**, scented bright **wallflower**, and **anemones**, whose seedheads resemble cotton swabs.

DWARF LUPINE
Lupinus lepidus ssp. caespitosus

This western slope denizen grows only 4 inches high and sports inflorescence shorter than its palmate leaves. Pressure, such as the weight of a bee on the clasped keel, ejects pollen from covert stamens. **Dwarf lupine** may be known as **stemless** or **cushion lupine**, and is a member of the pea family. Six hundred lupine species occur in North America.

A damp swale, marked by a curve of willows, dips the roadway past stately spires of **tall larkspur**. **Tall chiming bells**, **tall valerian**, **saffron senecio**, **curlyhead goldenweed**, and several species of sunny **cinquefoil** appreciate the moisture here, as did a pool of **wild iris** earlier in the season.

A small copse of quaking aspen on the left provides dancing shade for **lupine**, **mountain parsley**, lazy **white-flowered peavine**, and a clump or two of **blue columbine**. The road arcs to reveal an overhanging cutbank where extra moisture lets **Rocky Mountain phlox** bloom later. The sloped meadow above is habitat for **pink plumes**, whose trio of nodding urns pull erect with feathery seed plumes, validating other common names, such as **prairie smoke** and **old man's beard**.

Pass through ranks of lodgepole pine to enter a clearing. Up ahead is the West Portal of the Roberts Tunnel, which carries Dillon Reservoir's water to Front Range communities. Beyond the intake building, our route curves down to the right, passing long-blooming **golden aster** to reach a shingle generously referred to as "Dillon Beach." Consisting of broken shale, it provides a clean place to relax in the shade of lodgepoles. While you rest, enjoy a 180-degree Rocky Mountain panorama. To the northeast, look for 11,441-foot Tenderfoot Mountain; to the north, 12,498-foot Ptarmigan Peak; and, to the west, 12,777-foot Buffalo Mountain and 13,189-foot Red Mountain.

Leaving the hard rock beach, head south carefully along a low, shaley shelf above the lake, searching for lavender-blue **creeping penstemon**. Gravelly roadbed soil just west of the tunnel building may support **dwarf** or **littlebunch lupine**, whose finger-joint-high blooms nestle in velvet soft, gray-green, palmate leaves. To get back to your car, return the way you came.

*Wildflower
Hike 45*

Eccles Pass:
Meadow Creek Trail

Quiet meadows stretch towards 11,890-foot Eccles Pass.

Trail Rating	moderate
Trail Length	9.0 miles out and back
Location	Frisco/Eagles Nest Wilderness
Elevation	9,090 to 11,890 feet
Bloom Season	June to August
Peak Bloom	July
Directions	From Denver, take I-70 west to exit 203. Follow the roundabout at the exit to the second spur and a sign for Meadow Creek Trailhead on the right. Continue west to the road's end and the trailhead.

SITUATED IN EAGLES NEST WILDERNESS, the trail to spectacular Eccles Pass is well worth its 4.5-mile length and 2,800-foot elevation gain. On the north side of the pass, dozens of alpine species hang from rugged granite outcrops, and the vista from 11,890-foot Eccles Pass is simply and stunningly elegant.

A wildflower count of about 120 species puts this hike solidly in the "century" category.

Parking is adequate but fills up on mid-summer weekends, as Meadow Creek Trail shares its trailhead with that of popular Lily Pad Lakes. An early arrival secures a spot.

The trail begins at an information board covering the rules of wilderness etiquette and displaying an area map. Enter a mature quaking aspen grove where whites of **cow parsnip**, **yarrow**, **white geranium**, and **northern bedstraw**, along with yellows of **sneezeweed**, **shrubby cinquefoil**, and **sulphur paintbrush**, are all accented by **fireweed** and **monkshood**. Farther along, watch for a pair of petalless cousins: **Bigelow rayless senecio**, with sturdy turbans attached to thick flower stalks, and **nodding senecio**, with smaller yellow-green heads dangling on slim stalks.

In the filtered shade, **false hellebore** presents its toxic flowers. In the grasses along the ascending track, look for **sego** or **mariposa lily**, lavender **harebells**, and rambunctious **American vetch**. Complementing soft purple **aspen** or **showy daisies** are yellow **cinquefoils** and creamy **subalpine buckwheat**. The rough trail eases as it pulls up to the sound of Meadow Creek music.

Where aspens begin to mix with evergreens, **Parry goldenweed** puts forth late-blooming yellow stars on fresh greenery. Its rangy cousin, **western ragwort**, signals a gentler segment of trail, aided by a log footbridge. Look in the vicinity for **fireweed**, **cow parsnip**, and **lupine**.

Contour through an aspen parkland to encounter **sneezeweed** and **tall larkspur**. Smaller aspens frame **sulphur paintbrush**, **harebells**, **sneezeweed**, and **yarrow**. Mornings favor **wild blue flax**, opening ephemeral azure petals on stems tough enough to once have served Native Americans for cordage, nets, and snares.

Ubiquitous **yarrow**'s aromatic, fernlike foliage emits a medicinal odor, and indeed the herb is both a coagulant and an antiseptic. Proceed to a more moist habitat where aspen attain impressive girths and shelter intensely purple, acutely toxic **monkshood**. Colossal **cow parsnip** is a neighbor.

Where the trail rises again, ground-hugging mats of evergreen **kinnikinnick** and lush patches of **meadowrue** prosper. Lodgepole pine fingers in. When the lodgepoles fade and the understory vegetation resumes, watch for white **checkermallow** with its purple stigma. **Twinberry honeysuckle** displays red bracts cupping pairs of inedible black berries that began as dull gold tubes.

The stony trail returns to the shelter of aspen, passing **wild geranium** and **alpine milkvetch**. Golden **sneezeweed** and **cinquefoils** and purple **tall larkspur** and **aspen daisies** grow trailside. The route introduces soldier-straight **aspen sunflowers**, passing an old relic of mining days, a double tipple of small logs.

At a junction, stay left on Meadow Creek Trail. Head through mixed evergreens and leafy colonies of **heartleaf arnica**, which are frugal with their flowers. Approach a sign designating Eagles Nest Wilderness and ascend to a sagebrush meadow where **lupine, larkspur, pussytoes, harebells,** and lovely **sego lily** grow.

Reenter aspen to find **American vetch** and **orange agoseris**, or **burnt-orange false dandelion**. When you pass through a stand of lodgepoles, look for **one-sided wintergreen**. Damper environs bring on **twistedstalk** and **pink pyrola**.

Another sign reinforcing Meadow Creek Trail sends you into an even wetter environment. Travel a half-log walkway past alders and willow sheltering **cow parsnip**, yellow **bur avens, tall chiming bells,** and **triangle-leaf** or **arrowleaf senecio**.

Briefly ascend to a drier forested area suited to **pink-headed daisies** and **tall scarlet paintbrush**. An upcoming wetter zone is the perfect habitat for **white bog orchids** and **brookcress**.

Along a rocky sector, more **pink pyrola** blooms near a log footbridge. Wet, black rocks and frothing whitewater here frame lacy **cowbane**.

Another ascent brings on thinning pines sheltering **least wintergreen**. **Pink-headed daisies, sulphur paintbrush, tall scarlet paintbrush,** and even **heartleaf arnica** join in to celebrate the improved light conditions. **Alpine milkvetch, mountain parsley, golden aster,** and **goldenrod** also grow here, along with a clump or two of rich purple-blue **subalpine larkspur**.

When the forest opens to lumpy knolls, the trail turns a corner to meet blue **littleflower penstemon** and **yellow stonecrop**. **Fleabane daisies** dot the grasses, as does an occasional **Whipple penstemon**. On the margins, look for **tall false forget-me-not** in baby blue.

A small drainage presents **leafy aster**, whose ray petals range from radiant lavender-blue to vivid magenta-pink. **Tall larkspur** towers over **mountain death camas**. Rocky and rooty, the trail leads to an opening featuring creamy **Parry lousewort**, hairy **rayless** or **Parry arnica**, and **subalpine buckwheat**.

Narrowing considerably, the trail comes near the creek, where moisture-loving **white bog orchid, marsh marigold, queen's crown, cowbane, bistort,** and airy **brook saxifrage** flourish. **Tall chiming bells, brookcress,** and **Gray's angelica** are here as well.

Continue past annual **fringed gentian** unfurling royal purple tubes. **Mountain death camas** increases to showcase **horned dandelion**, a stocky native with dark phyllaries under its shaggy yellow head. Spruces and stumps curve the trail up to meet **little rose gentian** and, later, **Parry** or **Rocky Mountain gentian**.

Before an ascent, look for hairy **subalpine arnica**, native **Coulter daisy**, and white **stitchwort**. **Whipple penstemon** signals a trickle on the right where **white bog orchid**, cool pink **subalpine daisy**, and dainty **pink willowherb** grow under willows.

Paintbrush dominate the ascending trail, flanked by willows that open to unveil a snow-creased peak. Nearby, **sandwort** joins **orange agoseris** and **shrubby cinquefoil**, while **fringed gentian** aims hikers creekside in search of tiny-flowered blue **speedwell**, or **alpine veronica**, and fragrant, rosy globes of **Parry clover**.

A hefty half-log bridge signals a delightful wildflower garden featuring purple **monkshood** and plush-bracted **rosy paintbrush**. Peaty underfoot, the trail leads to dusky-purple **star gentian** and white **narcissus-flowered anemone**.

As you travel the south flank of Meadow Creek, look in the moist soil to your left for lots of **star gentians**, **little pink elephants**, and **rosy paintbrush**. Farther on, legions of pale-yellow **bracted lousewort** spikes greet **daffodil senecio**. Another meadow introduces the finely divided foliage and white umbellate heads of **fernleaf lovage**. Look under bushy willows for **subalpine arnica** and **subalpine daisies**.

Gravelly granite leads toward a little vernal pond where tiny **trailing butter-cup**, or **spearwort**, sprawls on the muddy edges. Spruce shade leapfrogs sunny openings, and the trail contours near a colorful army of **Parry primrose**, **black-headed daisy**, **tall chiming bells**, **Parry clover**, **rosy paintbrush**, **brookcress**, **brook saxifrage**, **cowbane**, and **bistort**.

Rise to a widening landscape of mountains and meadows. **Western paintbrush**, **mouse-ear**, **blueleaf cinquefoil**, and **alpine hawkweed** flourish among the grasses. To the north, note the crescent grin of Eccles Pass, about a mile and 500 vertical feet ahead. On the right is 12,777-foot Buffalo Mountain.

Venture briefly off the trail to stroll alongside the creek. Thick grasses overhang its calm, topaz water, providing ideal habitat for pink **subalpine daisies**,

PINK PYROLA
Pyrola rotundifolia ssp. asarifolia

Wintergreen family member pink pyrola decorates bare stalks with waxy parasols, each spouting a curved style. Its rounded, glossy leaves remain green under snow. This pretty plant spreads by rhizomes. Alternative names include **bog wintergreen** and **pink swamp pyrola**; both reveal its penchant for wet habitat. Another name, **shinleaf**, an old English countryfolk label, refers to its use as a healing plaster. Native Americans made poultices from the leaves. **Shy wood nymph** (*Moneses uniflora*) is related.

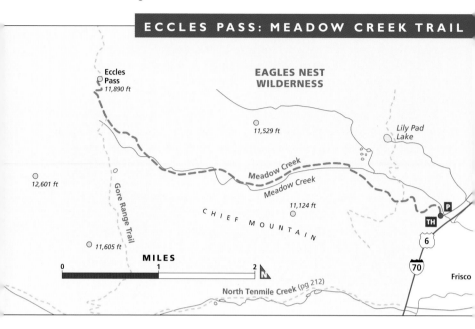

ECCLES PASS: MEADOW CREEK TRAIL

little pink elephants, queen's crown, fringed gentian, and monkshood. Tall chimin bells and bog saxifrage also bloom here.

When the spirit is ready and the body willing to follow, return to the trail and prepare to wander through acres of wildflowers before the push up to the pass. Granite peaks and outcroppings flank the gentle ascent through a broad, flowery basin.

Pass abundant mountain death camas before encountering a tributary displaying yellow monkeyflower, little pink elephants, rosy paintbrush, and ethereal brook saxifrage and cowbane. Cross the creek a few yards upstream of the trail on convenient stones. Brookcress and pink willowherb's fondness for wet places is evident here. White batons of American bistort wave above Coulter daisy and subalpine daisy. This is the type of floriferously resplendent open place poet Edna St. Vincent Millay might have had in mind when exclaiming, "I will be the gladdest thing under the sunset! I will touch a hundred flowers and not pick one."

Rough rock cairns direct the route, keeping you on the ascending path to Eccles Pass. Pass by abundant fernleaf lovage, whose small popcorn umbels top foliage that is very aromatic, reminiscent of celery leaves with medicinal overtones.

Cruising up to a sign mid-meadow, arrive at a junction with the Gore Range Trail, which goes left. Continue straight along the Meadow Creek Trail. Look ahead for a cascade of whitewater—Meadow Creek's beginnings. Trailside flowers include white willowherb and homely buttercup. Plentiful mountain

death camas still shows some budded specimens. As you continue northwest-ward, look for a string of beaver ponds below a slope of **paintbrush** and **sub-alpine arnica**. **Rocky Mountain gentians** cover a steep hillside. Ahead, stunted spruce islands float in a sea of pale **western paintbrush** lording over **mountain blue violets**.

Head up, passing shaggy-headed **horned dandelion** before dipping into small drainages where **little pink elephants, Parry primrose,** and **rosy paintbrush** think pink beside white **bog** and **brook saxifrages**. Yellow **arrowleaf senecio** pokes above low willows and **rosy paintbrush** grandstands on the left as the route traverses a steep slope. Also look for **alpine arnica** and **red paintbrush**.

The crushed granite trail switchbacks for the last push to Eccles Pass. Close to the top, look for **pinnate-leaved daisy, alpine avens, whiproot clover, Parry lousewort, dwarf goldenrod,** and **Whipple penstemon**. Nearby **alpine sandwort** hugs its five-petaled white blossoms to its foliage.

From the top of 11,890-foot Eccles Pass, the mountainscape panorama is simply stupendous. From the ragged Gore Range panorama to the south, turn north to view 13,189-foot Red Peak. The steep basin in the foreground rolls out like emerald velvet embroidered with conifer stands, dark ponds, and the thread of trail leading to Red Buffalo Pass.

Saddle outcrops to the left or west tuck a bit of **pink bog laurel** in moist pockets. Small slides of decomposed granite may turn up **mountain dryas'** eight creamy petals along with its twisted troll-hair seedheads. Further examination reveals crevices draped with needlelike mats of **spotted saxifrage** and cushions of pink **moss campion**.

The pass' secret rock garden adorns a sheer north face with late-blooming examples of tundra dwellers. Approach the precipitous outcrop cautiously—careful boot placement is not only a safety factor but protects vulnerable plants. Look for **rock or Fremonts senecio** and **Holms senecio. Mountain candytuft** and cousin **fernleaf candytuft,** or **Smelowskia,** as well as select yellow **drabas,** are all in the mustard clan. Check around for **king's crown, purple fringe,** and perhaps even a photogenic clump of pastel **blue columbine**. Fine-foliaged **snow buttercups** pop up where lingering snowbanks recently receded. The rocky heights are also home to marmots, pika, and mountain goats, any or all of which may put in an appearance. When you are ready, turn around and return the way you came.

*Wildflower
Hike 46*

North Tenmile Creek

*Subalpine larkspur casts purple tints along this hike
that boasts 120 wildflower species.*

Trail Rating	moderate
Trail Length	7.0 miles out and back
Location	Frisco
Elevation	9,070 to 10,050 feet
Bloom Season	June to September
Peak Bloom	mid-July to early August
Directions	From Denver, head west on I-70 to Frisco/exit 201. Take the underpass under I-70 to the parking area immediately on your left.

GARNERING a "century" trail designation with well over a hundred wild-flower species, North Tenmile Creek Trail is as floristically rewarding as it is a pleasant trek. Even if you hike only to the Eagles Nest Wilderness boundary and pause beside fast-moving Tenmile Creek, there is a sense of accomplishment. North Tenmile Creek Canyon is bounded by 10,855-foot Wichita Mountain on the south and 11,377-foot Chief Mountain on the north.

About 120 species of Colorado wildflowers greet hikers along this 3.5-mile trek, 70 of them within the first 2 miles.

Parking spots go quickly on summer weekends, so plan to arrive early to secure a place and complete the trek before afternoon thunderstorms conjure up flash and fury.

M id-summer is a wildflowerist's dream, with a big species count and montane beauty. Start the flower count at the parking area. Scattered among quaking aspen, **northern bedstraw**, **wild chamomile**, and **cow parsnip** are joined by **wild rose** and **fireweed**. Showy or **aspen daisy**, **harebells**, **narrow-leaved paintbrush**, and **creamy buckwheat** chime in. A whole glen of imported **oxeye daisies** interspersed with fragrant, and also imported, **red clover** creates a bucolic scene.

Disturbed road edges by the parking areas are home to addictively perfumed **wild rose** and prolific alien **yellow sweet clover**. **Dogbane**'s delicate-scented bells oversee the sparse, yellow heads of fresh-foliaged **Parry goldenweed** near a sign pointing North Tenmile Trail right (west).

Along the sandy trail, note low-growing **false box**, an evergreen subshrub. A water facility in a peculiar shade of acid green signals a rise where intensely pigmented **Rocky Mountain penstemon** grows in sturdy-stalked clumps. The rocky roadbed climbs through a mixed conifer-deciduous wood lit occasionally by **heartleaf arnica**.

At a fork—whose paths will rejoin—try the left path, which heads down to a rushing creek where the remains of an old wooden mining flume languish. A pile of lichen-encrusted rock provides a challenge to pioneering aspen, and the sound of a small waterfall calls you toward it. In late June, look here for **western red columbine** blooming alongside its cousins **green-flowered wintergreen** and **pink pyrola**.

Continue along, passing a seep that pampers **tall chiming bells**, **cow parsnip**, and a **green bog orchid** or two, not to mention whining mosquitoes. The trail curves near the clear creek, revealing old beaver workings and some **wild iris**. **Queen's crown**, a pink-headed sedum; **blue-eyed grass**, a member of the iris family; and **bog orchids** take you back to the main trail, where **wild rose** perfume encourages those sweet moments of life.

The level trail passes beaver ponds, which lead the way into willows harboring scented **white bog orchid**. Circumvent the mucky domain of **little pink elephants** and hot pink **shooting stars**.

Enter a plush meadow where legions of **pink pyrola**, purple **tall Jacob's ladder**, **white bog orchid**, and **white geranium** thrive. Arrive by the ore tailing piles of a mine rumored not to be the Square Deal its name implied. Check for real treasures at your feet when **wild strawberries** ripen in late July.

The trail cruises levelly, passing **golden aster** and **scarlet paintbrush**. Lodgepole pine forest, a miserly habitat for flowers, provides openings where **shrubby** and **silvery cinquefoil** grow. Parading **elephants** signal a seep on the right. Just uphill, a tiny chocolate-colored pond's outlet nurtures unusual **purple avens**, a lanky rose family member with bowed heads.

Beyond the boggy pond, spruce and fir shade the trail as it heads up into the domain of pea family members **American vetch** and **white-flowered peavine**. The ascent brings you to a lovely riverside meadow shadowed by 12,522-foot Uneva Peak. Look for **early blue daisy**, **mouse-ear**, and **cow parsnip**.

Pass through a section of forest. In the next meadow, look for cool **western paintbrush** and **creamy buckwheat** entwined by rambunctious **American vetch**. Ramrod-straight **aspen sunflower** lords over all.

Forest and meadow play leapfrog. The next meadow is home to dainty-flowered **subalpine valerian** and its chaperone, **false hellebore**, a substantial plant with pleated leaves. **False hellebore**'s toxic flowers may be lethal to pollinating bees.

Wild iris and **scarlet paintbrush** lead up to an Eagles Nest Wilderness boundary sign. Lively North Tenmile Creek flows just below. For those not wanting to challenge the rough, narrow trail beyond this point, this makes a good turnaround point. For those continuing on, the best is yet to be.

Pass into the wilderness area and curve down to where **brookcress** and **tall chiming bells** brighten the creek's edge. A damp hillside yields purple **monkshood** and subtle **purple avens**. A little farther on, a minimal seep nurtures **yellow monkeyflower**, **pink willowherb**, **arrowleaf senecio**, and more **monkshood**.

The trail climbs past a trickling tributary decorated with **monkeyflower**, **shooting stars**, **purple avens**, and dainty **brook saxifrage**. A bit of **green mitrewort** joins both **white** and **green bog orchids**. Moisture feeds tall **twistedstalk** and uncommon **twayblade**, a tiny green orchid with a cleft lower lip. A peeled log causeway leads to a clump of aspen framed by **white geranium** and **golden draba**.

BIGELOW RAYLESS GROUNDSEL
Ligularia bigelovii v. hallii

Hefty heads shaped like fluted drums define Bigelow groundsel or senecio. Though its blooms are often burnt maroon, they can occasionally be bright green. This flower thrives in montane and subalpine life zones. Both the genus and common names recognize Boston-based Jacob Bigelow, an 18th-century professor of botany.

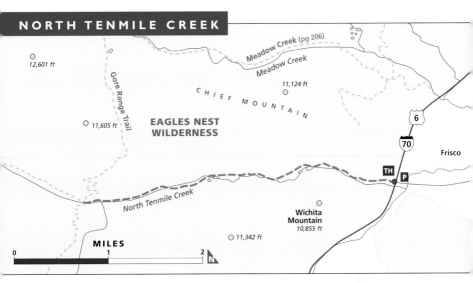

Twin seeps precede a deeply shaded spruce habitat supporting the wonderful, wildly fragrant **shy wood nymph**. Becasue this flower's wavy, margined white petals bow to the earth, it may take some determined "belly botany" to earn a sniff.

Pass through a dry, open area where **sego lilies**, **beauty cinquefoil**, and **creamy** or **subalpine buckwheat** prosper. Back in the cool shade of conifers, more sweet **shy wood nymph** shares the spotlight with **western red columbine**. A creek, crossed by stones, displays head-high **monkshood**, **cow parsnip**, and **tall chiming bells**.

Drifting down and briefly into the open, the rocky, rooty trail meets troops of **elephants** and **orchids** before returning to the forest. Look for toxic **mountain death camas**. Native Americans gave it an alternative moniker: **poison onion**.

Before the trail heads up, the main creek is crossed by a half-log bridge in view of a lighthearted creeklet. Uneva Peak points the way onto open, flowery slopes spattered with **sego lily**, **creamy buckwheat**, and **tall larkspur**.

Pass through a section of deep forest where several tricky and wet stream crossings are necessary. Return to open skies, bisected by a copse of quaking aspen. **White-flowered peavine**, **western paintbrush**, and **showy** or **aspen daisy** paint their understory.

Nearby **Bigelow groundsel** is worth a look. This flower has no petals; even its disk flowers are somewhat incognito. Compare its glossy foliage to the conspicuously hairy leaves of **rayless arnica**, another petalless denizen.

Partial to nectaring open-faced flowers, fritillary butterflies find **orange agoseris** exactly the same burnt-orange color as their wings. **Pink-headed daisy**, with its woolly buds, offers butterflies more landing pads.

Arriving at the junction with Gore Trail signals completion of the 3.5 miles of wildflowering. An optional left turn down to the creek may turn up some hybrid **rosy paintbrush**, **white catchfly**, and, at water's edge, vestiges of hot pink **Parry primrose**. When you're ready, retrace your steps back to the parking area.

Wildflower Hike 47

Piney River Falls:
Upper Piney River Trail #1885

Scarlet gilia's trumpets color the banks of Piney Lake.

Trail Rating	easy to moderate
Trail Length	7.0 miles out and back
Location	Vail/White River National Forest/Eagles Nest Wilderness/Vail
Elevation	9,360 to 9,920 feet
Bloom Season	late June to early August
Peak Bloom	mid-July
Directions	From Denver, take I-70 west to exit 176/Vail. Head straight (west) on North Frontage Rd. W and continue 1 mile. Turn right down Red Sandstone Rd./County Road 700. Continue for 7.2 miles. Where the road forks, stay straight on Meadow Creek Rd. and travel 4 miles. Park to your right, at the first wood gate.

TUCKED INTO A CURVE of south Eagles Nest Wilderness, Upper Piney River Trail #1885 begins at Piney River Ranch Resort, hugs Piney Lake, then follows Piney River to Piney River Falls, leaving no doubt, to the point of ennui, about the name. But the spectacular mountain scenery, abundance of still and moving water, great views, and 90 species of wildflowers guarantee that you will not sustain ennui but be exhilarated on this 3.5-mile jaunt. Those wishing for a longer hike may continue up Piney River Valley to—you guessed it—Upper Piney Lake.

Muddy places make boots a boon. Parking is to be found adjacent to the Piney River Ranch Bighorn-West gate and corral.

After driving many miles of gritty dirt road and potholes, setting off afoot feels good. National Forest Service Trail #1885 Upper Piney River starts off on the north side of the ranch road, inside a peeled rail fence. A red sandstone cliff, streaked with dark manganese and fringed with aspens, serves as a backdrop for **green gentian**, **pink plumes**, and **shrubby cinquefoil**, all wound about by climbing **American vetch**. A more unusual wildflower found here is **saffron senecio**, topped with bright red-orange buds. Also look for **beauty cinquefoil**, **littleflower penstemon**, **creamy buckwheat**, **tall valerian**, and **pink plumes**. By August, this natural garden presents royal blue **Rocky Mountain** or **Parry gentian**. Western valerian charmed early-season hikers.

Head east on a trail shared by horses, passing through a ranch gate. Piney Lake and the grand, rugged Gore Range come into view. A break in the fence continues the trail past an aspen copse and attendant **aspen sunflower** and **aspen** or **showy daisy**.

Below the open hillside, jade waters frame **harebell, orange**

PEARLY EVERLASTING
Anaphalis margaritacea

This member of the composite or sunflower family is notable for its papery flowers that make one think of strawflowers. Though the basal leaves wither, alternate woolly leaves grow along the erect stems. Clumps of this summer-blooming plant are formed by rhizomes. Pearly everlasting has myriad medicinal uses. Native Americans used it as a treatment for sore throats, upset stomachs, and dysentery. They also used it to make poultices that were applied to swellings, sores, and painful joints. Some tribes also prized it as a purifier. Others smoked the leaves, especially when dealing with lung issues. The Greek word *margarites* means "pearl."

agoseris, and sweet **wild rose.** The trumpets of **scarlet gilia** add panache. **Giant hyssop**'s smaller trumpets are tinted palest mauve. East-facing **aspen sunflowers** cast a golden touch.

At a casual junction a few hundred yards from Piney River Ranch, bear right along the lower segment. A cascade of blowzy-headed **cow parsnip** heralds moisture-loving willows, home to cowled **monkshood** and golden **arrowleaf senecio.**

Prefering drier habitat, **creamy buckwheat, yarrow,** and **showy daisy** appear before you arrive at another peeled-log fence. This one brings you into Eagles Nest Wilderness. While old beaver workings anchor the east end of Piney Lake, a platinum curve of peaks over 13,000 feet high prods the horizon.

Another trail junction appears, taking Upper Piney River Trail straight ahead. Spires of rubbery **green gentian** stud a meadow sustaining **pink plumes** and **valerian** cousins **western** and **tall.**

The sometimes-double-tracked trail travels beside meandering, willow-flanked Piney River. Look for **tall chiming bells, monkshood,** and pleated-leaved **false hellebore,** sometimes called **corn lily.** In the vicinity, native white **Coulter daisy** meets cousin **whiplash fleabane daisy** by a blister of smooth rock.

A decomposed red sandstone foot bed leads to complementary **littleflower penstemon** and **shrubby cinquefoil** overlooking clumps of **early blue daisy.** In the grasses, **American bistort** waves its long batons at **stemless evening primrose.**

Though the main trail pushes through a willow-bound morass, avoid muddy feet by heading right for the elephants, then weave through the grasses to a seep where **yellow monkeyflower** thrives. A **marsh marigold** may linger here. Now, head back up left to rejoin the still-muddy main trail.

The trail leads you to **white bog orchids** secreting a sweet fragrance; moisture-loving river birch's many-stemmed clumps shelter the orchids as well as **elephants.** Soon, a little side creek offers pristine white **brookcress.** Keep left at the next creek crossing for a distant vignette of peaks.

The valley closes in as the trail rises briefly through xeric soil featuring **pink pussytoes** and the wide chalices of **sego** or **mariposa lily.** Water returns to the scene, cascading over ledgy rock to introduce the green-tinged, white stars of **mountain death camas.**

Drift down briefly through an increasingly rocky landscape before heading up into aspen and finding a hidden creeklet. Rampant greenery and the large aspen here are highlighted by **pink-headed daisy, white geranium, mountain parsley,** and **Porter's lovage.**

An easygoing section of the trail passes large clumps of graceful ferns, aiming you toward those Gore Range rock ramparts. Where lacy waters thread a "v" in the rock, find an amphitheater of **fireweed** in late summer.

Lit by pink **tiny trumpets, yellow stonecrop, harebell,** and lavender **sego lily,** a steep, open slope is cloaked with lush vegetation. Navigate a great lump

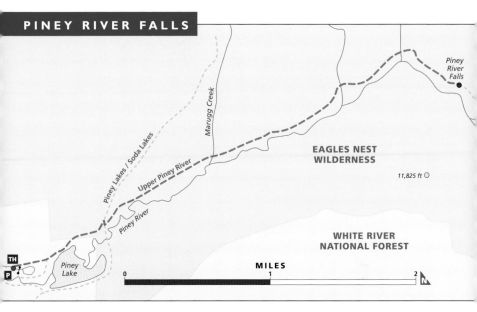

of rock to reach an even trail segment where a trickle nourishes delicate **brook saxifrage**. Next up, a picturesque seep harbors a garden of **yellow monkeyflower**, **monkshood**, **tall chiming bells**, **white bog orchid**, and **cow parsnip**.

The trail passes through aspen, then spruce, then aspen again. Pink granite and perfumed **wild roses** overlook the rushing creek. Meanwhile, muck takes the trail past **twistedstalk**'s dangling bells and **cowbane**'s lacy umbels. Next, look for **pearly everlasting** and **meadowrue**, or **false columbine**.

The next water crossing challenges dry boots. More challenging is the rocky, ascending trail as it passes through thickets of leafy but sparsely-flowering **thimbleberry**, where parasol-hung stalks of **pink pyrola** find shelter. House-sized boulders offer their surfaces to **dotted** or **moss saxifrage**. Grittier, rockier, and steeper, the trail climbs through evergreens. The last yellow and scarlet lanterns of early-blooming **western red columbine** linger here.

The steep pitch ends at an outcrop overlook decorated with rockbrake fern and **serviceberry**. On the far side, drop at about the same pitch to outcrops hung with **yellow stonecrop** and mats of **dotted saxifrage**. At the bottom of the hill, look for **false Solomon's seal**'s emerald-green, arched leafstalks.

At last, whitewater sound brings you through alders and mud to Piney River Falls. Shooting through a chasm of its own making and impeded by giant boulders, the frothing water courses down a flume of raw rock. Scan the shady far-side river wall for more **western red columbine**. When you are ready, retrace your steps back to your vehicle.

Cottonwood Pass South Knob:
Continental Divide Trail

Mid-summer finds abundant narcissus-flowered anemones on the saddles south of Cottonwood Pass.

Trail Rating	strenuous
Trail Length	1.0-mile reverse balloon loop
Location	Gunnison National Forest/Collegiate Peaks Wilderness/Cottonwood Pass/Buena Vista
Elevation	12,126 to 12,560 feet
Bloom Season	late June to July
Peak Bloom	mid-July
Directions	From Buena Vista, head west on County Road 306. Continue for 28 miles. Parking is to the left on the top of Cottonwood Pass.

BUILT AS A TOLL ROAD IN 1880, Cottonwood Pass Road, west of Buena Vista, straddles the Continental Divide at 12,126 feet. The lofty elevation is rewarded with expansive views of mountain range upon mountain range sweeping into the blue distance. If the altitude begins to affect you, turn around immediately and descend quickly.

Over five dozen alpine wildflower species spangle the trail along the 1-mile loop, which feels much longer due to the rarefied air. These high-altitude plants have only a six to eight week growing window, during which they must emerge, bloom, attract pollinators, and set seed.

The scenic road up from Buena Vista is paved to Cottonwood Pass. Parking at the pass is generous. Remember that on this exposed trail above treeline, lightning-charged afternoon thunderstorms build with unbelievable speed.

Head south along the Continental Divide Trail into the krummholz (German for "crooked wood") where the route travels west of the stark hump and leads straight, passing a small patch of krummholz nurturing **delicate Jacob's ladder** and pale lavender **one-headed daisy**. Step up stony tread to find deeply pigmented, matte blue **greenleaf chiming bells**. Glaucous-leaved **blueleaf cinquefoil**'s small gold cups join ubiquitous **alpine avens**, the dominant yellow flower of the alpine zone.

As the trail continues, look for **alpine paintbrush** and woody **mountain dryas**. The latter's eight-petaled, eggshell-hued blooms hug point-shaped scalloped leaves that are a choice ptarmigan food source. This prostrate subshrub roots wherever it touches soil, making it a valuable ally against alpine erosion. Later, its plumy seedheads will rise like windswept troll hair.

American bistort—also favored by ptarmigan—waves

ALPINE SMELOWSKIA
Smelowskia calycina

Inhabiting the highest places, especially along the Continental Divide, **Smelowskia** is also called **fernleaf candytuft**. Grayish pinnate leaves, including last year's curled at the plant's base, and four-petaled, fragrant white flowers that mature into short black seedpods characterize this mustard clan member. It is also found in Asia. Anchored by a long taproot driving into gravelly soil, this tundra dweller may also be known as **siberian smelowskia**. The name recognizes an 18th-century Russian botanist, Timotheus Smelowsky. Cousins **wild** or **mountain candytuft** (*Noccea montana*) and **wallflower** (*Erysimum capitatum*) prosper from foothills to alpine life zones.

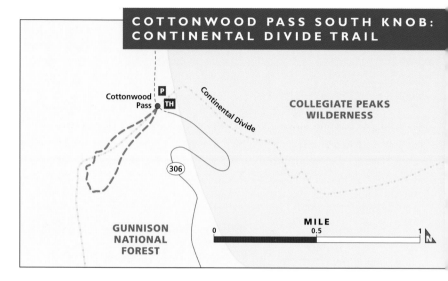

long-stemmed, bottle-brush swabs, each made up of myriad tiny flowers. Here and there, protected swales feature showy **narcissus-flowered anemone, moss campion,** and **alpine Smelowskia,** or **fernleaf candytuft.** Nearby, **snowball saxifrage** pops up lollipop heads that will elongate with the season.

Intent observers may spot **alpine** or **single harebell**'s purple trumpet aimed out over the grassy tundra. Charming **alplily,** each single tulip-like chalice translucent white, each tepal lightly striped, also takes a keen eye.

Rockier and steeper, the track passes golden **draba,** of mustard lineage, and gold-cupped **whiplash saxifrage.** Push uphill to reach lichen-encrusted tumbled stone, home to mats of fragrant **alpine phlox.** Delightfully scented, electric-blue **alpine forget-me-not** also blooms here.

The path levels somewhat near a boney krummholz where **king's crown** tucks itself in beside a boulder. Approach a divide and cross to the far side to ascend the looming summit ahead. The flat, stony area preceding the ascent supports pioneers such as **moss campion,** bicolored **whiproot clover,** azure **alpine forget-me-nots,** and the occasional **old man of the mountains.** Creamy **narcissus-flowered anemone** floods the saddle.

Ascend toward the knob ahead, taking time to check for easily missed and uncommon **snowlover**—a small, ivory-tubed penstemon relation partial to lingering snowbanks. This is a good area to find **one-headed daisy, Parry lousewort,** and those rich purple **alpine harebells.**

As you proceed, watch for tight-foliaged **alpine sandwort,** an exceptionally long bloomer that presses rounded white stars against a dense mat. Sweet pink starbursts of **pygmy bitterroot** cuddle in succulent, narrow basal leaves; white sports of this purslane family member are common. Look nearby for cousins

mountain candytuft and **alpine Smelowskia**. Note **dwarf** or **deer clover** as the trail ascends seriously through alpine flowerscape anchored with tufted grasses and sedges.

Straight ahead, a rock cairn on the horizon signals the approach to the well-earned summit of Cottonwood Pass' south knob. Easing slightly, the rugged track spreads through rock gardens displaying more deep-pink **dwarf clover** and azure **alpine forget-me-not**, which occasionally comes in white. The lichened rocks act as a foil for the red buds and blushed-white stars of **alpine** or **bigroot spring beauty**. "Bigroot" is an apt name, as the root may be 8 feet long, facilitating acclimation to shifts of the unstable rock slopes it inhabits.

One last pull for the crest heralds the flat summit. The tundra world here harbors **alpine phlox**, golden **pygmy tonestus**, **alpine cinquefoil**, a **sky pilot** or two, and a breathtaking 360-degree peak panorama.

Retrace the way back down to the saddle, cross it, and bear right, toward a narrow trail climbing the ridge ahead. Studded with rocks harboring lots of **forget-me-not** and **moss campion**, the path now follows the Continental Divide Trail up and over this rugged sample of the nation's backbone.

Upon gaining the ridge top, pause to search outcrop crevices for **blue columbine, dotted** or **moss saxifrage, alpine alumroot,** and **purple fringe**. After viewing massive fourteener peaks in the Collegiate Range, look on the west side of this stegosaurus-back ridge for the pretty combination of burnt-red **king's crown** and gold-coined **alpine avens**.

Continue north to find your parked vehicle below.

Wildflower Hike 49

West Maroon Pass Trail to Hasley Basin Junction

A mountain backdrop sets the wildflowers along West Maroon Pass Trail on display

Trail Rating	easy to moderate
Trail Length	5.0 miles out and back
Location	Maroon Bells–Snowmass Wilderness/Scofield Pass/Crested Butte
Elevation	10,400 to 10,900 feet
Bloom Season	late June to September
Peak Bloom	mid- to late July
Directions	From Crested Butte, head north on Gothic Rd./Frontage Road 317. Continue 7.7 miles to the almost-town of Gothic. Continue another 8 miles to Scofield Pass. The trailhead is 0.9 mile farther on the right.

A WILDFLOWERIST'S DREAM COME TRUE, West Maroon Pass Trail deserves every superlative that comes to a color-craving mind. The showstopper display in mid-July is not to be missed if you are in the Crested Butte area—justifiably called the Wildflower Capital of Colorado. Note that in some years lingering snowbanks block the road to Scofield Pass road far into summer.

The 2.5-mile trail is easygoing most of the way, following contours of a wide valley. The moderate trail-rating mention is attributed, mostly, to the elevation. West Maroon Pass Trail soon enters Maroon Bells-Snowmass Wilderness as it steadily gains altitude.

Fasten your wildflower seatbelts for about eight dozen species in countless quantities. To record the color spectacle, bring lots of film and oohs and aahs.

Parking is limited, so arrive early. Mountain thunderstorms are born big up here—don't underestimate their power, especially on summer afternoons.

Access the trail by heading east and entering a spruce forest. Wind past ivory **parrot's beak** or **ram's horn lousewort** sporting dark leaves. **Tall chiming bells, heartleaf arnica,** and **white geranium** add touches of color.

With the sound of shallow East Fork Creek comes a trail sign, followed by a creekside presentation of **rosy paintbrush, brookcress,** and **cowbane.** The keen eye may spot **green mitrewort**; an even keener eye, **sidebells mitrewort,** whose minuscule white snowflakes are aligned along a slender, erect stalk. A pocket meadow adds flat-topped, brick-red **king's crown.**

Verdant masses of **tall chiming bells** and **arrowleaf senecio** take the trail up to a bit of falling water. Bedded with multi-colored cobbles, the clear stream courses around an island of **rosy paintbrush** and **little pink elephants,** both accented by lacy white **cowbane.**

Curling away from the water, the trail passes three-paneled pods of very early blooming **glacier lilies.** Deep forest duff leads to a tumbledown cabin anchoring a flowery hillside where **orange sneezeweed** combines with **arrowleaf senecio** for a golden touch.

The track winds up around the sagging cabin to meet white **geranium** and **cow parsnip** entwined with scrambling **American vetch.** The gold of **cinquefoil** and the sky-blue of morning-blooming **wild blue flax** are tempered by **pink-headed daisy** and cool-tinted **sulphur paintbrush.** Nearby, **Porter's lovage** rises over ferny foliage. Later-blooming **fireweed** will soon inflame the open slope.

Ascend the stony track to a Maroon Bells-Snowmass Wilderness sign where early-season hikers noted **glacier lily.** Huge spruce harbors **mountain prickly currant.** Dip into a ravine to search for **pink** and **milky willowherbs. Tall scarlet paintbrush** and elegant **blue columbine** flank the trail with wild abandon.

Soldier-straight **aspen sunflower** aims you toward a junction. Follow the sign pointing West Maroon Pass Trail right. A wildflower-flooded creeklet carves its foot-wide way through sturdy **little pink elephants,** fragile-looking brook saxifrage, and stately **monkshood**. Stepping across the water, look north to catch **green bog orchid**, a tad of **yellow monkeyflower**, and the single pearl buds of bare-stalked **Parnassia**, which will soon open to pristine white cups.

The level hillside pathway exults in **wild blue flax** and blushing quantities of bushy **Engelmann aster**. Slopes steepen and go somewhat xeric as the wine-red, striated sandstone of the Maroon Bells peaks comes into view. Cruise past **golden aster**, **showy daisy**, **harebells**, and **dwarf sulphurflower**.

Dark blue **lupine** and a patriarch spruce prepare the way for pleated-leaf **false hellebore**, or **corn lily**. Plain-jane **tall valerian** is plentiful. Pagoda-like, **green gentian** rises above sun-struck prism colors. Late summer will witness royal blue chalices of **Parry gentian**. A lazy trickle nurtures **yellow monkey-flower**, **cowbane**, and richly pigmented **subalpine larkspur**. A muddy section flanked by wet-loving willows sheltering **meadowrue** is followed by a slate-bedded, mossy rivulet nurturing **little pink elephants**.

KING'S CROWN
Rhodiola integrifolia

Deep, brick-red **king's crown's** crowded heads consist of tiny, fragrant flowers. The flattish heads will darken with age, becoming almost black; in fall the thick, bluish-green leaves turn red. Found from Alaska to New Mexico, this member of the stonecrop clan is also referred to as **roseroot** for the scent of the rhizomes. The succulent leaves, once used by Native Americans as a headache remedy, were also eaten raw or boiled, though they become increasingly bitter with age. Pink-headed cousin **queen's crown** (*Clementsia rhodantha*) needs more moisture than **king's crown**.

Undulating and climbing slightly, the track passes moist habitats where **brook saxifrage**, **lupine**, **cowbane**, **tall chiming bells**, and **elephants** flourish. Look for **mountain death camas'** greenish-tinged white blooms and even more toxic **monkshood's** purple-hooded bloom stalks.

The trail drifts through flowering greenery, meeting lighthearted **lovage** and heavy-headed **cow parsnip**. Trickling over slate bedrock under overhanging willows, a moss-bordered rivulet heralds **king's crown**, **bracted lousewort**, and more **elephants**.

Pass blisters of worn, quartz-charged stone decorated with **Whipple penstemon**, **ballhead** or **clustered sandwort**, and yellow **parsley**. White **Coulter daisy** pops up here and there. Later-season hikers can expect to see notable **Parry gentian**. Early-season hikers found pale lavender **ballhead waterleaf**.

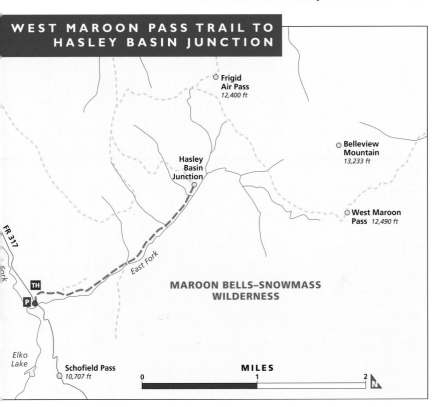

Coming up is a waterway of gray rock acting as a foil for **alpine** or **broadleaf fireweed**. Short, but showy, with vibrant rose-pink flowers and bluish-tinged stubby leaves, this less common cousin of ubiquitous fireweed is lyrically labeled **river beauty**.

The valley grows more willow-bound as it faces a glimpse of falling water and a wall of steep talus. Here a trail junction sign divides the trail, sending Hasley Basin Trail left and West Maroon Pass Trail right. For the sated subalpine wildflower lover, this juncture makes a good turnaround point.

Wildflower Hike 50

Dark Canyon Trail #830

Wild roses overlook an endless mass of quaking aspen west of Crested Butte.

AT THE PARKING AREA, huge quaking aspens serve as harbingers of the aspen-covered mountainsides seen from this hike's overlook goal. This easygoing route follows an old road for most of the way, facilitating side-by-side walking and relaxed enjoyment of the beaver ponds, open meadows, and majestic mountain vistas.

The 2 miles to Dark Canyon Overlook discover over six dozen wild-flower species, including passionately pigmented Grand Mesa penstemon. Even the 12-mile drive from Crested Butte is flower-lined.

The parking area is generous and includes horse trailer space.

Trail Rating	easy to moderate
Trail Length	4.0 miles out and back
Location	Raggeds Wilderness Area/Crested Butte
Elevation	8,890 to 9,400 feet
Bloom Season	June to August
Peak Bloom	early to mid-July
Directions	From Crested Butte, go west on Kebler Pass Rd./County Road 12 for about 12 miles. Parking and trailhead are on your right at Horse Ranch Park.

From the parking area, follow an old jeep road (#707) uphill, passing a wide meadow of **tall Jacob's ladder, aspen sunflower**, and **cow parsnip**. Look south for a panorama of the Anthracite Range, centered by 12,290-foot Ohio Peak. To the northeast, Ruby Dyke slices the Colorado sky as it crests toward the Ruby Range.

Refined **beauty cinquefoil**, a golden member of the rose family, blooms trailside, while **showy daisy** revels in the wide-skied meadow grasses alongside coarse but brassy **mule's ears**. Broad-girthed quaking aspens shelter **orange sneezeweed** and **false hellebore**. At the crest of a gentle hill, a sign welcomes you to Dark Canyon Trail #830.

A gentle decent follows, taking you past clumps of **Colorado blue columbine** drifting among mature aspen. **Cow parsnip** and **white geranium** match the white bark of the "quakies"—an affectionate term for these high-country trees. Moist shade is an ideal habitat for shoulder-high vegetation, which leads to level terrain overlooking a pond featuring a beaver lodge and slipways. East and West Beckwith Peaks command the southwest vista. At your feet, **wild blue flax** is as blue as a clear Colorado sky.

Continuing along this clover-flanked pack trail brings on fuzzy buds of **pink-headed daisy** and dolphin-shaped buds of **tall larkspur**. Bright pink **wild rose** wafts a seductive scent.

The trail becomes rockier, lifting among aspens. Look beneath the trees for slender purple **monkshood** and prolific **meadowrue**. The latter's small-leaved foliage mimics that of columbine. Male **meadowrue's** subtle flowers resemble daintily fringed parasols, while the female ones are sturdy green bursts. To compare this plant, sometimes called **false columbine**, with the real thing, watch for **blue columbine** growing nearby.

Avoid brushing against hairy-leaved stinging nettles, whose drooping cones of flowers look like packed greenish dots. As you pass deeper into the aspen cathedral, look for more **pink-headed daisies**.

Rise to reach a flat trail segment along a small meadow spattered with **blue flax**, **aspen sunflower**, and **sneezeweed**. In the early 1900s, sheepherders carved dates into the aspen trunks along here. In a verdant meadow below the track, grasses and sedges accent a pond's dark waters. A grand range of mountains creates a stunning backdrop.

GRAND MESA PENSTEMON
Penstemon mensarum

Grand Mesa penstemon, graced with hot-blue tubes suffused with violet, was first discovered east of Grand Junction on Grand Mesa—hence its name. This eye-catching endemic looks somewhat like Rocky Mountain penstemon (*P. strictus*), also a western slope inhabitant, but is brighter and sports hairless stamens. Clumps of Grand Mesa penstemon grow to be about 2 feet high. Each calyx is sticky, the flowers less so. The genus name, *Penstemon*, means "five stamens"; the species name, *mensarum*, means "of the mesa."

The trail continues along, flanked by cool **western paintbrush**. **Thimbleberry**, with its big maple-like leaves and few flowers, thrives in the shade, as does **heartleaf arnica** and a lantern or two of **western red columbine**. Umbellate **cowbane** laces a small stream, heralding a muddy section of trail. Plow through head-high **cow parsnip**, **tall larkspur**, and **monkshood**—the latter two are toxic cousins. Down to the left, tall and tropical-looking **Cases' fitweed**, or **corydalis**, sports braided racemes of spurred white to pinkish blossoms, each flaunting a purplish projection.

Alternating between level and ascending, the path wends through aspen. Magenta **American vetch** twines through the understory. A talus slide offers roothold to **wild raspberry** and **serviceberry**, whose green fruit will ripen to blue-black. The next incline introduces **giant hyssop**—check it for the square stem of the mint family.

An s-curve announces the sound of running water. The route grows rockier, passing little clouds of **northern bedstraw**. A little farther along, a brooklet refreshes noble stands of **cow parsnip**.

DARK CANYON TRAIL #830

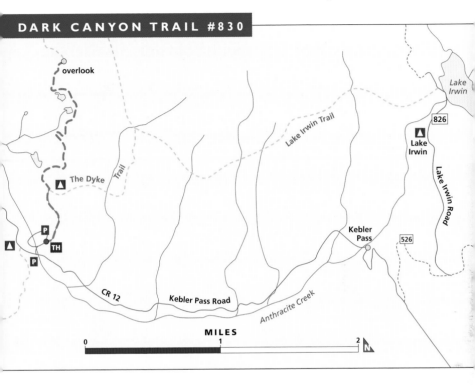

Pass through a meadow offering up shrubs of **twinberry honeysuckle**. **Wild roses, bedstraw, yarrow, snowberry,** and long-stemmed **western coneflower,** a rayless species with a bullet-nosed cone of purplish-brown disc flowers, also bloom here. In the backdrop, the Ruby Range's mahogany-red spires contrast with vivid, violet-blue clumps of **Grand Mesa penstemon**.

The trail brings you eye-level with a series of beaver dams to observe their construction. Pass **giant hyssop** and the daisy-like blooms of **sunspots,** or **goldeneyes,** before heading back into dappled aspen shade.

A few minutes more leads you to a short spur heading west to an awe-inspiring overlook of Dark Canyon. This rocky spot is the perfect place to absorb high-country glory. Even the **wild roses** here bow to the stunning panorama. Magnificent peaks, anchored by 11,348-foot Marcellina Mountain, and aspen-covered slopes course down, allowing you to imagine the flow of gold autumn brings.

If you can drag your attention away from the breathtaking views, check fissures in the outcrop you are standing on for **rockbrake fern, rock spirea,** and the neatly speckled stars of **dotted** or **moss saxifrage.** When you are ready, turn around and retrace your steps.

APPENDIX: *Hikes by Elevation* (IN FEET)

PLAINS

1. Well Gulch Nature Loop   5,500–5,860

PLAINS TO FOOTHILLS

12. Lichen Loop   5,900–6,280
13. Foothills/Hogback   5,550–6,400
    Ridge Loop
14. Mesa/NCAR Loop   5,800–6,160
15. Doudy Draw   5,850–6,100
27. Coyote Song/Lyons Back/   5,850–6,070
    Pass/Columbine/Cathy Johnson Loop

FOOTHILLS

2. Crosier Mountain East   6,600–7,360
9. Sleepy Lion Loop   5,940–6,650
10. Canyon Loop   6,000–6,600
    at Betasso Preserve
11. Anne U. White   6,040–6,540
19. Apex/Pick 'n Sledge/   6,150–7,150
    Sluicebox Loop
20. Rawhide/Longhorn/Maverick/Sawmill/
    Mustang/Belcher Hill Loop 7,500–7,800
21. Red Rocks/   6,200–6,730
    Morrison Slide Loop
22. Beaver Brook West   6,600–7,400
28. Castle/Tower/   7,700–7,850
    Meadow Loop
29. Hummingbird/   7,200–7,400
    Songbird Loop
30. Elk Valley/   6,100–7,205
    Carpenter Peak Loop
31. Mesa Rim Loop   6,400–6,500
32. Indian Creek   6,800–7,480
33. Spruce Mountain Loop   7,100–7,605
37. Wildflower Path/Stratton   6,240–6,480
    Springs/ Lower South Suburban/
    Ridgeway Loop
38. Meadow-Redrocks Loop   6,500–6,800
39. Zook/Sundance/Talon Loop 6,200–6,400
40. Canyon Loop at   6,432–6,880
    Aiken Canyon Preserve

FOOTHILLS TO MONTANE

3. North Fork/Dunraven   7,960–8,160
    to Deserted Village
16. Forgotten Valley   7,800–8,200

23. Meadow/Meadow View/   7,760–8,120
    Elkridge/Sleepy "S" Loop

MONTANE

5. Lily Lake Loop   8,880–8,900
6. Cascade Creek   8,340–9,500
8. Ceran St. Vrain Trail   8,000–8,300
17. Raccoon Loop   8,800–9,250
24. Grass Creek   8,700–9,400
34. Puma Point Nature   9,502–9,440
    Trail Loop
35. Hornbeck/Twin Rock   8,320–8,880
36. Outlook Ridge/   9,280–9,680
    Geer & Lost Ponds Loop
44. Dillon Peninsula   9,070–9,230
47. Piney River Falls: 9,360–9,920
    Upper Piney River Trail #1885
50. Dark Canyon #830   8,890–9,400

MONTANE TO SUBALPINE

25. Tanglewood   9,250–10,440
45. Eccles Pass: 9,090–11,890
    Meadow Creek Trail
46. North Tenmile Creek   9,070–10,050

SUBALPINE

18. Loch Lomond   10,360–11,200
42. Kenosha Pass West/   19,960–10,400
    Colorado Trail
43. Peak 8 SuperChair   11,059–11,440
    Nature Walk Trail
49. West Maroon Pass Trail 10,400–10,900
    Hasley Basin Junction

SUBALPINE TO ALPINE

4. Mount Chapin   10,640–11,580
    Vista Overlook
7. High Lonesome/   11,220–11,671
    Betty & Bob Lakes
41. Black Powder Pass   11,481–12,159

ALPINE

26. Geneva Knob   11,669–11,941
48. Continental Divide   12,126–12,560
    Trail/ Cottonwood Pass South Knob

Index

About the Author and the Photographer

AUTHOR PAMELA IRWIN has been a volunteer naturalist at Roxborough State Park since the early 1980s. Her extensive background in and love of wildflower identification has earned her the certified title of Native Plant Master from Colorado State University. Pamela is also a member of the Rocky Mountain Nature Association, the Rocky Mountain Chapter of the American Rock Garden Society, Windflowers Garden Club, and the Audubon Society.

PHOTOGRAPHER DAVID IRWIN purchased his first 35mm SLR camera as a teenager and has been behind a lens ever since. His favorite subjects include people of foreign lands, the remnants of past civilizations, and the textures of western terrains.

Avid hikers, Pamela and David enjoy combining their talents to produce beautiful guidebooks detailing hikes in their home state. Previous collaborations include *Colorado's Best Wildflower Hikes Volume 1: The Front Range*, *Colorado's Best Wildflower Hikes Volume 2: The High Country*, and *100 Best Day Hikes: Denver Area & Front Range*. They also maintain an extensive slide library and have given slide-illustrated talks for various organizations including the Colorado Mountain Club. Additionally, many of David's photographs and Pamela's watercolors are now in private collections.